The Complete Handbook of

BUSINESS MEETINGS

The Complete Handbook of
BUSINESS MEETINGS

ELI MINA

WITHDRAWN

AMACOM
American Management Association

New York • Atlanta • Boston • Chicago • Kansas City • San Francisco • Washington, D.C.
Brussels • Mexico City • Tokyo • Toronto

This publication is designed to provide accurate and authoritative information in regard to the subject matter covered. It is sold with the understanding that the publisher is not engaged in rendering legal, accounting, or other professional service. If legal advice or other expert assistance is required, the services of a competent professional person should be sought.

Library of Congress Cataloging-in-Publication Data

Mina, Eli.
    The complete handbook of business meetings / Eli Mina.
        p.   cm.
    Includes index.
    ISBN 0-8144-0560-6
    1. Business meetings.   I. Title.
    HF5734.5.M566   2000
    658.4'56—dc21   00–038625

Printing number

10 9 8 7 6 5 4 3 2 1

I dedicate this book to my wife, Michelle, in recognition of her continued support and her tolerance of our lengthy and lively discussions. I also dedicate it to my clients and seminar participants, for their many questions, for the unique and challenging assignments that they have given me, and for supporting and sustaining my business. Without them, this work would not have been possible.

Contents

3. Preventive and Visionary Planning — 55

4. Empowered and Proactive Members — 100

5. A Masterful Facilitator — 110

6. Surviving the Contentious Meeting 149

7. Rules of Order That Make Sense 167

8. Accurate and Useful Minutes 245

Preface

This book presents a collection of insights and ideas, gained in the course of more than 15 years of practice, consulting, and training on meeting dynamics and rules of order. It responds to persistent client requests for meeting planning and management tools, derived from an approach that is sensible, practical, results oriented, inclusive, and relevant to today's realities.

I feel truly fortunate and blessed to have had the opportunity to serve my clients in this field. The feedback on my work has been humbling and gratifying. It has convinced me that the approach I have developed is unique, has broad applicability, and stands to make a difference beyond my established client base. I firmly believe that the common-sense approach to meetings and rules of order can help you free your organization from procedural difficulties, build internal consensus and harmony, and focus more effectively on fulfilling your mandate and on serving your stakeholders. This approach is bound to increase the returns on the large investment you often make in meetings.

Since starting this work in 1984, I have often wondered (as have members of my family) how a quiet and shy person, formally educated as an engineer, succeeded in developing a unique approach that has earned accolades from many civic and corporate leaders. Perhaps there is a message here for you: You don't have to be loud and outspoken to do great things in meetings or elsewhere. All you need is a set of principles and tools, and a healthy dose of common sense.

I sincerely hope that you and your organization will benefit from this work. No one deserves the pain and agony of a boring and monotonous meeting or one that is chaotic, disorderly, and adversarial. Given your expenditure of time, money, and other resources in a meeting, you deserve a substantial return on investment. Insist on it!

The Complete Handbook of

BUSINESS MEETINGS

Introduction

The Complete Handbook of Business Meetings is intended to assist you and your organization in having meetings that are more productive and more inclusive, leading to wiser and better collective decisions. It provides practical and proven tools for the planning and management of meetings. For the more formal meetings, the book demystifies and humanizes the rules of order. It should induce creative thinking, questioning of entrenched practices, and the adoption of alternative approaches to collective decision making. Ultimately, this book stands to help you in increasing the returns on the substantial investments made in a meeting.

This book will serve the following readers:

- Meeting chairs who need tools to better manage time, issues, and people in meetings
- Meeting attendees who need tools to participate more effectively and to assert themselves without getting angry
- Chief executive officers who need tools to work more effectively with their governing boards
- Staff who record minutes, design agendas, and coordinate meeting logistics

This book provides tools to plan, chair, or participate in a variety of meetings: small or large, informal or formal, harmonious or controversial. It is assumed that there is a desire or a requirement to involve members in meaningful discussions and decision making (otherwise why waste their time in a meeting?). Among others, the methods apply to:

- Informal meetings of staff committees or larger staff gatherings
- Formal meetings of governing boards, councils, and commissions
- Large meetings of members of nonprofit organizations, cooperatives, or home owners
- General meetings of shareholders of public companies
- Public meetings and hearings sponsored by municipal and other statutory bodies

In more than 15 years in practice I have noted the consistent frustration of my clients with books on meeting dynamics and rules of order. Complaints have included: "This is such a thick book. Less than 1% of it applies to us, and it would take a detective to discover the 1% that we need." "The rules of order are mechanical and artificial, and they stop the free and creative flow of ideas." "How can a person who was elected president be expected to memorize this many rules?" "The structure appears to constrain us and slow progress down."

In response to these comments, I have ventured to give you proven tools and ideas for today's meetings. The focus is on advice that is practical, relevant, and readily usable. This advice can save you time and money and can help you build organizational consensus and harmony. As a result, you should be able to use much more than 1% of this book's content immediately, and you should not have to rely on a parliamentary expert to find or interpret what you need.

In this book, I question the "conventional wisdom," and challenge you to think and operate "outside the box." By doing so, you will look beyond mechanics and will examine fundamental principles and broad perspectives. I question common practices and dispel myths, as well as make suggestions for discarding procedures that waste time and don't make sense. You will learn ways to shift to a simpler and more user-friendly approach.

You may be an experienced chair, or you may be a new and

anxious member of a board. Regardless of your level of skill and experience, this book will have something for you. You will likely benefit from some or all of the following:

- Underlying principles and philosophies for shared decision making
- Assessment tools for your organization and its meetings
- Preventive measures and remedial interventions to cure meeting ailments
- Overall scripts for meetings (formal or informal)
- Ad-hoc scripts for chairs, members, and staff to address specific challenges in meetings
- Answers to the most frequently asked questions about rules of order

Here are some things this book will not give you:

- As a leader, are you accustomed to always having your way? If so, this book does not offer tools with which to manipulate, deceive, dominate, or coerce your members. Instead, a genuinely inclusive approach to shared decision making is presented. Many leaders are at first uncomfortable and anxious about letting go of control and allowing democracy to prevail. It is my view that a good leader is one who knows when to make decisions and when to facilitate decision making.
- Are you looking for a bouncer for a rough meeting? I do not offer you a list of security guards or tools to overpower disruptive members. Although the adversarial approach may bring short-term gain, it will likely yield long-term pain. The principled approach in this book has the potential of converting members from critics to creators, and from passive observers to active contributors.
- Are you looking for an all-inclusive encyclopedia of ideas? As tempting as it may be, I refuse to claim a monopoly on ideas. I do not address every single challenge that you will face and some of my solutions will be inappropriate for your group. I outline a sensible approach, several key principles, and examples

of solutions that have worked for my clients. You will need to customize this approach to your group's needs.

▪ Are you a scholar of parliamentary procedure? Sorry to disappoint, but a comprehensive and complex procedural guide would be intimidating, confusing, and of limited use.

▪ Are you looking for legal advice? I have no legal expertise and therefore refuse to argue with lawyers or speculate on what the courts would do in the event of a procedural violation. Instead, I focus on nonlegalistic common-sense principles for procedures and rules of order, and on preventive and remedial measures to address problems in meetings.

Chapter 1 covers general concepts that apply to meetings and collective decision making. The cost of meetings and how to maximize return on investment are discussed. Shared decision-making principles and models are included.

Chapter 2 outlines the ten key ingredients of a successful meeting. It offers assessment tools and numerous ideas on how to have a productive meeting.

Chapter 3 teaches preventive medicine: how to use visionary and proactive planning to facilitate good meetings, and how to prevent common meeting ailments.

The roles of individual members between and at meetings (as separate from the roles of the chair) are covered in Chapter 4, which includes helpful scripts for members to express concerns without getting angry.

The roles, ethics, and rights of the chair are given in Chapter 5. Interventions and sample scripts are provided to assist both novice and experienced chairs in handling challenging scenarios during meetings.

Chapter 6 addresses the unique challenges of planning and facilitating a contentious meeting.

Chapter 7 humanizes and demystifies the rules of order for formal meetings. It shows how to use the rules in a simple and user-friendly manner to facilitate progress.

Assistance to those who take minutes of meetings is offered in Chapter 8.

Chapter 9 discusses virtual meetings, or those less costly

alternatives to conventional meetings (i.e., meetings in writing, teleconferencing, and videoconferencing).

Chapter 10 is a troubleshooting guide. It identifies ailments in meetings, and suggests remedial medicine to cure those ailments and preventive medicine to avoid them in the future.

Eli Mina's Guiding Principles for Meetings and Consensus Building

- A meeting's success is ultimately measured by the quality of the decisions made in it.
- Fairness, equality, common sense, and principle must always be in the forefront.
- Always assume people are reasonable, and this will likely become a self-fulfilling prophecy.
- Never attribute to malice what can reasonably be attributed to a misunderstanding.
- Rules of order are intended to facilitate progress, not to impede it.
- To truly gain control, leaders must know how to share control and build partnerships.
- It is much easier to be a critic than a creator.
- God gave us two ears and one mouth so that we could listen at least twice as much as we speak.
- Diversity of opinions is healthy. An opposing view or criticism should not be interpreted as a threat but just as another piece of the bigger truth on which wiser decisions can be based.

1

Healthy Meetings and Effective Decision Making

In this chapter, the following subjects are covered:

- The costs and impacts of meetings, and a return on investment
- The prerequisite to healthy meetings: a healthy organization
- General concepts relating to collective decision making
- The three decision-making models: autocratic, majority-based, and consensus
- Principles for curing meeting ailments

The Costs and Impacts of Meetings

Is Your Return on Investment as Good as It Can Get?

Meetings are generally held to exchange information and ideas, as well as for collective problem solving and decision making. Face-to-face meetings still dominate shared decision-making processes. However, teleconferencing, videoconferencing, fax machines, and the Internet are emerging as viable and less costly vehicles for sharing information and building group consensus.

The financial and time investments in meetings are often far greater than most people realize. Thus, it is imperative to raise these obvious questions: Are there sufficient returns on the investment of money, time, and effort? Are these returns as good as they should be? These simple questions are often overlooked as meetings are planned and facilitated.

The direct costs associated with a meeting include wages and expenses of participants and support staff, facilities (meeting room rentals, catering, audiovisual aids), preparation efforts, paper production (minutes, notices, agendas, reports, presentation materials), and more. In addition to the direct costs of meetings, their impact and the indirect costs to which they can lead should be considered, including impacts on organizational decisions and on people.

Impacts on Organizational Decisions

If a meeting is run well, the decisions made are likely to be wise and responsible, and to work well for the organization. In contrast, if a meeting is run poorly, flawed decisions are likely to be made. The costs may not be immediately obvious, but they will be incurred in the short and long terms. The return on investment will be nonexistent or even negative.

If the issues at hand are controversial, a well-run meeting will lead to closure, healing, and reconciliation. The meeting should facilitate the realignment of the organization's resources on achieving its mandate and serving its stakeholders. Improperly handled controversies will undermine an organization and may even lead to adversarial action against it. Lawsuits are a drain on resources, distract from the organization's mandate, and can be expensive.

Impacts on People

When you leave a well-run meeting, you typically feel energized and invigorated. You have a sense of achievement and a renewed commitment to the organization. You sense that your time was well spent and that you made a difference. You look forward to the next meeting, and you will prepare for it by fulfilling commitments that you have made. You are enthusiastic about the organization and your work. Of course, this attitude can lead to financial gains.

In contrast, if a meeting is run poorly, you leave it with a sense of confusion and frustration, questioning why you needed to be there and what was truly accomplished. You wonder why your busy schedule had to be disrupted and you can think of ten worthwhile things you could have done instead of attending this meeting. Your energy level and enthusiasm for the rest of the day diminish. Reduced productivity and a negative financial impact are likely.

It is difficult to attach monetary values to the human impacts of a meeting. But it is clear that the indirect or soft costs of a meeting can be substantial.

Assessing Returns on Investment

Given the direct and indirect costs of meetings, it is logical to conduct a cost-benefit analysis to determine:

- How much of an investment a meeting requires
- What returns should be received on this investment
- Whether the actual returns are substantial enough to justify the investment

A cost-benefit analysis can be done before a meeting to determine whether it should be called, and, if so, to establish how the returns can be maximized; or after a meeting to check whether the expected returns have materialized, and, if not, why. This analysis can be done:

- On the meeting as a whole (a *macro* basis), to assess the returns on the entire meeting.
- On each agenda item (a *micro* basis), to assess the returns on this item, and, based on this assessment, to determine how much time and effort, if any, should be invested in it. This way you will be less likely to spend 90% of your meeting time achieving 10% of the results that matter.

The cost-benefit analysis should consist of four steps as discussed next.

Step 1: Adding Up the Costs of a Meeting

When assessing costs, make sure to add everything, including:

- *Monetary Costs:* Salaries, fees for speakers and advisers, travel, accommodation, meals, meeting room, electricity, paper, delivery of documents, preparation time, meeting time.
- *Nonmonetary Costs:* Distractions created by the meeting, stress and reduced productivity as a result of it, and so forth. Attach a monetary equivalent to these nonmonetary costs. For example: If it takes several hours for a meeting attendee to recover from the impact of the meeting, or if someone else is required to attend to his or her duties, add the lost wages to your indirect meeting costs. If members are demoralized or become unproductive or quit as a result of a bad meeting, add the cost of lost productivity or the cost of finding and training new replacement staff.

When you finish adding up the costs (X), estimate the total time for the meeting (T), and divide the total costs by the total time allocated to the meeting. This will give you the investment for each minute of the meeting (Y). For example: If the total cost for a 3-hour meeting $(T = 180$ minutes) is \$1800 (X), the cost per minute (Y) is \$10.

Next, estimate the time required for each agenda item (I), and multiply it by Y. This will give you the investment required for each agenda item (Z). For example, if an item requires 30 minutes $(I = 30)$, the investment in it $(Z = Y \times I)$ is \$300.

Step 2: Adding Up the Returns on Investment

When assessing returns on investment, consider tangible and intangible benefits, both in the short term and in the long term, for each agenda item. The potential returns on investment may be:

- Sharing new information and answering questions directly, thereby preventing costly misunderstandings and saving time, money, and aggravation
- Resolving issues and making collective decisions
- Developing ideas that will save money, lead to a better use of resources (time, human, other), and increase organizational effectiveness (i.e., ideas on working smarter, not harder)
- Developing ideas that will make money and advance the organization's mandate
- Building consensus on difficult issues, thereby reducing costly tensions and stress, creating internal alignment and harmony, and increasing the commitment to the organization

Attach a monetary value to the potential benefits from each agenda item and then add them up, to calculate the total return on investment. The result of this analysis will be the following numbers:

- Returns on the meeting as a whole (your entire portfolio, or A)
- Returns on each agenda item (or B)

Step 3: Comparing the Costs to the Benefits

To determine whether you had a positive return on investment you need to ask:

- Is A greater than X? If so, your investment in the overall meeting can be justified.
- Is B greater than Z? If so, your investment in the respective agenda item can be justified.

However, if the costs exceed the benefits, you need to take action to increase the returns on investment. This action may pertain to the overall meeting or to specific agenda items.

Step 4: Considering Your Options

Having completed your cost-benefit analysis, you will need to consider your options. Suppose that once all costs are added your meeting (or an agenda item) is projected to cost $1000. Imagine yourself standing at a store where you can purchase the purported benefits of this meeting. Would you write a check in the amount of $1000 to pay for these potential returns?

If your answer is yes, go ahead and hold the meeting. If your answer is no or maybe, you may want to consider one of these three options:

1. *Negotiate more value.* Keep the investment unchanged, but look for ways to increase the benefits. For example, search for more benefits from the same agenda items, delete or allocate less time to less profitable agenda items, and make more time available to profitable ones.

2. *Negotiate a lower price.* Reduce the investment to achieve the same or higher returns. For example, invite fewer members, invite advisers for only a part of the meeting, make the meeting shorter, and work to reduce the human tolls (e.g., make the meeting more engaging so that instead of being tired members will leave rejuvenated and motivated for other tasks that day).

3. *Go to another store.* Cancel the meeting (if you can) and look for less costly ways of achieving the same returns. For example, send information by letter, fax, or e-mail, and solicit feedback, ideas, or questions; or hold a meeting by teleconferencing, videoconferencing, or on the Internet. For a variety of ways to share ideas and build consensus, see Chapter 9 on less costly alternatives to "real" meetings.

Prerequisites for Successful Meetings

Examining the Health of Your Organization

Seeking to heal meeting ailments by themselves is like treating symptoms of a disease without examining its root causes. Dysfunctional meetings often reflect dysfunctional organizations, with outdated mandates, flawed decision-making processes, internal fragmentation and power struggles, a top-down autocratic leadership, an organizational culture that perpetuates dependency and stifles individual initiative, finger-pointing, and low commitment levels. A prerequisite to having truly good meetings is having a healthy organization.

When assessing the health of an organization, several performance indicators should be examined:

- Clarity, relevance, and entrenchment of organizational mandate
- Leadership effectiveness
- Commitment levels of individual members
- Clarity of roles and responsibilities
- Organizational culture
- Conflict prevention systems
- Conflict resolution systems
- Relationships with internal and external stakeholders

The remainder of this section contains questions that will help you assess the health of your organization in the above areas.

Compelling Organizational Mandate

- Is your organization's mandate clearly defined?
- Is it broad and flexible, while being specific and unique?
- Is the mandate logical, current, meaningful, and relevant to today's realities?
- Is the mandate engaging and compelling?
- Do internal and external stakeholders know and understand the mandate?
- Does everyone support the mandate? Reluctantly, passively, or enthusiastically?

Visionary and Principled Leadership

- Is the organization's governance structure logical and sensible?
- Is your governing board large enough to represent a

broad range of skills, knowledge, and views, and is it small enough to facilitate the meaningful involvement of all directors in decision making?

- Are leaders able to articulate their vision for the organization in a clear and compelling manner?
- Are leaders in tune with the needs of internal and external stakeholders?
- Are leaders crisis driven (reactive), or are they proactive, creative, and visionary thinkers?
- Are leaders autocratic (top-down), or do they build internal consensus (bottom-up)?
- Do leaders maintain tight control, or are they prepared to share it?
- Do leaders embrace necessary change? How attached are they to the status quo?
- Do leaders practice what they preach? Are they good role models for followers?
- Do leaders engage followers in activities that challenge them, take advantage of their unique talents and skills, and give them opportunities to excel and make a difference?
- Are individual directors guided by narrow interests or by the broad organizational mandate?
- Does the governing board work as a cohesive and coherent team?

High Commitment Levels of Individual Members

- Are the members passive observers, or are they empowered and motivated contributors?
- Are they critics or creators?
- Are they involved because they have to be (out of duty and obligation) or because they want to be?
- Do they wait for someone else to tell them, or do they make it their business to know how their work fits within the organizational mandate and how it affects others?
- Do they do only what is required, or do they seek to excel, deliver quality results, and go beyond the call of duty?
- Are they consistent and reliable?

- Are they accountable for their actions or do they point fingers at others?
- Do they act with honesty, integrity, and due diligence?
- Are they sensitive and respectful toward others?
- Are they open to learning from other points of view?
- Do they share feedback (both the positive and corrective varieties)?
- Do they know when to speak up and when to be quiet and listen?
- Do they welcome feedback and treat it as an opportunity to learn?
- Are they open to necessary change, or are they inclined to resist it?
- Are they team players? Do they accept that a chain is only as strong as its weakest link?

Clarity of Roles and Responsibilities

- Are the roles and responsibilities of the governing board, the officers, and the staff clearly defined in writing? Is this definition understood and supported by all?
- Are the terms of reference for committees clearly defined, understood, and accepted?
- Are the authority and accountability of governing bodies, committees, and individuals clearly defined and established?

Organizational Culture

- What values and principles are entrenched within the organization (excellence, quality work, results orientation, achievement, accountability, creativity and innovation, "thinking outside the box," respect, high service levels, listening, fairness, equality)?
- What is acceptable behavior and what is not tolerated?
- How do people talk, listen, and make decisions?
- How do people treat one another?
- How are customers and other external stakeholders treated?

- How are resources (money, time, talents) treated? Are they used effectively or squandered?
- How commonplace is honest, open, and direct communication?
- Is the organization fun?

Conflict Prevention Systems

- Is there an inclination to deny the existence of conflict?
- Is conflict treated as something to eradicate or as something to examine and learn from?
- Is corrective feedback shared regularly and openly, or is it delayed until things are unbearable?
- Is feedback only shared during scheduled periodic evaluations or also on an ad-hoc basis?
- Is feedback treated defensively, or is it welcomed as an opportunity to learn?
- Is feedback limited to the corrective variety, or is it balanced by recognition of efforts and contributions (privately and publicly), as well as celebration of successes?
- Are there early warning systems to anticipate conflict and address it proactively?

Conflict Resolution Systems

- Are there any procedures for resolving interpersonal and interdepartmental disputes?
- Is conflict resolved in a direct and principled manner? How common are plotting and discussions behind people's backs?
- Are disputes settled directly (by full disclosure of feedback, focusing on issues, not personalities) and informally (by mediation and negotiation) or by adversarial means (threats, intimidation, manipulation, undermining individuals who are deemed problematic, or even costly litigation)?

Relationships with Internal and External Stakeholders

- Do decision makers consider the impacts of their actions on internal stakeholders (staff, volunteers) and external stakeholders (customers, suppliers, the general public, government agencies, and others)?

- Is there an effort to engage stakeholders in a meaningful and timely exchange of information?
- Are stakeholders informed of decisions only after they are made, or is there an effort to keep them informed early?
- Are stakeholders consulted regarding initiatives that would have significant impacts on them? Is their feedback taken into account before decisions are finalized?
- Is there a tendency to trivialize and minimize the significance of complaints, or is there an effort to find out more about them (recognizing that for every person who complains, there may be ten others who experience the same difficulty but who do not take the time to complain)?

Collective Decision-Making Concepts

Meetings are typically held to facilitate collective decision making. In this section several concepts that relate to collective decision-making processes are explored.

Substantive Decisions versus Procedural Decisions

Commonly, group consensus is sought on substantive issues, for example, a decision to adopt a new policy, or to embark on a new project, or to approve an expenditure. In my experience, it is rare for groups to invest time in examining the way they make decisions together. However, if you examine substantive initiatives that failed at the implementation stage, you will often discover an interesting fact: The initiative failed not because it lacked merit but because of the way the decisions were made. Consider the following:

- Members resist an important initiative because it is presented as a done deal. They had no opportunity to give feedback on it at an early stage.

- An important decision is pushed through by a narrow and aggressive majority, with little debate. This rushed process causes the minority members to feel stifled. Some of them leave the organization. Others become demoralized, and still others seek to undermine the implementation. Had they only been given an opportunity to debate the issues, their opposition might have been softened: "We disagree with the decision, but we accept the verdict of the majority."

Individuals are becoming increasingly reluctant to blindly and obediently follow authority. It is therefore essential for groups to discuss not only substantive issues but also procedural issues. They may need to make collective decisions about issues such as:

- How will we work and make decisions together?
- How will we avoid the perception of winners and losers?
- How much discussion is reasonable to have before voting on a proposal?

Without collective decisions on process issues, the preceding questions are typically settled by:

- The leader (autocratic regime, or monarchy)
- The most outspoken and assertive members (anarchy, or the tyranny of the minority)

Conversely, empowering members to make process-related decisions collectively is the democratic way to go. This approach will reduce tensions, increase members' control over how meetings are conducted, and enable them to deal more effectively with substantive issues.

Eight Criteria for Good Decision Making

The success of a meeting is ultimately measured by the quality of the decisions made in it. A good decision reflects intelligence, responsibility, credibility, and durability. Decisions should be:

1. Supportive of organizational needs and broad mandates
2. In the best interests of the stakeholders that the organization is intended to serve

3. Beneficial in the short and long terms
4. Realistic and possible to implement
5. Focused on fundamental problems (root causes) rather than surface issues (symptoms)
6. Concerned with impacts on all resources (time, people, money, facilities, etc.)
7. Creative, holistic, and reflective of visionary thinking "outside the box"
8. Based on the courage to question the status quo, and, when needed, to let go of entrenched traditions

Dynamics of the Deliberations

Quality decisions require a certain amount of group deliberation. Whereas routine decisions can be made with little or no discussion, substantive or contentious decisions need a more measured and deliberate approach. Consider the following aspects of deliberation dynamics:

■ *Lateral Movement and Forward Movement.* Good decision making requires a healthy balance between lateral movement (creative, informal, and free-flowing discussion) and forward movement (summary of progress, identifying areas of agreement and issues that still need to be resolved). With a deliberate approach, lateral movement will precede forward movement.

■ *Problem Mode or Solution Mode.* Far too often, groups rush into solutions without first asking what the problem is. This is especially true in groups that insist no discussion can take place until there is a motion (solution mode) on the floor. This approach may work well for simple decisions that have little impact. However, in the case of complex issues, rushing to solution mode is likely to produce shortsighted solutions that do not stand the test of time. It tends to focus on symptoms rather than root causes. "Solved" problems come back to haunt you later.

■ *Self-Fulfilling Prophecies.* In his book *Illusions* (New York: Delacorte Press, 1978), Richard Bach offers this thought: "Argue in favor of your limitations, and sure enough, they are yours." If the deliberations are focused on all the reasons why something cannot be done, it will not be done. If, instead, ideas are explored with an open mind and subjected to objective criteria, wiser and more visionary decisions are bound to be made.

■ *Opposing or Proposing.* When controversial proposals or unexpected new ideas emerge, many members are predisposed to criticize and raise their objections first. Raising concerns is important. However, it is not enough to say what is wrong with a proposal or oppose it. Opponents should be challenged to propose solutions or better alternatives.

A Success Story: To Oppose or to Propose

A member of the board of directors of a large national organization was alarmed by a proposal that was to be considered at the next board meeting. The proposal was to relocate the headquarters to new premises, at a substantial cost. Her objections arose from the following issues:

■ The need to relocate was questionable. It appeared to have been driven by the depressed real estate market and by the persistence of an aggressive real estate agent.
■ The board was not well focused on fulfilling the organization's mandate and serving its members, and too much money was being spent on side issues (a wrongful dismissal lawsuit, a malfunctioning computer system, and this proposed relocation).
■ The member could identify at least ten mandate-related initiatives that could have been launched for the same cost of relocation to the new premises.

The member requested advice on how to fight this proposal. The suggestions were as follows:

■ Prepare a written analysis of the relocation proposal indicating its various flaws.
■ Prepare an alternative proposal to pursue the ten mandate-driven initiatives.
■ Circulate the written analysis of the proposed relocation and the alternative proposal to other board members and invite

them to discuss the documents by phone prior to the meeting.

- Arrange to have the alternative proposal scheduled on the board meeting agenda.

Remember that the strength of an advocate of a proposal depends on three main factors:

1. The strength of the argument. Opposing a motion and indicating its weaknesses is one thing. It is quite another thing to propose a more credible, principled, creative, and visionary alternative, and to do so in a convincing and compelling manner.
2. The strength in numbers, especially in the face of potential opposition. The member needed to convey the benefits of an alternate proposal and recruit supporters for it.
3. The strength in procedural knowledge. In this case, the board member needed to know how to write a motion, how to schedule it on the agenda, how to present and debate it, and how to withstand the procedural obstacles that she might have encountered.

With this approach, the member's participation at the meeting was more credible and compelling, and she was able to convince the board to take a second look at the proposed relocation.

Because it is easier to oppose than to propose, there are many more critics than creators. But if you want to increase your credibility and influence within the organization, don't settle for the weaker position of opposition.

A Better Approach to Making Difficult and Significant Decisions

In the case of complex, controversial, or significant decisions, the following six-step approach to problem solving should replace the mad rush to solution mode. It will likely yield better results:

1. Discuss the real problem and avoid being trapped by symptoms or surface issues. The symptom may be that an es-

tablished policy is not followed by a few "culprits." The real problem may be that the policy is outdated and is incompatible with today's realities. Rushing to punish the culprits would achieve nothing.

2. Establish the criteria and principles to look for in a solution, for example, fairness, equality, fiscal responsibility, enforceability, and consistency with organizational mandate.

3. Search for options for solving the underlying problem. At this stage, have a creative and free-flowing discussion (lateral movement) and avoid a detailed analysis of each idea. List all options that emerge, even those that appear senseless or outright bizarre (clearly "outside the box"), since they may induce novel ideas. Resist the temptation to quickly trivialize suggestions with: "We already tried it in 1977," or "Pat will never agree to this."

4. Evaluate the options according to the established criteria. This is the time to raise concerns and be a devil's advocate. This is also the time to be brave, take risks, and consider measured departures from the status quo.

5. Select an option. By now the most logical and holistic option will emerge, and a motion in support of it can be made, debated, and voted on.

6. In order to ensure follow-up, the group should decide on implementation schedules and duties: Who will do what and by when? How will progress be measured?

Pros and Cons of the Three Collective Decision-Making Models

Collective decisions are made by one of three decision-making models, or a combination thereof:

1. Autocratic decision making
2. Majority-based voting
3. Consensus

The Autocratic Model

Under the autocratic model, someone is given or assumes the unilateral power to make certain decisions without consulting the other members. This model is efficient, expedient, and simple. Decisions are made quickly and without the time-consuming efforts to consult affected parties.

The primary disadvantage of the autocratic model is that members or stakeholders are excluded from decision making and therefore may not support the decisions. Worse yet, they may undermine the implementation of decisions, as some resource companies and government agencies find out when they approve controversial projects without consulting affected communities.

The autocratic model is appropriate for:

- Routine decisions of a purely administrative nature
- Urgent decisions, when there is no time to consult members and build consensus among them

This model is not appropriate for decisions on significant initiatives or policies, or decisions that are bound to have a substantial impact on the members and stakeholders of the organization.

Even when an individual (e.g., a chief executive officer) or a corporate body (a board of directors) has unilateral decision-making power, it is often wise to involve affected parties in decision making in some way. At the very least, they should be given sufficient notice of an impending decision. If possible, their input and feedback on the initiative should be requested before finalizing the decision. Such efforts would likely increase the legitimacy of the decisions and lead to greater acceptance of them.

The Majority-Based Model

Under the majority-based model, decisions are made by the members, generally on the basis of one member one vote, and require a majority vote (i.e., more than half of the votes cast).

Parliamentary procedure is based on this model (see Chapter 7).

The majority-based model is more inclusive than the autocratic model. Conversely, it is more efficient than the consensus model, since a proposal would only require more than half of the votes cast to be adopted. However, if the majority uses its power to stifle debate, and force contentious decisions prematurely, this process can leave deep divisions and an adversarial climate within an organization ("We win, you lose"). This situation may create enough harm to offset the benefits of expediency.

The majority-based model is appropriate when inclusion of members in decision making is mandated or needed, and when it is not practical to achieve more than half the votes in favor of a proposal. This model is not appropriate for use as a tool to rush through a poorly crafted proposal, or when there is a need to develop wiser and more broadly based solutions.

The Consensus Model

The *Random House Collegiate Dictionary* defines consensus as "general agreement" or "majority of opinions." However, consensus is often interpreted as a broad level of agreement, larger than a majority of the votes cast. Some groups have even viewed consensus as unanimous support of a decision. In other groups a consensus on a proposal is deemed to have been reached when each member is prepared to either support it or stand aside and not block it (i.e., accept it as an imperfect compromise).

The consensus approach is more inclusive than the majority-based approach. In its ideal use, it can preclude win-lose solutions and soften adversarial climates within an organization. It can force decision makers to listen to one another and act only when a full understanding of the diverse interests has been reached. The consensus approach has the potential of addressing more needs and interests, thereby yielding wiser and more holistic decisions.

Consensus has two chief disadvantages:

1. It is more time-consuming and requires more efforts and creativity than the autocratic and the majority-based models.
2. It can become the tyranny of the minority, with a few members having the power to block the decision-making process (especially when consensus is interpreted as unanimous approval).

The consensus model is appropriate when there is time to develop it. It is also the preferred model when issues are complex and when the decisions are bound to affect a variety of stakeholders, especially when each stakeholder is capable of frustrating the implementation of the decisions by adversarial means such as court action and civil disobedience.

Consensus is not appropriate if a decision must be made quickly. It is also inappropriate if the decision is of a routine nature and has little impact on the members and the organization, in which case the time and effort invested in reaching consensus would be disproportionately high when compared to the potential returns on this investment.

The following table summarizes the advantages and disadvantages of each of the decision-making models.

Model	Pros	Cons	Appropriate Situations
Autocratic Decision Making	■ Expeditious. ■ Simple.	■ Not inclusive. ■ Lacks the benefit of a broad perspective. ■ Potential for a lack of commitment by followers, or even undermining of the decision by them.	■ Routine, administrative, or noncontroversial decisions. ■ Urgent decisions that cannot wait for collective decision making.

(continues)

Model	Pros	Cons	Appropriate Situations
Majority-Based Voting	▪ Inclusive, yet efficient. ▪ Potentially measured and deliberate. ▪ Unanimity is not required, and hence disputes can be settled by a vote. ▪ If minorities are at least heard, the decisions are likely to be viewed as legitimate, and are therefore more likely to be respected and implemented.	▪ Potential for creating winners (majorities) and losers (minorities). ▪ Potential for important decisions being pushed through by impatient majorities, possibly causing ``losing minorities'' to leave the organization, or stay but undermine the implementation.	▪ Complex decisions that stand to benefit from broad input. ▪ Controversial decisions that affect people and stakeholders in a significant way. ▪ Decisions that cannot wait, where the number of options is limited, and where a middle ground between positions is hard or impossible to find within the available time. ▪ No time is available to obtain much more than a simple majority support for a proposal.
Consensus (more than a simple majority)	▪ Broad support for an initiative is generated.	▪ Time-consuming, slow, tedious.	▪ Complex or controversial initiatives, where time is

Model	Pros	Cons	Appropriate Situations
	■ The decisions reflect a broad spectrum of views, and are more likely to endure. ■ Decisions are viewed as legitimate, and are less likely to be undermined.	■ Risk of becoming subjected to "the tyranny of the minority" (stubborn "holdouts"). ■ Risk of a proposal being so diluted (to accommodate all interests) that it becomes meaningless.	available and where it is important to get much more than a simple majority to endorse and support the implementation of an initiative.

Semantics or Principles?

The last thing you want to do is spend precious time arguing about semantics: Are we using majority or are we using the consensus model? The label is less important than the principles to which your group adheres. Key questions to consider are:

- How much of an impact will this decision have?
- Will the organization's best interests and mandate be better served by broader support for this decision, or should the decision be made expeditiously, saving time for more important issues?

If the impact of the decision is small, it should be made quickly or delegated to an individual or a committee. If the impact is substantial and the issues are complex or sensitive, it would be wise to invest the time and effort needed to explore the problem and look for the most holistic and inclusive solution possible. In some instances, motions should be made and formal votes taken, with the minority accepting the majority's wishes. Other times, a broader level of support should be sought, and a more flexible, informal, and creative approach (consensus) should be used.

General Concepts for Curing Meeting Ailments

This book offers many ideas on how to cure common meeting ailments (see Chapter 10). In this section some of the principles and concepts relating to interventions are discussed.

Treating Symptoms or Root Causes

When faced with a difficulty or a disruptive behavior in a meeting, people often wish for a simple solution for it. They look for quick fixes that will enable the members to move on. It is better to resist giving quick answers. Instead, ask the question: What is at the root of the difficulty or the disruptive behavior? Pausing to assess the cause of the problem tends to yield better and longer-lasting results. The following examples are proof.

EXAMPLE: A Side Conversation

In one meeting, the facilitator noted that two individuals were talking to each other. To address the distraction, he asked them to stop the side conversation. Later, the reason for the side conversation became apparent: One of the members experienced physical discomfort and needed the other to attend to it. The facilitator's intervention came across as harsh and inappropriate. The lesson? Do not prescribe the same remedy to all situations that appear similar, since the same symptom may be attributed to a different root cause. Just like in medicine, some apparent ailments may not be ailments at all—some situations may be resolved without intervention (as the latter would have), others may require ``an aspirin,'' and only a few may require ``major surgery.'' In the above case, the facilitator should have paused and asked, ``Is there a problem?'' before taking any remedial measure.

EXAMPLE: No Quorum

What would you do if you had consistent difficulties achieving a quorum at membership meetings? Most boards would introduce a bylaw amendment to reduce the quorum requirement. This solution seems appropriate when the quorum requirement is unreasonably high. However, this solution is not appropriate if the lack of a quorum is due to low member commitment or to boring and wasteful meetings. In the latter cases, you need to address the root causes by raising member commitment levels and by making your meetings more interesting, relevant, and engaging. Try inviting a popular guest speaker on an interesting topic.

How to Use the Two Types of Meeting Ailment Interventions

Once you've identified the root cause behind the symptom, you need to cure the ailment. As illustrated in our troubleshooting guide (Chapter 10), there are two types of interventions:

1. *Remedial Intervention:* What to do when a problem occurs
2. *Preventive Intervention:* How to prevent the problem from occurring at the next meeting

Noting that "An ounce of prevention is worth a pound of cure," preventive interventions are preferred. However, in reality, you will need both. No one can anticipate and prevent all possible ailments.

EXAMPLE: Rush-Hour Syndrome

Thirty minutes before the meeting is scheduled to end, you realize that you are far behind on the agenda. There are ten significant items to be concluded. Rush hour has arrived. As a more effective remedial measure, you can facilitate decisions on each of the remaining agenda items by choosing from the following:

- Doing it (i.e., concluding a discussion at the same meeting)
- Delaying the decision (postponing it to a future meeting)
- Delegating the job (referring it to a committee for study)
- Dropping the issue (withdrawing the proposal altogether)

Typical but ineffective approaches are as follows:

- You rush through the remainder of the agenda and risk making bad decisions in the process.
- You continue the meeting past the closing time, with some members leaving and others staying but resenting the imposition on their time.

You need to plan to avoid the rush-hour dilemma the next time. Your preventive interventions may include:

- Prioritize items and be more selective when placing them on the agenda: Are they ready for informed discussions and decision making, or should they wait? Do they fit within your group's mandate or should they be dropped?
- Estimate and allocate time to major agenda items, facilitate a decision at the beginning of the meeting to approve the time allocation, and give members periodic progress statements relating to time (''We have 10 more minutes for this item'').
- Place important items at the top of the agenda.
- Schedule last-minute additions to the agenda at the end of the meeting, unless the group decides that they are urgent and need to be addressed sooner.

Procedural Interventions or Informal Interventions

From time to time, the chair or a member introduces parliamentary procedure as a way of addressing a problem. In the absence of a shared understanding of rules of order and what they are intended to accomplish, the formal approach can be confusing, time-consuming, and counterproductive.

EXAMPLE: Calling the Question

Discussion of a motion is repetitive and you notice that some members are looking at their watches.

■ *Procedural Intervention.* You say: "I will allow two more speakers and then I will call the question." You probably mean to say that after two more speakers you will close the debate. You don't realize that you have just made yourself a monarch and that under parliamentary procedure you have no authority to impose such a decision on the members.

■ *Common-Sense Intervention (also consistent with the rules of order).* You say: "I am noting that our discussion is becoming repetitive. In light of our busy agenda, would it be acceptable to close the debate after the two members at the microphone have spoken?" Or: "Given our busy agenda, does anyone have anything to add to the discussion, and, if not, shall we proceed to the vote?"

Informal common-sense interventions tend to be softer, clearer, less intimidating, and more compelling than formal interventions. See Chapter 7 for more information on the principled and effective use of parliamentary procedure and rules of order in meetings.

2

The Ten Key Ingredients of a Successful Meeting

It has been said: "If you don't know where you are going, any road will take you there." If all you know is what you do not want to see in a meeting, this negative focus is likely to become a self-fulfilling prophecy. To make a good meeting happen, you need an affirmative vision of what it looks like and a set of principles and criteria with which to measure its success.

This chapter presents the ten main ingredients of a successful meeting:

1. Clarity of mandate, purpose, issues, and process
2. Order and decorum
3. Productivity and forward movement
4. Flexibility and creative thinking
5. Quality decision making
6. Openness, listening, and collaboration
7. Balance, inclusion, and equality
8. Shared responsibility
9. Variety and a light touch
10. Logistical support

These ten ingredients are accompanied by:

- An explanation of what you should generally look for
- A list of symptoms indicating the absence of an ingredient in a meeting

- Premeeting interventions—that is, how to plan for the ingredient to be present at the meeting
- Remedial interventions—that is, what to do during the meeting if the ingredient is missing

At the end of the chapter there is a section on how to use the ten key ingredients as an assessment tool to measure and enhance the quality of your meetings.

Clarity of Mandate, Purpose, Issues, and Process

For a meeting to succeed, several things must be clear:

- *Group's Mandate and Jurisdiction.* Why was the group formed? What was it mandated to achieve? What decisions is it authorized to make? What decisions are outside its jurisdiction?
- *Purpose of the Meeting.* Why is this meeting being held? What specifically needs to be accomplished in it? How is this purpose tied to the group's overall mandate?
- *Issues and Proposals.* Which agenda items are for information only and which ones are for decision making? What proposals need to be voted on? What is the impact of voting yes or voting no on a proposal?
- *Process.* What votes are required (e.g., majority vote, two-thirds vote) for different proposals to pass? What procedural options do members have if they want to modify, delay, or delegate an agenda item, or drop it altogether? What decisions are made by the chair and what decisions are made by the members? How are proposals, amendments, and other procedures handled?

Indicators of a Lack of Clarity

- There are issues on the agenda that are outside your group's mandate.
- Members are angry about a committee or an officer exceeding their authority.

- You are unsure about why a meeting was called or why you were invited to be there.
- You are uncertain as to why an item is on the agenda and how it will be processed.
- Members digress from the agenda.
- Members are not sure about what exactly they are voting on.
- You find yourself confused by technical terms and abbreviations.
- Members argue about the precise wording of a proposal instead of its substance.
- Members argue more about rules of order and procedures than about substantive issues.

Premeeting Interventions to Increase Clarity

- The group's mandate is emphasized in all premeeting documents and communications. In the case of a committee, the terms of reference are in writing and are given to each member.

- Proposed agenda items are screened and prioritized, and only those that fit within the group's mandate are placed on the agenda. It's okay to say no. The agenda is not a free-for-all.

- All necessary research is done and communicated to the members in advance of the meeting.

- Members receive reader-friendly documents and review them before the meeting.

- Proposals or motions are concise, unambiguous, and complete and are circulated to members prior to the meeting to avoid the dreaded and time-consuming "wordsmithing" at the meeting.

- The agenda indicates whether an item is for information, for discussion, or for decision making.

- Members participate in orientation programs, discussing the group's mandate, members' roles and responsibilities, lines of communication and accountability, and meeting procedures.

Remedial Interventions at the Meeting to Ensure Clarity

- The group's mandate and the purpose of the meeting are articulated at the beginning of the meeting and are reinforced whenever needed as the meeting progresses.
- The chair or any member feels free to question how an agenda item fits within the group's mandate.
- Members insist that proposals be concise, complete, and unambiguous before they are voted on.
- The chair repeats the proposals under discussion and verifies that members understand them.
- Technical jargon and abbreviations are explained.
- Meeting procedures are explained and are applied in a people-friendly manner (see Chapter 7).
- Members insist on clarity of procedures.

Order and Decorum

For a meeting to make logical progress, there must be order, civility, and decorum. The general principles that should be upheld are:

- Only one member speaks at a time (after being recognized to speak).
- Vocal or visual distractions should be minimized or eliminated.
- Members should be able to speak without being interrupted as long as they observe time limits and rules of debate.
- Members must remain courteous and use appropriate language.
- Members must keep their comments to the issues, and avoid personal criticisms or speculation on the motives of other members.

Indicators of a Lack of Order and Decorum

- There are side conversations or mini-meetings within the meeting.

- Several members speak at the same time.
- Members speak without getting permission to do so. Whoever has the loudest voice and the most assertive manner prevails.
- Members interrupt one another in midsentence (the "Yes, but" syndrome).
- Members pretend to listen but are busy forming their rebuttals.
- Members use profanities, attack personalities, and speculate on the motives of others.
- Speakers with unpopular views are heckled.
- Cellular phones and beepers go off.
- Members are distracted by outside noises.
- Members arrive late and leave early.

Premeeting Interventions to Ensure Order and Decorum

- Rules of order and decorum are established and communicated to members before the meeting.
- Private discussions are held with frequent offenders, and they are offered direct and principled feedback.
- If necessary (e.g., for a large meeting), the main rules of order and decorum are printed, circulated to members before the meeting, and reviewed at the beginning of the meeting (see Chapter 3 for discussion guidelines and for the chair's overall script for a meeting).

Remedial Interventions at the Meeting to Ensure Order and Decorum

- A motion to approve the discussion guidelines or rules of order can be presented and approved at the beginning of the meeting.
- The chair can make decisive, firm, courteous, and principled interventions to establish and reinforce order and decorum (see Chapter 5 for examples).
- Members should complain if a rule of order or decorum is not observed (if the chair doesn't intervene).

Productivity and Forward Movement

A good meeting moves forward at an appropriate pace, allowing the members to make timely progress along a predefined agenda. At the conclusion of such a meeting, members will leave with a sense of purpose and accomplishment, and with renewed enthusiasm and commitment to the group and its mandate.

The general premise is that time is money and that meetings are expensive. They should be planned and run in a way that maximizes returns on investment. Both the meeting as a whole and each agenda item should provide value.

Indicators of Low Productivity

- The agenda is not completed within the available time.
- Significant agenda items are scheduled at the end of the agenda and are rushed through at the end of the meeting (the rush-hour syndrome).
- Meetings habitually run later than their scheduled closing time (or no closing time has been established).
- No decisions are made.
- Decisions are made, but implementation duties are not assigned.
- Issues that are not ready for decision making consume time.
- Much time is spent on side issues at the expense of substantive issues.
- The discussion is repetitive, rambling, and unfocused.
- Members digress from the agenda.
- Members discuss several issues at once without bringing closure to any of them, leaving many loose ends behind.

Premeeting Interventions to Increase Productivity

- Teach members to communicate briefly and clearly. Tell them what you will discuss, substantiate your argument in point form (point 1, point 2, point 3), and then summarize what you told them.

- Establish a realistic scope and time frame for the meeting.
- Allocate time for main agenda segments and prepare timed agendas (see Chapter 3).
- Schedule high-priority items at the beginning of the meeting.
- Prepare decision-oriented documents and reports, clearly identifying options, proposals, and motions in a concise and reader-friendly manner.
- Have private discussions and offer feedback to members who consistently ramble and repeat themselves. Tread carefully and watch for those egos, but with clarity and with principled discussions you should do just fine.
- Delete agenda items that are not "ripe" for productive discussion.
- Analyze time consumption at a meeting on a per issue and a per member basis and share the results with the members. Do you spend 90% of the time achieving 10% of the results? Do 10% of the members consume 90% of the available time?
- Establish time constraints with guest speakers and indicate to them how they will be alerted when their time is about to expire.

Remedial Interventions at the Meeting to Increase Productivity

- When the meeting begins, agree on the agenda and the time frame.
- Give periodic progress reports on time.
- Give concise progress summaries on issues (e.g., "The main points raised so far are: 1, 2, 3. The issues that we appear to agree on are: 1, 2, 3. The unresolved issues are: 1, 2, 3").
- Use visual aids to summarize and illustrate progress.
- Address rambling, digressions, and repetitions with courteus but firm interventions (e.g., "Are we ready to move on?"). See Chapters 4 and 5.

- Question the need to spend more time on a side issue at the expense of more significant issues.
- Use creative ways to enforce time limits (e.g., an hourglass, a cowbell, a light timer, or even a train whistle). Some of these may not be appropriate to all situations.
- Use creative ways to deal with being deadlocked and making no progress (e.g., taking a break, going for a walk with persons holding the opposing view and trying to advocate their positions for a change).

Flexibility and Creative Thinking

To produce good decisions, a meeting needs to have a good balance between:

- Structure, formality, efficiency, and a sense of purpose (forward movement)
- Flexibility and opportunities for free and creative thinking (lateral movement)

The degree of structure and formality needed will vary from group to group and from issue to issue. If a meeting is large or deals with controversial or complex issues, more structure will likely be needed. Conversely, if a meeting is small and the level of collaboration is high, less structure will be needed, and too much of it would likely be oppressive and counterproductive. Formality and structure should only be used in a manner that frees the members to be creative and make good collective decisions, rather than constraining and frustrating them.

Establishing the structures for a meeting (agenda, time frame, and rules of order) is important. At the same time, departure from a predetermined plan or formal procedure is the best thing to do when a group is bogged down and is not making progress. For example:

- If an approved agenda is proving to be unworkable, the group should be able to change it as long as such a deci-

sion is made by the group and not by one vocal and demanding member.
- If rules of order are proving to be too oppressive, the group should be free to have informal and unstructured discussion for a while, without any motions, as long as fundamental principles are being adhered to and basic rights are protected (see Chapter 7).

Indicators of a Lack of Flexibility and Creative Thinking

- Time limits being enforced too rigidly, with discussions ending abruptly and prematurely
- Excessive use of rules of order (usually at the insistence of one vocal member and without serving any useful purpose)
- Members being intimidated by rules of order or time limits, and therefore hesitating to speak
- Decisions seeming predictable and lacking a creative touch

Premeeting Interventions to Increase Flexibility and Creative Thinking

- Present the timed agenda as a flexible guideline that can be modified by the group.
- Plan diverse discussion methods to stimulate creativity and thinking outside the box (small group discussions, case studies, etc.).
- Have private discussions with "closet parliamentarians" who insist on procedural accuracy when it is not necessary (see Chapter 7 for more help).

Remedial Interventions at the Meeting to Increase Flexibility and Creative Thinking

- Monitor the mood of the meeting when the time allocated for an agenda item has expired, and, if needed, facilitate a decision to extend the discussion time (with the group knowing that this would take time away from other issues).

- Strive to expand the range of possible solutions when complex or contentious decisions are being made, to encourage creative thinking instead of locking into the first and most obvious solution.
- Introduce more options than just voting for or against a motion if consensus appears to be elusive—for example, postponement, referral to a committee for study, or withdrawal of the proposal.
- Deformalize the discussion by having fewer motions.
- Protect members whose unpopular or unusual ideas are criticized or trivialized too quickly.
- Discourage points of order on procedural violations of a purely technical character that do not appear to cause any harm (see Chapter 7).

Quality Decision Making

The success of a meeting is ultimately measured by the quality of the decisions made in it. The more complex and controversial the issues are, the more important it is to ensure that the decisions:

- Are in the organization's best interests and support the attainment of its mandate.
- Are logical, wise, responsible, and compelling.
- Take into account the needs of internal and external stakeholders.
- Are made after consideration of all known data.
- Are made after considering all their impacts (short term, intermediate, and long term).
- Reflect courage, creativity, and visionary thinking "outside the box".
- Solve real problems rather than surface issues.

Indicators of Low-Quality Decisions

- Important reports are circulated at the meeting itself and not in advance.

- Some members open the precirculated envelopes containing documents for the meeting just before the meeting begins. (How likely are they to make informed and intelligent decisions?)
- Much time is spent clarifying issues instead of discussing them.
- Much time is spent on semantics instead of fundamental principles and impacts.
- Members routinely "rubber stamp" committee or staff recommendations without questioning.
- Insufficient time is allocated to significant issues.
- Members are guided by past precedents and hesitate to question the status quo or the "prevailing wisdom."
- Decisions are rushed through by aggressive majorities, or by dominant chairs or members.

Premeeting Interventions to Enhance the Quality of Decisions

- Conduct orientation programs to entrench the notion that members must prepare for meetings and review all documents.
- Hold private discussions with members who consistently do not prepare sufficiently for meetings.
- Conduct a full analysis of the problem and the impacts of proposed solutions before the meeting if the issues are significant, complex, or contentious.
- Allocate the appropriate amount of time to substantive issues.

Remedial Interventions at the Meeting to Enhance the Quality of Decisions

- Encourage questioning and healthy scrutiny of proposals ("There is no such thing as a stupid question or comment").
- Send the message that it is okay to question prevailing wisdom and challenge the status quo.

- Focus the discussion on bottom-line problems and away from surface issues.
- Question the introduction of issues that are relevant only to narrow interests.
- Intervene to caution about the impact of hasty decisions.

Openness, Listening, and Collaboration

Frequently, members come to meetings with their minds already made up on key issues. If this is the case, why have a meeting and why place such issues on the agenda? Why would you invest time and money in a futile endeavor that makes no difference and yields no return?

If time is to be spent in a meaningful way and if the debate is to stand a chance of truly making a difference, members must come to the meeting with an open mind. They must be prepared to set aside their personal biases at least temporarily, learn from others no matter how new to the organization they are (in fact, the newest member may have the most interesting and helpful insights), and work together with adversaries to advance the mandate of the organization.

Indicators of a Lack of Openness, Listening, and Collaboration

- There are frequent interruptions, often in midsentence.
- Members are driven by narrow interests rather than the broad interests of the organization.
- Members are intimidated by the adversarial tone of the discussion and hesitate to participate.
- Arm-twisting and bartering occur before the meeting, with efforts to build a majority in favor of or against a proposal.
- Members attack other members' personalities or motives.
- There is little or no tolerance for fresh or unusual ideas.

Premeeting Interventions to Increase Openness, Listening, and Collaboration

- Have private discussions with dissident members or groups to seek collaboration at the meeting.

- Entrench the notion that representatives of subgroups must place the broad interests of the organization ahead of the interests of their respective subgroups.
- Involve members from all sides of a dispute in meeting assignments, thereby turning them from critics to active and constructive contributors.

Remedial Interventions at the Meeting to Increase Openness, Listening, and Collaboration

- Intervene firmly and courteously to keep members listening and working collaboratively to serve the broad interests of the entire organization.
- Encourage critics to become creators. Challenge them to propose solutions instead of criticizing and complaining.
- Entrench the following notions:

    —*On Listening:* "God gave us two ears and one mouth so that we may listen at least twice as much as we speak." Remind your members of this phrase when they are quick to trivialize other arguments ("We've already tried it," or "This won't work because Bernie won't like it") and when they interrupt one another with "Yes, but" statements. "Yes, but" acts as a verbal eraser, especially when the "but" part is delivered with great passion, making the "yes" part appear as a gesture of tokenism.

    —*On Collaboration:* "Instead of you against me, can we work on the basis of you and me against the problem?" Collective decision making is not about one side winning and one side losing but about making the best decisions for the entire organization.

    —*On Divisive Issues:* "Debate must be hard on the problem and the principles, but soft on the people." And: "Diversity of opinions is what makes us a strong organization. A different opinion should not be seen as a threat but as a different piece of the truth. If we listen carefully, we will be able to make intelligent decisions based on the bigger truth."

Balance, Inclusion, and Equality

It is amazing how many bright and insightful individuals sit through a meeting without uttering a single word. Conversely, many meeting chairs express the wish and hope that they could overcome apathy and engage quieter members in discussions.

Hoping for equal participation in a meeting is laudable, but hope alone won't do it. Concrete steps must be taken to achieve balanced participation, or else the most outspoken, assertive, or knowledgeable members will dominate. Without broadly based input, the quality of the decisions will likely suffer.

Balance means creating an even playing field where each member has the same opportunity to speak, share insights, and influence decisions. It means that the meeting is structured in a way that makes it easy, convenient, and safe for all members to express their views. With this approach, more pieces of the truth will emerge and the quality of the decisions will rise dramatically.

Indicators of Unbalanced Participation

- The same members speak and establish the direction for discussions every time.
- Discussions and decisions are predictable, and there is a sense of sameness.
- Most members say nothing or very little at the meeting.
- Follow-up assignments are usually taken by the same people.
- The wishes of the majority succumb to the passions of individual members (anarchy).

Premeeting Interventions to Ensure Balanced Participation

- Contact quieter members between meetings, asking for their input, giving them specific tasks, encouraging them to raise questions and concerns, and alerting them that you might just call on them for input even if they don't raise their hands.

- Contact dominant members, asking them to make room for others to participate and alerting them that you will intervene to prevent domination and ensure balanced participation.
- Design the agenda so that as many members as possible take lead roles at the meeting.

Remedial Interventions to Ensure Balanced Participation

- Ensure that members speak by raising their hands and waiting to be recognized by the chair. If many members wish to speak, establish a speakers' lineup.
- Establish the rule that first-time speakers receive priority over second-time speakers.
- Solicit responses from members who may be quieter but are knowledgeable and insightful. Even if they do not ask to speak, you could say, for example, "Can you help us out with this issue, Frank?"
- Vary the discussion activities to engage more members (see later in this chapter for examples).
- Assign follow-up tasks to new volunteers.
- Measure the approximate percentage of meeting time consumed by each member and share the statistics.

Shared Responsibility

Who is responsible for the success of a meeting? Typically, if anything goes wrong, the finger of blame points in one direction: the chair. Why is the chair so disorganized and so hesitant to enforce the rules and establish order, or, conversely, why is the chair so dictatorial and impatient? Other times, the finger of blame points to a dominant or disruptive member: Why is he so stubborn and inflexible? Why won't she listen? Why is he such a nitpicker?

The maxim to consider is this: Every time you point the finger of blame at someone else, you fail to consider the three fingers pointing in your direction. Blaming others means that you trivialize the impact that your participation can have on the quality of a meeting and the welfare of your organization. You, your colleagues, and your organization deserve better.

Shared responsibility means:

- Empowered members know when to speak up and when to sit back and listen.

- Proactive members maintain high commitment levels to the organization and contribute willingly and actively to achieving its mandate without waiting for someone to ask them to help. (See Chapter 4 for more details on the roles of the member in a meeting and between meetings.)

- Suffering is optional. If the meeting is not going well and the chair is doing nothing about it (or maybe the chair is the worst culprit), members don't just sit back and suffer quietly. They raise procedural and substantive concerns, and seek to have them addressed. For example, if members are digressing from the agenda and the chair is doing nothing about the problem, it is quite acceptable and legitimate for a member to say: "Excuse me, but where are we on the agenda?" After all, time is money, and the organization deserves a good return on its substantial investment in a meeting.

Many members find it uncomfortable to interject and state a concern about the way a meeting is going. However, if you dare to interject, you may discover that you are not alone: Other members who share your concerns will likely thank you for your intervention, and may be motivated to follow your example and do the same in future meetings.

Indicators of a Lack of Shared Responsibility

- Members suffer quietly and don't complain when the meeting is run poorly.
- There is silence when a vote on a proposal is taken, but during the coffee break the real discussion takes place and major concerns are raised about an unwise decision.
- Members criticize others when they are absent and offer no constructive suggestions.

- There is little interest in assuming leadership positions or taking on implementation duties.
- Members miss meetings or come late and leave early.
- Members are at the meeting but are busy doing something else.

Premeeting Interventions to Increase Shared Responsibility

- Conduct orientation programs to empower the members and entrench the notions of due diligence and shared responsibility.
- Have private discussions with members who refuse to take on any duties, do not perform their assigned duties, or do a consistently poor job.
- Develop a recognition program to highlight unique and special contributions, thereby encouraging and perpetuating constructive and proactive participation.
- Invite and welcome feedback from each member between meetings.

Remedial Interventions at the Meeting to Increase Shared Responsibility

- Remind members periodically that suffering is optional. Encourage them to raise substantive or procedural concerns.
- Take member feedback humbly and nondefensively— that is, examine its merits with an open mind and take appropriate action.
- Thank members for expressing a concern, especially when it enhances the quality of the decision or the productivity or climate at the meeting. Consider giving them tangible tokens of appreciation.

Variety and a Light Touch

Are your meetings boring and monotonous? Do members sit in the same chairs, talk to the same people, drink the same coffee, and say the same things at every meeting? Do you sometimes wonder if you've been to this meeting before? Doesn't this monotony and predictability sometimes make you want to avoid meetings altogether?

Meetings don't have to be dull, monotonous, and predictable. They can be varied, dynamic, engaging, and invigorating. They can even be fun. Remember that suffering is optional. Variety should be implemented so that people look forward to meetings. It can be task-oriented (i.e., related to the discussion and the substantive issues and decisions that need to be made) or non–task-oriented.

Task-Oriented Ideas for Variety

- Invite a guest speaker to address a subject related to your organization or an issue on your meeting agenda. If this is too serious for you, consider an entertaining speaker on a subject related to the organization.

- Invite a staff member to make a presentation at a board meeting, explaining his or her roles and the challenges that relate to implementing your board's policies.

- Introduce case studies of other organizations trying to solve similar problems.

- Ask members to work on their own for a few minutes and jot down their thoughts on a selected question. Then call on quieter members to share their thoughts. They will have no excuse to say: "I had no time to think about it."

- Try breaking a complex task into smaller subtasks, then assign each subtask to a smaller discussion group. Have the smaller task forces report back on their findings (say 10 minutes later). If it is a warm day, some task forces could have meetings outside.

Non–task-Related Ideas for Variety

These ideas were actually tried by my clients, some even by conservative organizations:

- Change the seating arrangement so that members get to sit next to someone new at every meeting. Try printing name tags with names on both sides. Then designate a different member at each meeting to arrive early and decide who will sit where.

- Try mild aerobic exercise, which is especially useful for long meetings.

- Provide different and unexpected refreshments or meals.

- Celebrate a member's birthday with a cake. This will yield such benefits as personally recognizing a member, boosting morale, and lightening things up at the meeting.

- Acknowledge and possibly reward a member for a special effort. You may consider having several such accolades ready and interspersing them on the agenda to allow some down time, giving the members a mental break from serious business.

- Hold the meetings at different locations. How about an out-of-town location to avoid distractions? How about branch offices or even field locations (instead of the head office), with different subgroups designated to organize the logistics for each meeting?

- Change the sequence of items on the agenda. One group even tried a "backward" meeting, with adjournment first and approval of the minutes last.

- Rotate the chair. A different member organizes and chairs each meeting. In addition to variety, this can also increase the sense of shared responsibility while cultivating future leaders (a good succession plan). This approach may not be appropriate in more formal boards (e.g., a municipal council, where the mayor is expected to preside over meetings).

- Try a stand-up meeting, with no chairs, no tables, and no sitting on the floor. You may find the meeting time reduced by 40% to 50%.

Creative Ways to Deal with Difficulties in Meetings

- To deal with three members who consistently sat in the same corner of the meeting room and had loud side conversations, the chair tried this: One meeting he arrived early and positioned himself in the corner where the trio would sit. When they arrived and seemed puzzled, he said: "I suppose you're wondering why I am here, in your favorite corner. Well, I couldn't help but notice that you were having a wonderful time here, so I thought I would come and check out what was so special about this place." They got the message.

▪ To facilitate a timely start for meetings, a board scheduled premeeting dinners, with different ethnic foods served each time. The dinners would end just in time for the meeting to start.

A Word of Caution about Variety

Make sure your ideas for variety are appropriate to your group and its culture. In fact, the best ideas for variety will come from your own members. To solicit their ideas, try this approach:

It's been suggested that our meetings are very focused and productive but that they are also somewhat monotonous and predictable. It seems like some variety and a light touch could make our meetings more engaging and more fun. Ideas that others have tried are: _____. What do you think? Do any of these ideas sound interesting? Does anyone have any other ideas to add variety to our meetings and lighten things up a bit without reducing our productivity? If you don't have any ideas now, would you please contact me after the meeting if you think of some?

Logistical Support

Nothing is worse than wasting precious meeting time on fighting logistics battles. Do members who traveled long distances deserve to be kept waiting while a speaker figures out how the overhead projector works, or how to correct the microphone's high-pitched sound?

In a good meeting, no one notices the logistical details. Everything is there when and where you need it. The room setup is just right. The temperature is comfortable, the ventilation works, and the lighting is suitable. The room offers privacy and a quiet and distraction-free environment. The overhead projector, flip chart, and microphones function like clockwork. The refreshments and meals are tasty, healthy, sufficient (not excessive), and are served unobtrusively when needed.

Some Indicators of Poor Logistical Support

- The room is too dark, too cold, or too hot, and no one knows how to adjust the levels.
- The overhead projector's lightbulb is burned out and there is no backup.
- The microphones don't work, or there aren't enough of them.
- A noisy disco or swimming pool next door opens for business halfway through the meeting.
- The chairs are too hard or too soft.
- The coffee is cold or stale, and the soft drinks and juices are warm.
- The meals arrive late and the sandwiches have a lot of butter and very little filling.
- Corky the vegetarian was served a platter with a huge steak and no vegetables.
- There is an overflow crowd and fire regulations do not allow more people in the room.

Premeeting Interventions for Smooth Logistical Support

Logistical requirements must be fully considered and all details should be addressed before the meeting. See Chapter 3.

Using the Ten Key Ingredients as Assessment Tools

The ten key ingredients of a successful meeting are based on common-sense principles and can yield substantial returns on the time, money, and efforts you invest in meetings. Concrete steps must be taken to entrench these principles by:

- Visionary and preventive planning (see Chapter 3)
- Constructive participation by empowered and proactive members (see Chapter 4)
- Masterful facilitation of meetings (see Chapter 5)

It would be difficult or impossible to have successful meetings without the support of your members. You will need to share your vision of success and its underlying principles with them. Explain to them what it can accomplish and seek their input on how current practices can be changed.

Use this vision as an assessment tool for your collective decision-making processes. Periodic assessments will facilitate discussions on process issues and raise a question that is rarely considered by groups: How do we work together and how do we make collective decisions?

Periodic Assessments

Using the ten key ingredients as periodic assessment tools, you can follow these steps:

1. Use the evaluation form at the end of this chapter to rate your meetings on a scale of 1 to 10, 1 being poor and 10 being excellent. Do some soul searching on your own to determine what is working and what needs improvement.

2. Send the same evaluation form to your members along with an explanatory letter. Ask them to assess your meetings: What is working well, what could be working better, and what are their ideas for improvement?

3. Have a meeting to compare notes and exchange ideas on the results of the evaluation, or add it to the agenda of the next scheduled meeting.

4. Ask your members to prioritize their ideas and then seek to implement them one or two at a time. This way, progress is gradual and ongoing, as it should be. The moment change stops, you risk stagnation and complacency.

5. Use the same checklist periodically (e.g., every 6 months) to determine where you have made progress and where more improvement is needed.

Ongoing Assessments

Using the ten key ingredients as ongoing assessment tools, try the following:

- Schedule a 15-minute segment at the end of every meeting for members to comment on what went well at the meeting, what did not go well, and what should be improved next time.
- Invite members to give you feedback after the meeting by phone, memo, or in person. Honest and direct feedback is sorely needed in organizations. To encourage it, recognize good ideas and their originators publicly. How about rewards for unique and helpful ideas (e.g., free monthly parking or credit toward the purchase of a personal computer)?

Sample Assessment Form

Measuring the Effectiveness of a Meeting

On a scale of 1 (poor) or 10 (excellent), rate your meetings in these areas:

1. Clarity of mandate, purpose, issues, and process   ____
2. Order and decorum   ____
3. Productivity and forward movement   ____
4. Flexibility and creative thinking   ____
5. Quality decision making   ____
6. Openness, listening, and collaboration   ____
7. Balance, inclusion, and equality   ____
8. Shared responsibility   ____
9. Variety and a light touch   ____
10. Logistical support   ____

3

Preventive and Visionary Planning

With professional planning and attention to detail, a good meeting is more likely to occur. Planning may be tedious and time-consuming, but it is time well invested.

In this chapter, the following subjects are covered:

- Planning principles
- The "Whys" of planning
- The "Whats" of planning
- The "Whens" of planning
- The "Whos" of planning
- The "Wheres" of planning
- Discussion guidelines
- Premeeting communication and conflict management
- Meeting day checklist
- The chair's script

Planning Principles

It is amazing to see how casually the planning of a meeting is often treated. A manager might call a meeting on a moment's notice to solve an urgent problem without a clear idea of what the problem is, whether it is ready for informed and productive discussion, and whether it justifies taking members away from their busy schedules. There might not be an agenda, background material, or a designated time frame to accomplish the issue at hand. It is no wonder that many people view meetings with cynicism and contempt. They think the phrase "productive meeting" is an oxymoron.

A productive meeting happens by design. Planning efforts are carried on "off line" (before the meeting) so that "prime time" (meeting time) can provide the greatest possible returns on the substantial investment in the meeting.

Eleven Questions Typically Missed by Meeting Planners

1. How substantial will the investment in the meeting be? How can the returns on this investment be maximized?
2. Do you need a meeting at all? Could the same or even better results be achieved by less expensive means, for example, exchanging information and building consensus by memos, fax, e-mail, teleconferencing, or videoconferencing (see Chapter 9)?
3. Should agenda items be screened to exclude those that are not related to the group's mandate or those that are not ripe for discussion and decision making?
4. Should time be budgeted for the main agenda items?
5. Should you invite to the meeting only those who have a valuable contribution to make?
6. Have sufficient opportunities for meaningful participation been created?
7. Should potential proposals or motions be precirculated to members before the meeting?
8. How much time should be allocated to an invited speaker's presentation? How will he or she be notified that time is running out?
9. Should a condensed list of discussion guidelines or rules of order be prepared in anticipation of a contentious meeting?
10. Should you attempt to address tensions among members proactively before the meeting?
11. Are there any potential distractions that could disrupt the meeting?

General Planning Considerations and Principles

- Anticipate and ask "what if" questions. The moment you think you have everything handled, something else will need attention.
- The planner's greatest enemies are assumptions. It is tempting and easy to assume that things will just fall into place. Some things may, but others won't unless you make sure they do.
- Necessary planning efforts will increase with the size of the meeting, and with the complexity and divisiveness of the issues to be addressed.
- Planning a meeting should not be a solitary task and efforts should be made to involve members in it. The team effort will enhance the quality of the meeting and increase the sense of ownership and shared responsibility. In addition to delegating certain planning tasks (e.g., logistical details), members can be contacted to ensure that they are making progress on assigned duties and to solicit their feedback on the proposed agenda.

The "Whys" of Planning

Your planning activities should be guided by:

- The group's mandate and jurisdiction (the global "why")
- The purpose of the meeting (the specific "why")

Group's Mandate and Jurisdiction

The first factor to consider when planning a meeting is the group's mandate, as defined in its governing documents, for example, bylaws, terms of reference, and mission statement. Advancing the group's mandate is an important return on the investment of time, money, and efforts in a meeting.

Related to the mandate is the issue of the group's jurisdiction. For example:

- A committee should not assume spending authority and other powers unless they were clearly specified in its terms of reference.

- A governing board should concentrate on governance issues (policies, goals, and priorities for the organization). Precious board meeting time should not be consumed by micromanaging the organization and becoming involved in operational or administrative issues. Those should be attended to by the staff under the chief executive officer's direction.

- Members or shareholders in a large general meeting cannot make binding decisions in areas that are within the exclusive jurisdiction of the governing board.

To achieve clarity and a sense of purpose, plan to make the group's mandate prominent. Consider the following ideas to emphasize the group's mandate before and during a meeting:

- Question the need for agenda items that seem to be irrelevant to the group's mandate.
- Display the group's mandate in large print behind the person chairing the meeting or in another prominent place.
- State the group's mandate at the opening of the meeting.
- Read the organization's main purposes or mission statement at the beginning of a meeting.

Planning to entrench the group's mandate will make the meeting better focused. It will give importance to a few vital questions that are often ignored during meetings:

- Why are we here?
- What are we trying to accomplish?
- Who are we serving?
- What values do we seek to uphold?

With this sense of purpose and direction, the likelihood of the often unasked question: "Why are we wasting our time discussing the issue?" will diminish.

The Purpose of the Meeting

The broad mandate will give you the long-term view (or *macro* agenda) of the group's work. With this perspective, you'll need to assess the *micro* view, determine the purpose for each meeting, and plan it accordingly. Ask:

- What is this meeting called for—to inform the members of new developments or progress, to receive and discuss reports, to make decisions, or a combination thereof? What issues need to be addressed? What questions need to be given collective answers?
- How far will this meeting advance the group's mandate or the macro agenda?
- Given the purpose of the meeting and what it is expected to achieve, are the projected returns on investment substantial enough to justify the costs of holding the meeting? Can the same or better results be achieved in a virtual meeting (see Chapter 9)?

The "Whats" of Planning

The agenda is your master plan or road map for the meeting. It reflects your vision of how the meeting will unfold step by step to accomplish its purpose. This section presents the following aspects of agenda design:

- Who should design the agenda?
- Screening and prioritizing agenda items.
- Estimating and allocating time to agenda items.
- Establishing the order of agenda items.
- Activities and flow in connection with each agenda item.
- Using consent agendas to move things along.
- Including proactive agenda items to make the meeting more interesting and meaningful.
- Other ideas for agenda design.
- A sample agenda.

Who Should Design the Agenda?

To promote shared responsibility, members should be given opportunities to help design the agenda. This will increase their sense of ownership and commitment to the agenda and its completion. At the same time, there is a need for central management of the agenda. To balance member input with global management, the following system could be established:

- A preliminary meeting agenda is designed by an individual designated by the group, for example, the chair, or a designated member, or a staff person.
- Members have a channel through which they can request that certain agenda items be added: They can contact the agenda designer, or the agenda designer can poll them for requests.
- The agenda designer is given the authority to screen proposed agenda items and determine whether they will be scheduled (see next section on screening criteria).
- Before the meeting the agenda designer informs proponents of agenda items on whether their proposed items have been included, and, if not, why.
- A preliminary agenda is circulated to the members along with support documentation.
- Time permitting, members are given an opportunity to offer feedback and suggestions on the preliminary agenda. If possible and advisable, adjustments to the agenda are made.
- At the start of the meeting, individual members may propose that unscheduled items be added to the agenda (e.g., items that were turned down by the agenda designer). They should be ready to explain the nature and urgency of such items, and how much time they will require. The group may agree or refuse to accommodate such requests: If a member objects to the inclusion of an unscheduled item, the group votes on whether it should be included.
- Prescheduled items are generally addressed before last-minute additions, except if the group decides that an unsched-

uled item should be addressed sooner—that is, the group deems it to be more urgent than the items that it will precede.

- Note that it is best to let the group settle disputes related to the agenda. This approach is fairer and more democratic than giving the chair the power to settle such disputes (monarchy) or allowing the proponent to dictate his or her wishes (anarchy).

Screening and Prioritizing Agenda Items

The following screening criteria should be used to determine whether an item will be placed on the agenda, and, if so, what priority it should be given:

- Does the item fit within the group's mandate and the overall purpose of the meeting?
- Is there a real need to place it on the agenda, or has it been scheduled on past agendas because of traditions and the force of habit? Is it worthy of the time invested in it?
- Is the item ripe for productive discussion and informed decision making?
- Must the item be addressed at this meeting or can it be delayed?
- How urgent and significant is this item when compared with others?
- What work and what documents are needed to prepare the item for a productive discussion and informed and focused decision making? Is there enough time to do it?
- Who will lead the discussion of this item (make a presentation, take questions)?
- If the item belongs on the agenda, how much time will it require (see next section on allocating time to agenda items)?
- Is the item confidential and should it be scheduled for an in-camera (closed) meeting (e.g., sensitive contract negotiations, advice from the solicitor, personal privacy issues)?

After a preliminary screening of agenda items, the scope of the meeting and the time required for it will become evident. Given this information, decide on one of the following actions for each agenda item:

- Deal with it—that is, leave it on the agenda.
- Delay it—that is, put it on the agenda for the next meeting.
- Delegate it—that is, designate a committee or staff to study it or look after it in some other way.
- Drop it—that is, decide it is outside the group's mandate or is not worthy of any action.

If the scope of the meeting seems too narrow, consider these tough questions:

- Is there a need to spend time and money on this meeting?
- Is the work of this group completed or diminished? If so, should the group be disbanded?
- Is the group delegating too much of its power, leaving it with too little to do?

Do not dismiss too quickly the need to have a meeting even if at first look the gains appear to be small. Meetings can provide intangible benefits by binding a group together and turning it into a more cohesive team. A weekly staff meeting is a good habit to perpetuate, but it needs a basic structure that will provide benefits. For example, members should report on progress and share ideas and concerns, the manager should present updates, and some decisions should be made.

In some cases, a meeting is required by the governing statute or bylaws (e.g., the annual meeting of a company or a society) and canceling it is not an option. Remember that suffering is optional and consider adding items to the bare-bones agenda to make the meeting more interesting and appealing. You could:

- Have a keynote address relating to the group's mandate. Make sure to let guest speakers know how much time they will have and how you will let them know that time is running out.

- Plan small group discussions to collect ideas on issues that affect the organization, thereby building a sense of community and involving members who refuse to speak in public.
- Consider some activities on the lighter side, for example, an entertaining presentation when the formal business is over, door prizes, or creative refreshments such as international desserts.

Estimating and Allocating Time to Agenda Items

Meetings are costly (see Chapter 1) and should be budgeted for with caution. The time required for each major agenda item or category of items should be estimated proportionately to the returns on the time invested. Here are some suggestions:

- Estimate realistically based on your analysis of agenda items.
- Avoid planning so tightly that you have no room to maneuver. Provide for contingencies in case you underestimated the time required.
- Allocate less time for routine and noncontroversial items.
- Allocate more time for items that attract intense interest or are controversial.
- Allocate more time for complex proposals to allow the members to absorb technical details and make informed decisions.
- If in hindsight it appears that you underestimated or overestimated the time needed for certain agenda items, apply the lessons learned when designing future agendas.
- Avoid scheduling too many items on the agenda and consolidate related items. For example, a client was about to deal with thirty proposals in 2 hours. The establishment of a resolutions committee to consolidate or eliminate proposals was suggested. The number of proposals was reduced to ten.

- With the proposed time allocations, map out the agenda. Start with the opening time (say 7 PM), continue with a few interim milestones (e.g., 7:30 PM personnel report, 8:15 PM finance report), and end with the projected closing time (say 9 PM). This will enable you to measure the progress of the meeting (see the sample agenda at the end of this section).
- Avoid a minute-by-minute synopsis of the meeting (e.g., 7 PM start, 7:01 PM minutes, 7:02 PM chair's report), since it is unrealistic, constraining, and hard to enforce.
- Avoid putting down durations (e.g., budget 30 minutes, personnel report 15 minutes, etc.), since the members will have to add up the numbers to find out if they are on time. Instead, put down fixed times (e.g., 7:20 PM budget, 7:50 PM personnel report).
- Make it clear that the allocated times are only a flexible guideline to ensure that there are not many unfinished items at closing time, thus avoiding the rush-hour syndrome.

Establishing the Order of Agenda Items

Most groups follow a standard agenda and do not give themselves permission to depart from it. I suggest that you avoid being held prisoner to past practices. There is nothing scientific or magical about standard agendas, so feel free to experiment and see what sequence works best.

Consider the following when determining the sequence of agenda items:

- Deal with routine items first (e.g., approval of minutes and routine updates and reports), provided that they do not consume excessive amounts of time. Spending large amounts of time arguing about such items at the expense of more substantive items is a waste of time.
- Schedule items that must be concluded early or for a time when it is certain that a quorum will be present.
- Schedule items that require creativity when the best concentration can be achieved, for example, early in the meeting and not after a heavy lunch (which should be avoided anyway).

■ Avoid scheduling too many substantive items in succession and intersperse lighter items to give the brain a rest. For example, break the continuity by recognizing special efforts or acknowledging a member's birthday. Lighter items need not be placed on the official agenda but can be saved for use on an as-needed basis.

■ Leave room at the end of the agenda for new business to allow for unscheduled items to be addressed. Note that the group should be allowed to decide informally or by a formal vote to agree or refuse to consider an unscheduled item, or to give an unscheduled item a special priority and deal with it earlier on the agenda.

■ Avoid predictability and feel free to experiment with the sequence of agenda items with the group's permission. For example, switch the order of reports or even have a backward meeting (i.e., starting with the item that is ordinarily last).

■ Remember that there is more than one right way to run a meeting. As long as the business gets done and the expected benefits materialize, no harm is done by experimenting with different sequences of agenda items.

Activities and Flow for Each Agenda Item

As a planner, you need to determine the most effective way for each agenda item to unfold. Some will require simplicity whereas others will require more elaborate treatment. Ask:

■ Is the item of a routine or housekeeping nature?
■ Is the item for information only, or does it require debate and decision making? If it is the latter, what questions need to be answered and what decisions need to be made?
■ Is the item simple or complex? Do many technical terms need to be explained?
■ Is it an issue on which there is broad agreement or is it a controversial one?

Examples of agenda items that do not require elaborate treatment are:

■ *Minutes of Previous Meetings.* All that's needed is to check if the minutes are an accurate reflection of what took place in a meeting (see Chapter 8). There is no need to rediscuss the decisions made in previous meetings. Any follow-up or progress on past decisions can be discussed under the appropriate report on the agenda.

■ *Routine Items and Reports for Information Only.* A brief update in concise point form and an opportunity to ask questions are sufficient. Avoid the painful practice of having the entire report read out loud. Ensure that report presenters recognize this procedure before the meeting. There is also no need to vote on the report if it contains no recommendations (see Chapter 7).

If an agenda item requires decision making, a more elaborate treatment will be needed. In order to properly frame the discussions, an individual or a committee can be assigned to prepare an analysis for circulation prior to the meeting. The analysis should address these questions:

■ What exactly is the problem to be solved?
■ What are the fundamental issues, needs, and interests that must be addressed?
■ What are the criteria for a good solution?
■ What are some of the options that could be considered?
■ What motions might be needed to facilitate the debate and decision making?

When considering how the discussion and decision-making process will unfold, try to balance expediency with member involvement. Also seek to introduce variety, to avoid monotony and repetitiveness, and to keep the members engaged and interested. For the more substantive items, discussion activities may include:

■ Summaries by designated lead presenters followed by discussions of key points.

■ Plenary discussions that involve the entire group around the same table addressing clearly defined questions, followed by problem solving and decision making.

- Breakout groups or task forces with different questions considered by different groups (in parallel) for a specified amount of time. This is followed by task force reports and discussions by the full group.

- A short time frame (e.g., 2 minutes) when individuals work on their own and jot down their answers to a specific question. At the end of the specified time, members may be surveyed at random or everyone may be polled for a brief comment. This procedure encourages participation from quiet members.

- Analysis of case studies (e.g., what other organizations did in a similar situation).

- Presentations by senior staff members on selected topics.

- Presentations by outside experts and consultants.

- Other creative methods of engaging the members in discussions.

EXAMPLE: An Unusual Discussion Activity

To build consensus on an organization's priorities, a facilitator listed ten of them on separate sheets of paper and placed them on the walls around the room. Members were given three small stickers each and were asked to place one sticker on each of their favorite priorities. They were also asked to discuss the priorities with others. After 30 minutes, the charts with the largest numbers of stickers indicated the highest-priority items. Additionally, members were energized from walking around the room instead of sitting. Even the quiet members were engaged in the process. Thus, there is more than one way to reach consensus, so why not give your group permission to experiment?

Using Consent Agendas to Move Things Along

To expedite progress and save time, routine and noncontroversial items can be grouped into a consent agenda so that they can be addressed as one package. The procedure for handling the consent agenda at the meeting is as follows:

- Members who believe that an item on the consent agenda requires separate consideration can request to take the item out.
- The items that remain in the consent agenda are voted on as a package.
- The items taken out of the consent agenda are treated separately.

In meetings with large volumes of business to address and with many members in attendance, it may be desirable to place limits on members' ability to take an item out of the consent agenda, for example, a request by at least 10% of the members present would be needed to do so.

Adding Proactive Agenda Components

You may get the sense during a meeting that you are doing everything that you have to do (i.e., agenda items dictated by the outside world, by some crisis, or by established routines) and none of the things that you want to do (i.e., issues that relate to the organization's mandate and future, and lend themselves to being creative and visionary. If so, your meeting agenda probably includes reactive components but no proactive components. To make your group's work more interesting, meaningful, and engaging, you need to deliberately schedule visionary or proactive items on the agenda for every meeting. You can try the following steps:

1. Dig out that long-range strategic plan that has been gathering dust on the shelf. If you don't have one, gather your group and create one. Call this long-term plan the macro agenda.
2. Divide the macro agenda into smaller components called proactive components.
3. Schedule at least one proactive component per meeting agenda.
4. Call each meeting agenda a micro agenda.
5. Make sure the micro agenda has two parts: a reactive component (what you have to do) and a proactive com-

ponent (what you want to do). Dedicate enough time to the latter, and make the discussions engaging and meaningful.

The following questions can be addressed in the proactive part of the agenda:

- How can we serve our members or customers better?
- What creative fund-raising methods should we consider?
- How can we keep our members informed and consulted about new initiatives?
- How can we work more effectively with government agencies?
- How can we influence legislative change at the various government levels?
- How can we collaborate with similar organizations to help further our mandate?
- How can we improve our communications with the community and the general public?
- How can we improve our relationship with the news media?
- How can we capitalize on the skills, knowledge, and experience of our staff and volunteers?
- How should we recognize and reward individual achievements and contributions?
- How can we celebrate our collective successes?
- What can we do to facilitate the regular and ad-hoc exchange of feedback?
- What can we do to anticipate internal disputes and prevent them from escalating?
- How can we enhance the quality of our meetings?

Other Ideas for Agenda Design

An agenda can be enhanced by indicating next to each item or on the support documents:

- Whether the item is for information only, for discussion, or for decision making.

- Who is responsible for presenting the item and taking questions on it. Try to spread the work and get more members involved.
- What support documents are attached.
- What the options are for decision making.
- What motions are needed for closure. Include at least preliminary wording to save time at the meeting. If more than one motion is possible, include the wording for all of them.
- A numbering system for agenda items (e.g., 00-05-16-06, being the sixth agenda item at the May 16, 2000, meeting).
- A numbering system in the minutes of the meeting that is consistent with the agenda items so that members can cross-reference from the agenda to the minutes.

It has been said: "The human mind will absorb only as much as the human seat will endure." Don't forget to schedule a refreshment break every 1½ to 2 hours, or when a significant milestone has been reached.

A Sample Agenda

Information Technology Department Meeting (April 4, 2000)

12:45 PM: Registration, refreshments, networking
1 PM sharp: Meeting begins
4 PM (or sooner): Adjournment
Location: Committee room number 1, head office

1 PM sharp:

1.	Opening remarks	Libby Smith	
2.	Agenda, activities		
3.	Approval of minutes		
4.	Reports:		
4.1	Finance	Derek Ng	For information only

| 4.2 Personnel | Joan Smith | Proposal: Hire a new secretary |

2:30 PM: Refreshment break

2:40 PM:
  5.   Unfinished business:

| 5.1 Computer upgrade | Norm Sutton | Proposal: Option A (see report) |

3:20 PM:
  6.   New business
       (proactive component):

| 6.1 Staff recognition program | Everyone | Brainstorm for ideas |

4 PM: Adjournment

Notes
1. There will be refreshments (coffee, soda, desserts) and informal networking at 12:45 PM.
2. We will start at 1 PM sharp. We must conclude the meeting no later than 4 PM to enable members to attend to other commitments. Thank you in advance for your support.
3. Please contact Libby Smith at local 2223 if you want to:
   a. Raise a question or concern about the agenda.
   b. Propose an item for the "New Business" portion.

The "Whens" of Planning

This section discusses:

- Choosing the time frame for a meeting
- Planning to start on time
- Planning to end on time or sooner

Choosing the Time Frame for a Meeting

The time frame for a meeting should be chosen after considering the schedules of members. Yes, it is impossible to accommodate everyone all the time, but to avoid poor attendance it's a good idea to consider the following questions:

- Will members be able to be there on time and stay for the full duration of the meeting?
- Is an important event being held at the same time you're considering for the meeting?
- Do some members have to catch flights or be concerned with a public transportation schedule?
- Is the proposed meeting time during rush hour, which would make it difficult to predict whether members would make it on time?
- Is it lunchtime or dinnertime, and, if so, should you arrange a light meal?
- Is it happy hour or another significant social-gathering time?
- Should the meeting be on a weekday or a weekend? During the day or in the evening?
- Are your members most alert in the morning or later in the day?
- Are there additional costs or constraints associated with a particular month, day, or time (e.g., overtime costs for a weekend, busy convention facilities in the spring or fall)?
- Is a suitable meeting room available at the proposed time?
- Will you have access to the room before the meeting starts so that you can test audiovisual equipment? Is another meeting scheduled in the same room immediately afterward?

Once the date and time frame of the meeting have been chosen:

- Inform members of the timing of the meeting.
- Confirm that they will be there for the full duration of the meeting.
- Plan to start on time and end on time or possibly sooner (see the next sections).

Planning to Start on Time

Starting a meeting late means that precious time is wasted with no return on investment. Waiting for latecomers or taking time to summarize progress for them is unfair to those who make the effort to arrive on time. Here are some ideas for facilitating a timely start for a meeting:

- Schedule the meeting to start at a realistic and reasonable time.
- State the starting time in the notice and on the precirculated agenda, for example, 7 PM sharp.
- State the importance of arriving on time and being there for the duration of the meeting.
- Schedule a premeeting meal or another activity that will entice members to arrive early, and put it on the agenda, for example, 8:30 AM: Networking and refreshments. 9 AM sharp: Meeting begins.
- Put an interesting item early on the agenda, possibly something that would be fun and that the members would not want to miss.
- Confirm the starting time with the members in writing and by phone if necessary.
- Entrench the notion that those who arrive on time deserve to have the meeting started on time.
- Alert the members that the meeting is about to begin a few minutes before the scheduled start time: "It is now 8:57. The meeting will begin as scheduled at 9 AM, so please get your coffee and take your seat."
- Never underestimate your ability to facilitate change. Even if past meetings always started late, you can start a new trend. And please don't give up after the first attempt!

Some of the more creative ideas that clients have used to achieve promptness are as follows:

- Giving prizes for consistent early arrivals and for good attendance records.
- Imposing a fine system, whereby each member pays set

amounts for tardiness, early departures, or being absent from a meeting (except in the event of sickness or family emergency) with the money raised being given to charity or used for a fun event at the end of the year.

Planning to End on Time or Sooner

To increase the likelihood of ending the meeting on time or sooner:

- Ensure that your overall agenda and time allocations are realistic.
- Indicate on the agenda the closing time and a few interim milestones so that progress and timing can be monitored during the meeting (see sample agenda earlier in this chapter).
- Have the agenda and time frame approved at the beginning of the meeting to create a shared commitment for a timely closure on issues.
- Reinforce the time allocations in the chair's opening script: "You'll note that we are scheduled to end the discussion on the budget at 10, then have a break, and then carry on with the systems report. We are scheduled to conclude the agenda by noon. I know that some of you need to leave right at noon for another meeting, so we'll need to work together to stay on track and on time."
- Give periodic updates on timing as the meeting moves along, for example: "We have 5 minutes left for this item," or "It is 11:50 and we need to do the following things before our lunch break."
- Facilitate a decision by the members on extending the time if more is needed for an item (informally, by asking: "How much more time do we need for this item? Is it acceptable to continue until 10:15?" or formally, by taking a vote on a proposed extension).
- Notify guest speakers and advisers in advance of the meeting how much time they will have and how you will let them know when they need to end (e.g., passing a note or giving an appropriate visual signal).

- Establish an appropriate pace for the meeting so that the group can reach closure on issues without rushing the decision-making process.
- Discourage rambling, repetition, and digressions from the agenda.
- Facilitate a decision to postpone an issue to the next meeting if progress seems impossible, or a decision to refer it to a committee for detailed consideration.
- Be prepared to intervene if time is spent unproductively (see Chapters 4 and 5).

The "Whos" of Planning

In this section the following questions are examined:

- Who should be invited to a meeting?
- Who should not be invited to a meeting?
- How should mandatory attendance be handled?
- Who should attend an in-camera (i.e., closed or confidential) meeting?

Who Should Be Invited to a Meeting?

Invitees to a meeting may include some or all of the following:

- The voting members of the group
- Those who have useful information to offer
- Outside experts or advisers on key issues
- Guest speakers
- Those who will be affected by decisions made at the meeting
- Those who will be involved in implementing the decisions
- Those who have the power to block or undermine the implementation of a contentious decision and who might work against it if they are not kept in the loop

As you invite individuals to attend the meeting, you'll need to clarify the rights and roles of the various parties:

- Who is entitled to speak?
- Who is entitled to make motions?
- Who is entitled to vote?

Who Should Not Be Invited to a Meeting?

There should be a legitimate reason for someone to be at the meeting. Consider the following suggestions:

- If the only reason for inviting someone to a meeting is to keep him or her informed, the same goal can be achieved via a follow-up memo or report.
- Resist the temptation to invite those whose contribution to the meeting is likely to be minimal, or those whose contribution could be offset by the negative impacts of their presence.
- The possibility that someone will be offended by not being invited should not be a factor in deciding whether that person should be there. This is not a popularity contest. The object is not to please everyone but to maximize the return on the substantial investment in the meeting.
- It may be wise to exclude authority figures if their presence could stifle the discussion.
- Clearly, the toughest meeting to chair is one that your boss attends and is predisposed to dominate. Consider carefully whether this person should or should not be invited. If he or she is to be invited, then the two of you will benefit from principled discussions before the meeting begins.

How Should Mandatory Attendance Be Handled?

In some instances, attendance in a meeting is mandatory (e.g., it is ordered by senior management). The commitment levels of members to such meetings can be low, which can make them inefficient and aimless. Even though it is possible to mandate attendance, it is impossible to legislate commitment, enthusiasm, and collaboration.

But don't give up hope. Accept what you cannot change (i.e., the mandatory attendance) and change what you can (i.e., how the meeting will be run). Together with the participants, find a meaningful purpose for the meeting. You can achieve this outcome by asking these questions:

- What do we have in common?
- How could our time together be well spent?
- What benefits could the sponsoring organization derive from this meeting?

Who Should Attend an In-Camera Meeting?

Your invitation list will shrink if the meeting needs to deal with items that require confidentiality. Such meetings are referred to as executive sessions or in-camera meetings. Those who are entitled to attend such meetings are:

- The bona fide members of the group (usually referred to as voting members)
- A confidential secretary to take minutes (unless a member of the group does it)
- Advisers or staff members that the group members agree (informally or by a formal vote) to invite to attend the meeting (or only a portion of it)

In-camera meetings should have their own agendas and minutes. Such meetings are often held after the adjournment of the open meeting. Nonmembers who attend the open meeting are excused as soon as it is adjourned and the closed meeting can then be called to order.

Issues that require confidentiality may include:

- Sensitive contract or labor negotiations, when the organization's economic interests could be harmed if the discussion is held in an open meeting
- Receiving and discussing legal advice, which is subject to attorney-client privileges
- Issues whose public discussion would be an unreasonable invasion of personal privacy
- Other matters as stipulated in the organization's govern-

ing documents (statute, bylaws, terms of reference) or as determined by the members of the group

Here are a few additional points to consider for closed meetings:

- Unless the governing documents stipulate otherwise, the members present at a closed meeting can make decisions. They should not be required to ratify those decisions at an open meeting, since this practice would defeat the object of confidentiality.
- Minutes of a closed meeting should be approved at another closed meeting and not at an open one. Again, to do otherwise would undermine the required confidentiality.
- If, at an open meeting, it becomes apparent that an item requires confidentiality, it should be removed from this meeting's agenda and placed on the agenda of the next closed meeting.
- At some point after a confidential issue has been dealt with, the voting members may agree to declassify it. For example, a contract that was approved at a closed meeting has been signed and it is now public knowledge. The minutes that relate to this issue can then be made public (see Chapter 8 for information on minutes).

The "Wheres" of Planning

Logistical problems can be a minor annoyance or they can worsen an already bad situation. Here are a few examples:

- In a contentious meeting, attended by several hundred angry members, the first half hour is spent determining who is to blame for the microphones not working.
- A hot and stuffy room in the summer or a freezing room in the winter demotivates even the most enthusiastic participants.
- A guest speaker discovers that the overhead projector needed for his or her presentation does not work.

- A planner forgets to check who prefers tea over coffee and who has special dietary needs.

This section covers the main logistical aspects that may require attention when planning a meeting. The list is by no means complete and some of the items are unlikely to apply to small and informal meetings. Specifically, the following topics are discussed:

- Facility selection
- Room setup
- Seating arrangement
- Audiovisual aids
- Catering arrangements
- Registration logistics
- Teleconferencing or videoconferencing

Facility Selection

Ask these questions when choosing the location of the meeting:

- Should the meeting be held on your premises or would an off-site location work better? Your own office might intimidate some members, thereby inhibiting participation.
- Is the facility conveniently located? Is it easy to find? Is it accessible by public transit? Is there sufficient parking?
- Is the room sufficiently large to accommodate the participants? Conversely, is it too large?
- Is the room too narrow? Does it have pillars that will block the view of some members?
- Do you need contingency plans in case of an overflow crowd (e.g., a nearby room with a public address system and video projection capability)?
- What is the facility's track record in hosting similar meetings?
- Are there any potential distractions (e.g., an adjacent pub, a swimming pool, or a noisy fan)? Is a noisy event scheduled next door during the meeting?
- Does the room have windows? Is the lighting level appro-

priate? Do the air-conditioning, heating, and ventilation systems work? Can they be turned off or adjusted easily?
- Are reliable audiovisual aids available? Have they been tested recently? Are electrical outlets conveniently located and is there power in them? Are extension cords needed?
- What are the facility staff's levels of professionalism, responsiveness, and attention to detail?

Room Setup

The room setup can have a significant impact on the climate at the meeting. Here are a few tips:

- With small groups, it is advisable to have a room setup where members can see and hear one another. Try a U-shape or a circle.

- For larger groups, I generally advise against "classroom" or "theater" style, since it tends to perpetuate a lecture mode and "we against you" discussions. Instead, try a set of round tables, which will present the advantage of some informality, a physical sense of community, and the ease of breaking into small group discussions, thereby deformalizing the meeting.

- Try running some meetings without any chairs or tables (stand-up meetings). You'll be amazed at how much faster they progress. If the weather is suitable, have meetings outside.

- Set the room up so that latecomers or catering staff will not distract the group.

- Ensure that projection screens and flip charts are visible from every corner of the room.

Seating Arrangement

In many meetings, members walk to the same corner, talk to the same people, drink the same coffee, and make the same comments almost every time. The meetings become predictable and monotonous. Logistical monotony can translate into substantive monotony—that is, entrenchment in fixed positions on issues—and is therefore an enemy of creative thinking out-side the box.

Try to discourage sameness by facilitating variety in the seating arrangement, which may have the following benefits:

- Members will be working alongside different people every time.
- In a symbolic way, it might reduce entrenchment in the status quo. This symbolic flexibility may translate into substantive flexibility and get people thinking outside the box.
- It might promote higher degrees of creativity and collabo-ration.

Here are a few ideas on facilitating variety in the seating arrangement:

- In a small meeting, print name tents, with names in large letters on both sides, and assign the seats just before the meet-ing begins or delegate this task to the first member who comes to the meeting.

- In a large meeting, use round tables and suggest infor-mally in your opening remarks that the purpose of the meeting is to share ideas on some tough issues and to learn from one another. To enable everyone to learn more about different view-points, suggest sitting at a table with unfamiliar people.

- If the meeting is lengthy, suggest that members move to a different seat after each break. The change in seating can in-duce a change in the pace of progress.

- If two members are inclined to argue against each other, avoid having them seated opposite each other (an adversarial setting). Instead, have them seated next to each other (a collab-orative setting).

- If two members are likely to conduct distracting side con-versations, see if you can seat them away from each other.

Some people will not want to change seats (e.g., they may need to sit in a certain place to hear better), so don't fight them.

Also, if you sense that there might be resistance to changing seats, get members' support for this approach before you try it.

If the room setup or seating arrangement does not feel right, make it your business to make it right. Even after the meeting has begun, it is not too late to ask the members to help you switch to a setup that would be conducive to a better meeting.

Audiovisual Aids

Rarely does Murphy's Law prove so potent as it does in connection with audiovisual aids: overhead projectors, microphones, video equipment, or flip charts. The antidote to Murphy's Law? "An ounce of prevention is worth at least a pound of cure." You need to take steps before the meeting to prevent problems:

- Check whether your members or outside presenters need audiovisual equipment, and, if so, what specific requirements they have.

- Stress the importance of reliability when ordering the equipment. And do not hesitate to ask the supplier to repeat and confirm your requirements.

- Arrive early, test audiovisual equipment, and ensure that it is set up and operates as required (or designate an experienced and reliable person to do that). Consider things from the perspective of the presenters and the members, and check even the smallest details, for example, whether the felt pens have ink.

- Never assume anything and never rely on someone's re-assurances, such as: "We have great acoustics. You won't need a microphone." You need to consider soft-spoken speakers as well as members who have difficulties hearing and may hesitate to complain. Your job is to prevent prime time from being wasted on logistical details.

Catering Arrangements

Here are a few ideas on catering arrangements:

- Costs may be an obstacle to providing refreshments. At the same time, investing a small amount may result in happier and more comfortable members, and could positively affect the meeting outcome. The investment may very well pay for itself.

- As a minimum, insist on cold water (bottled if tap water is highly chlorinated). As extras, consider coffee, tea, soda, and juice. Remember to include the decaffeinated, herbal, and diet varieties.

- Consider light pastry for the morning and fresh fruit for the afternoon. Check if the hotel would object to the delicacies that one of your members offers to bring.

- If you arrange lunch or dinner, avoid heavy meals (e.g., creamy pastas and rich desserts). Keep your members awake and alert, with vegetable trays, soup, sandwiches, and fresh fruit.

- Avoid alcoholic drinks before a working session (even if you can afford them). If you have them at all, save them as a reward after all business has been concluded. But encourage moderation and remind the members not to drink and drive!

- Check if members have special dietary needs and do your best to accommodate them.

- Communicate your expectations clearly and fully to the catering staff: What is required, at what time, and through which door? Where will the beverages and food be placed? Will you need refills, and, if so, when? How will disruptions to the meeting be minimized? Do you want leftovers removed immediately or left behind?

- Give the catering staff feedback. Start with accolades and then give the corrective feedback. If they've done a good job, consider acknowledging their efforts in front of your group.

Registration Logistics

In large membership or shareholder meetings, you will need to register members at the door. Logistical details to consider may include some or all of the following:

- Separate registration tables for members and for guests
- Up-to-date lists of voting members or shareholders (in-

cluding, where applicable, records of proxy assignments) divided, if necessary, into sublists (e.g., A to K, L to R, S to Z)
- A senior staff member or adviser to address voting eligibility disputes
- Registration packages containing such items as meeting agendas, basic rules of order, voting cards, secret ballots, minutes and reports, motions, and parking validation tickets
- A way of preventing uninvited persons from attending in the case of closed or restricted attendance (e.g., security guards at the door)

Teleconferencing or Videoconferencing

Teleconferencing or videoconferencing are valuable ways of saving time and money by avoiding the travel costs and the inconvenience involved in bringing all members to a meeting. They should be considered for urgent decisions that cannot wait for the next scheduled meeting. When planning teleconferencing or videoconferencing:

- Confirm which members will be available at the designated time (at least a quorum) and that their phone lines will not be busy.
- Coordinate with the telephone operator and start the meeting only when every participant is included in the call.
- Establish rules on how members will identify themselves and be recognized to speak. Speaking without permission from the chair should generally not be allowed.
- Emphasize that members should feel free to interject if they cannot hear or understand what is being said so that everyone can properly be included in the discussion.

See Chapter 9 for more on virtual meetings.

Discussion Guidelines

The larger the meeting gets and the more sensitive or complex the issues are, the greater is the need for structure and formality. A level playing field should be established so that each member will have the same opportunity to participate in debate and decision making and so that the principles of order, decorum, civility, equality, fairness, and common sense can be entrenched. The language and tone of these basic discussion guidelines or rules of order can be modified to fit the level of formality, size, or culture of your group:

- If you want to speak, please raise your hand (or go to a microphone), wait for permission to speak, and open by identifying yourself. Only voting members may speak, make motions, and vote. Others may speak if granted permission to do so by the members.

- On each issue, each member will be entitled to speak up to two times, each time for no longer than 3 minutes (or a different time limit, as appropriate for the group). Additional speaking opportunities may be granted by informal agreement or by a formal vote.

- A member who wishes to speak for the second time on the same issue will wait until those who wish to speak on it for the first time have spoken.

- Discussions must be related to the issues at hand. Members must avoid discussions of personalities and speculation on the possible motives of previous speakers.

- Members who wish to propose motions are required to submit them to the chair in writing before introducing them.

Discussion guidelines can be established and reinforced by some or all of the following methods:

- Have the basic guidelines printed in a one-page summary.

- Include the summary in the premeeting package.

- Restate the main guidelines in your opening remarks (see chair's script at the end of this chapter).

- Ask if the members have any concerns about the guidelines, especially if you are using them for the first time. It may be wise to take a vote on these guidelines at the start of the meeting.

- Arrange for the necessary tools to monitor time and enforce discussion guidelines if necessary (e.g., a stopwatch). Feel free to be creative and soften the impact of your interventions (being fair but firm; see Chapter 5).

Premeeting Communication and Conflict Management

The success of a meeting largely depends on the quality of your communication with the members before the meeting. Related topics covered in this section are:

- Information given to members
- The quality of circulated reports and documents
- Information collected from members
- Premeeting conflict management
- Communications with guest speakers and advisers

Information Given to Members

Information given to members before the meeting may include:

- The place, date, and time of the meeting.
- The proposed agenda including opening time, closing time, and interim milestones.
- Discussion guidelines or basic rules of order.
- Documents that the members need to review before the meeting.
- Requests and reminders, for example, arrive on time, read enclosed documents, be ready with questions and ideas, complete tasks assigned to you.
- Guidelines on how agenda items can be added, deleted, or modified. It should be clarified that requested additions will not be automatically accommodated but will be subject to such factors as compliance with the group's

mandate, time constraints, priorities, urgency of proposed items, and their readiness for informed debate and decision making.

The Quality of Circulated Reports and Documents

Reports sent to members should be relevant, clear, concise, complete, and reader-friendly so that they can be reviewed with relative ease. Consider the following suggestions:

- Lengthy paragraphs should be replaced by a concise point format.
- Technical terms should be explained (consider a glossary of terms and abbreviations).
- Lengthy documents should start with a table of contents and an executive summary, and should have a section and page-numbering system.
- Key points and options should be highlighted (bolded, underlined, etc.)
- Minutes of previous meetings should be concise, accurate, action oriented, and reader-friendly. For more information on minutes, see Chapter 8.

Information Collected from Members

Communications from members to the planner of the meeting may include:

- Confirmation of attendance and commitments made for the meeting (e.g., facilitating a discussion or introducing a guest speaker)
- Reports and documents for inclusion with the premeeting package (submitted in time so that they can be sent to members for meaningful review and scrutiny)
- Confirmation of the amount of time needed for a presentation (including follow-up discussion)
- Confirmation of audiovisual equipment and other requirements for a presentation

- Requests to change the agenda
- Suggestions on how the meeting should be conducted

Premeeting Conflict Management

To the extent possible, the planner should anticipate and attempt to address conflict and tensions before the meeting, so as to minimize adverse effects on its progress. Such tensions can be addressed by informal discussions with individual members or by mediative action.

EXAMPLE: A Premeeting Discussion of Concerns

An impartial facilitator met with two disputing factions before a meeting to discuss concerns about how the meeting would be conducted. The result of these discussions was that mutually acceptable discussion guidelines were established and tensions were substantially reduced. The meeting itself, which was estimated by some to last 4 hours and achieve nothing (as was the case in previous years), ended with a constructive resolution after only 1 1/2 hours.

Communications with Guest Speakers and Advisers

If guest speakers or advisers are invited to the meeting, ensure that their presentation is as beneficial as possible:

- Give them information about your group and the challenges that it faces as they relate to the speaker's areas of expertise.

- Establish the questions that need to be addressed by the speaker.

- Establish when the speaker will start, how much time has been allocated for the presentation, how much time is available for questions, and how you will indicate that time is about to run out (e.g., verbal or nonverbal warnings that 5 minutes is left). Be respectful but unapologetic: It is your meeting and the speaker cannot assume that he or she can take up all the time.

- Interview speakers and prepare brief introductions of their background and experience as they relate to the issues at hand. Give this introduction just before they speak to the group.

- You can invite them to stay for the full meeting, but clarify what portion of time they can expect to be paid for.

- At the meeting itself, introduce advisers at designated times. Don't keep them waiting. It's unfair and can be expensive if they bill by the hour.

Meeting Day Checklist

On the day of the meeting, the chair and the meeting planners should arrive early at the location with a checklist of items to address before the meeting begins. The following is a sample checklist to be customized to your needs.

The Room

✓ Is the room set up according to the plan? If not, who can help make adjustments?
✓ Is the room temperature and ventilation comfortable?
✓ Are there any distractions that need to be taken care of?

The Seating

✓ Is the seating arrangement acceptable?
✓ Are there enough chairs and tables? Are there any broken chairs?
✓ Are name tents set up?

Catering

✓ Have refreshments been provided in accordance with specifications?
✓ Is the coffee hot? Are the soft drinks cold?
✓ Are any last-minute adjustments required?

Audiovisual Equipment

✓ Has audiovisual equipment been set up as specified?

√ Does the overhead projector work? Is there a spare light-bulb?

√ Do all microphones work? Can you be heard from the back of the room?

√ Is the flip chart set up? Is there enough blank paper? Are there marker pens with ink?

√ Does the video equipment, slide projector, or other equipment need to be tested?

Registration Arrangements

√ Are registration tables set up as planned? Are they sufficiently staffed?

√ Is there an up-to-date list of members?

√ Have voting cards and ballots been prepared? Are they properly secured?

Documents

√ Agenda?

√ Rules of order?

√ Minutes of previous meeting?

√ Reports, summaries, other documents?

√ If documents were precirculated, are spare copies available?

√ Where is the closest photocopying facility?

Communications

√ Have guests and advisers been welcomed? Do they need any logistical or other support?

√ Do any last-minute details need to be confirmed with individual members?

The Chair's Script

Preparing a script for the chair is one of the best investments in a meeting. A good script will enable the chair to follow the agenda, manage the meeting, bring closure to issues, and set an appropriate tone and climate for the meeting. A script is a must in controversial meetings.

Naturally, following a verbatim script would not be practical, since the chair's primary role is to manage the meeting and not to give the members an extended lecture. Some parts of the meeting are possible to predict and they can be scripted. In others, communications are on an ad-hoc basis.

A good script should combine text with prompts for action to be taken by the chair or designated members (i.e., Who will take a lead on an agenda item? Who will make a motion?). The overall script for the meeting can be supplemented by ad-hoc scripts for procedural and substantive interventions (see Chapter 5).

Script Checklist

The following is a list of items that the chair's script may include. You will need to customize the list to suit the level of formality and complexity of the respective meeting:

Opening Portion

√ Call the meeting to order, welcome the members, and introduce yourself.

√ Explain the purpose of the meeting and how it relates to the mandate of the group.

√ State the notice and quorum requirements and whether they have been met.

√ Give opening greetings and comments, as needed.

√ Review the agenda and how the meeting will unfold: State the main items, the projected closing time, and major interim milestones to be reached.

√ Ask if there are any questions or concerns about the agenda. Then facilitate informal agreement or a formal vote on the agenda.

√ Review the main guidelines for the meeting (e.g., speaking by raising hands, observing time limits, avoiding domination) and the principles that they are intended to uphold (equality, fairness, common sense).

√ Ask if there are any questions or concerns about the rules of order.
√ If deemed beneficial, take a formal vote to approve the rules of the meeting.
√ Proceed to the first substantive item on the agenda.

Body of the Script

√ Announce items according to the agenda, briefly outlining the parameters for each item and mapping out how it will unfold. Is it for information only? Is there a decision to be made in connection with it? If so, is there a motion in the member's package to start the discussion? How much time is allocated for this agenda item?
√ Invite individuals to present reports or introduce proposals or motions.
√ Facilitate the discussion and initiate closure on issues (see ad-hoc scripts in Chapter 5).
√ Periodically review the progress and the timing of the meeting (see ad-hoc scripts in Chapter 5).

Closing of the Script

√ Check if there is further business to be addressed. If not, you can proceed with closing.
√ Indicate that the agenda has been completed.
√ Review the purpose of the meeting.
   Summarize the overall progress made at the meeting.
√ Concisely recap agreements on key issues and acknowledge the work still to be done.
√ Review any follow-up action: What's next? Who will do what and by when?
√ Remind members of the date and focus of the next meeting.
√ Thank the members for their attendance and participation.
√ Declare the meeting adjourned. The formality of a motion to adjourn is not needed if there is no further business to be transacted.

Sample Chair's Script

You can modify this sample script to fit the circumstances of your meeting. Note that several decisions are made without the formality of a motion, for example, approval of the agenda, approval of rules of order, and approval of previous minutes.

6:57 PM: Alerting members that the meeting is about to begin

Would the members please take their seats? We will start the meeting on time, at 7 PM.

7 PM sharp (the scheduled opening time)

The meeting will please come to order.

Good evening everyone and welcome to the annual general meeting of the University of Wisdom Faculty Association. My name is Johnny Educator, the president of the association and the chair of this meeting.

Notice, Quorum

The notice of this meeting was sent to all members on June 9, 2000, and the 14-day notice that section 4.2 of our bylaws requires has been met.

Section 7.6 in the bylaws states that a quorum for membership meetings is 25 members in good standing. We have 65 members present and therefore this meeting is duly convened.

I remind the members that we require a quorum to be present for the full duration of the meeting, so please stay until the meeting is adjourned.

Opening Remarks (insert welcoming remarks, as needed)

Agenda

The agenda for the meeting has been included in your member's package. On it we have a few housekeeping items, then a few reports, then the election of directors, and then new business.

It has been suggested that we establish a 9:30 PM target closing time for this meeting to enable you to return home at a reasonable hour. The proposed closing time is intended as a preliminary target and not as a rigid restriction. If at 9:30 there is a need to continue with the meeting, a motion to extend the time will be in order. On the other hand, if we conclude our business sooner than 9:30, we will adjourn at that time.

If members have new items for discussion, they will be placed under the new business section. In the interests of maintaining clarity and efficiency, we ask that you let us know of such items in advance. If you have a motion to make, we ask that you write it down and pass it to the chair before making it so that I can read it to the members and have it recorded in the minutes.

Is the proposed agenda acceptable to the members? (Pause.) Is there any objection to the agenda, with a projected closing time of 9:30 PM? (Pause.) There being no objection, the agenda is approved, with 9:30 PM as the projected closing time for the meeting.

Rules of Debate

The next item is the rules of debate. A copy of the rules for this meeting was included in your package. These rules are designed to help us run a meeting that is fair and inclusive, and, at the same time, efficient, civil, and orderly. I will now review the main rules that you will need to be aware of:

- First, if you want to speak, please approach the microphone, wait for permission to speak, and open by identifying yourself. Only voting members may speak, make motions, and vote. Others may speak only if granted permission to do so by the members.
- Second, on each issue, each member will be entitled

to speak up to two times, each time no longer than 3 minutes. Additional speaking opportunities may be granted by the members.
- Third, a member who wishes to speak a second time on the same issue will wait until those who wish to speak on it for the first time have spoken.

Are there any questions or concerns about the rules of order?

The only rule that requires approval is the one on the 3-minute time limit. Is there any discussion on this rule? (Pause.) If not, we will take a vote. Those in favor of limiting comments to 3 minutes each, please raise your hands. Thank you. Those opposed to this rule, please raise your hands. Thank you. The 3-minute time limit has been approved.

Approval of Minutes

The next item of business is the approval of the minutes of last year's annual general meeting. The minutes were circulated to the members and we assume that you have read them. Are there any corrections to these minutes? (Pause.) If not, the minutes are approved as circulated.

In connection with the approval of minutes: It has been noted that members do not always remember what took place a year ago and that it is more logical to have minutes of annual meetings approved sooner than the next annual meeting. The recommended practice is that the board of directors be authorized to approve minutes of general meetings and that the approved minutes be made available to members upon request. To change our practice, we need to authorize the board to approve minutes of annual meetings. Is there such a motion? (Pause.)

It is moved and seconded that the board be authorized to approve the minutes of annual meetings. Is there any discussion on this motion? (Pause, take comments.) If not, we will take a vote on the motion that the board be authorized to approve the minutes of annual meetings. Those in favor of this motion, please raise your hands. Thank you. Those opposed, please raise your hands. Thank you. The affirmative has it and the motion is carried.

Reports (for information only)

The next item of business is the board's report. The report has been circulated. As president, I will highlight only the key points and will then take a few questions. (Report is presented.)

Are there any questions on the board report? (Take questions.) Any further questions? There being no further questions, the board report will be placed on file. (Proceed similarly with other ``for information'' reports: Note that no motion is required to have the reports received or filed. Such a motion is meaningless; see Chapter 7.)

Reports Containing Recommendations

The next item of business is the report of the Continuing Education Committee. The report will be presented by Don Carey. (Report is presented and Don concludes by making a motion.)

It is moved and seconded that a change management seminar be added to our continuing education program. Is there any discussion on this motion? (Take discussion.)

There being no further discussion, we will vote on the motion that a change management seminar be added to our continuing education program. Those in favor of this motion, please raise your hands. Thank you. Those opposed, please raise your hands. Thank you. The affirmative has it and the motion is carried.

Treasurer's Report

Next we have the treasurer's report. I will invite our treasurer, Jean Morrow, to present this report.

(Highlights of the report are presented.)

Are there any questions on the treasurer's report?

Approval of Audited Financial Statements

If there are no further questions, is there a motion that the audited financial statements be approved? (The motion is made and seconded.)
It is moved and seconded that the audited financial statements be approved. Is there any discussion on this motion? (Take comments.)

There being no further discussion, we will vote on approving the audited financial statements. Those in favor of this motion, please raise your hands. Thank you. Those opposed, please raise your hands. Thank you. The motion is carried.

Appointment of the Auditor

Next we have the appointment of the auditor. The chair will entertain a motion that Coopers and Company be appointed as the auditor for the association for the next fiscal year and that the board be authorized to fix the remuneration for the auditor. (Motion is made and seconded.)

It is moved and seconded that Coopers and Company be appointed as the auditor for the association for the next fiscal year and that the board be authorized to fix the remuneration for the auditor. Is there any discussion on this motion? (Pause, take comments.)

There being no further discussion, we will proceed to the vote.

Those in favor of appointing Coopers and Company as the auditor for the association for the next fiscal year and authorizing the board to fix the remuneration for the auditor, please raise your hands. Thank you. Those opposed, please raise your hands. Thank you. The motion is carried.

Election of Directors

Next on our agenda we have agenda item number __, the election of directors. There are three openings on the board, each for a 3-year term. The Nominating Committee has proposed the names of Donna Ng, Russ Baker, and Cindy O'Day for the position of director.

Are there any nominations from the floor for the position of director?
(Take more nominations. There is no requirement to ask three times if there are more nominations from the floor. Just wait long enough to give the members a reasonable opportunity to nominate. Ask nominees whether they will serve if elected. It may be necessary to check whether nominees meet eligibility requirements stated in the bylaws.)

There being no further nominations, nominations are now closed. Please add the names of the nominees from the floor to the ballot and do not mark your choices yet. We still need to hear from the nominees and there will be some voting instructions.

We will now hear a statement from each nominee, up to 3 minutes each. (Nominees speak.)

You have heard the nominees speak and it is now time to vote. Please mark your ballot with up to three names. It is acceptable to choose less than three names. But if you mark more than three names, your ballots will be declared invalid. When you finish, please fold your ballot and raise it so that it can be collected. (Wait.)

Have all ballots been collected? (Pause.) If you have not handed in your ballot, please raise it so that it can be collected. (Wait.) Thank you. While the ballots are being counted, we will carry on with the new business portion of our meeting. (Carry on with new business.)

Election Results

We now have the election results. They are as follows:

- A total of 63 ballots were cast.
- 1 ballot was invalid.
- Donna Ng received 43 votes.
- Russ Baker received 22 votes.
- Cindy O'Day received 38 votes.
- Jeff Young received 37 votes.

Donna Ng, Cindy O'Day, and Jeff Young were elected for a 3-year term each. Congratulations!

Closing Portion

Is there any further business to come before this meeting?

If not, before adjourning this meeting, I would like to thank you for attending and for participating. Having concluded its business, this annual general meeting of the University of Wisdom Faculty Association now stands adjourned.
(There is no need for a formal motion to adjourn if there is no further business to address.)

4

Empowered and Proactive Members

In this chapter the ethics of individual members and their roles in helping to make the vision of a successful meeting (see Chapter 2) a reality are discussed. Specifically, the following topics are presented:

- How members lose their power or give it up
- The benefits of shared responsibility and empowered members
- Three examples of how one individual made a significant difference in a meeting
- The "suffering is optional" motto
- How a member can make a difference between and during meetings
- How members can assert themselves without getting angry
- How to induce a shift toward greater member empowerment

How Members Lose Their Power or Give It Up

When a meeting runs well, the credit typically goes to the chair. Similarly, when it goes poorly, the chair gets all the blame. The individual members are all but forgotten. Is this a healthy balance? The answer is clearly and unequivocally *no*. Why should the weight of an entire organization rest on the shoulders of one leader? Wouldn't this notion be a disincentive to serving as chair ("I can't possibly handle this much responsibility")? Wouldn't it attract to the chair's office mainly those who like the power and prestige associated with it, and deprive the organization of good talent? The important question is: Who is to blame for this prevailing imbalance in favor of the chair? This blame can usually be divided among the individual members, the chair, and the group's culture—that is, the set of basic norms, assumptions, and expectations within the organization.

Far too often, the members themselves underestimate and trivialize their potential impact. Common notions that inhibit and impede members from expressing themselves include:

- "I am only one member. How much of a difference can I make?"
- "It's a silly question and I will only get embarrassed by asking it."
- "It's not my job to do that. What do we have a chairperson for?"
- "My concern is not that important. Things are not so bad."
- "Asserting myself is not nice. It would undermine and embarrass the chair."

Individuals can become their own worst critics and the above notions can become self-fulfilling prophecies. If you truly believe that you cannot make a positive difference, you probably won't.

It has been said that there are three types of people:

1. Those who make things happen
2. Those who watch things happen
3. Those who have no idea what happened

Which of these three types describes your participation in meetings?

Apathy and acquiescence are not only the individual member's fault. A chair might make condescending remarks and make it difficult for members to speak up. The chair might rebut every statement made, show favoritism, and have difficulty letting go of control. Indeed, some chairs view member empowerment as a threat to them and to their status and power.

Benefits of Member Empowerment

One of the key ingredients of a successful meeting is shared responsibility (see Chapter 2). With this ingredient, the weight of leadership and decision making is divided among the members of the group. With empowered and proactive members, the chair is only a first among equals.

When considering collective decision making, envision true democracy, not monarchy. Instead of a train, where the engineer makes all the decisions and the passengers sit back and watch, envision a rowboat, where the leader gives directions and guidance, but the members are the ones who row. Everyone must pull their weight or the boat will go in circles. Remember that a chain is only as strong as its weakest link.

Of course, an organization could work just fine with only a few individuals carrying most of the load and making all the decisions. But think about the added value if each member is transformed from a passive observer to an active, enthusiastic, and conscientious contributor. Here are just a few of the benefits of proactive, empowered, and motivated members:

- *Equalized Distribution of Work.* With more members sharing the load, the likelihood of burnout and exhaustion among key contributors is reduced. Tasks are assigned based on talent, skill, and potential, and not by who volunteers first. As a result, tasks receive more dedicated attention.

- *Greater Accountability.* With empowered and conscientious members, personal accountability increases, and the futile and wasteful finger-pointing is minimized. Instead of criticizing the imperfections and errors of others, members focus on their own performance and contributions.

- *Increased Teamwork.* There is less concern with the structured and regimented assignment of duties and more concern with getting things done.

- *Better Decisions.* With members studying issues more carefully, sharing unique and creative ideas, expressing legitimate concerns, and asking the right questions before voting, decisions are bound to be wiser, more responsible, and more durable—that is, they will stand the test of time.

- *Better Returns on Investment.* With more disciplined members, meetings are more efficient, less repetitive, and better focused on the issues at hand. The organization's mandate and its best interests are better served.

- *Succession Planning.* With empowered members, leadership is shared and there is less dependency on the talents and expertise of a few officers. There is also more interest in leadership duties. At election time, the group is bound to have more potential leaders from whom to choose and to be able to balance the need for continuity with the need for rotation in leadership.

Three Success Stories

Do you ever underestimate how much of a difference one person can make? Here are just three examples of how one individual made a significant difference in a meeting:

- At an annual meeting of a credit union, a proposal was made to increase the minimum share requirement for new members. This was intended to strengthen the institution's capital position and thereby make the members' funds more secure. But vocal opponents of the proposal were much more effective than management in presenting their arguments (which were largely based on myths and misconceptions). The proposal seemed destined for defeat. Just before the vote, one member made a brief, logical and dispassionate statement in favor of the proposal. You could almost feel the temperature in the room change. The vote in favor of the proposal was overwhelming.

▪ A new member was concerned about a proposal. At first he hesitated to interject, but then he mustered some courage and did so anyway. The chair resisted the input and tried to enlighten the member on the benefits of the proposal. The member did not give up and requested that other members be polled for their opinions. A majority shared the member's concerns and modified the proposal before approving it. The member's intervention facilitated an important shift from monarchy to democracy. It gave the members the power that they had lost (or given up) to a dominant chair.

▪ A meeting suffered from digressions, repetitive discussion, and slow progress. Despite her nervousness, a member complained and requested a more disciplined approach to the meeting. The meeting got back on track and became more focused and efficient. Other members approached this member after the meeting to say how much they appreciated her intervention and indicated that they would consider doing the same in the future.

The "Suffering Is Optional" Motto

The underlying notion for members should be that suffering is optional. If something is not working at a meeting and no one is doing anything about it, you can indeed opt to suffer. But you can also opt to consider what you can do (or stop doing) to help remedy the situation. Depending on your style, you may need to start doing the things that you have been reluctant to do, or stop doing the things that you have been accustomed to doing. For example:

▪ *Taking Corrective Action.* If there is a distracting side conversation at the meeting and the chair is not intervening, you can end the suffering by saying: "I am having trouble concentrating when we have two meetings at the same time. Can we have some order, please?"

- *Refraining from Action.* If you find yourself anxious about getting your point across and becoming defensive and argumentative, you can tone down your passionate and stubborn advocacy, avoid dominating the discussion, stop trying to set the record straight on every point, stop forming your rebuttals halfway through other statements, and start listening to others with an open mind.

Making a Difference between and during Meetings

Between meetings you can make a difference in these ways:

- Complete all assignments that were assigned to you.
- Review documents that are relevant to the meeting.
- Introduce items that should be included on the next meeting's agenda.
- Raise substantive and procedural concerns with those who can take corrective actions.
- Offer to help the chair and the members in getting pre-meeting assignments completed.
- Offer feedback to the chair on her or his facilitation style (suggestions for improvement are fine, but don't forget the compliments).

During meetings you can make a difference in these ways:

- Attend meetings regularly.
- Arrive on time and be there for the full duration of the meeting. Be there in body and in spirit.
- Speak up and offer insights and ideas.
- If you tend to be dominant, hold your comments back and make space for others to participate.
- Raise valid concerns, even at the risk of sounding stupid or being unpopular. The meeting is not a popularity contest but a collective effort to make the best decisions for the organization.

- Insist on clarity of the wording of proposals when votes are taken.
- Insist on logical and deliberate decision making.
- Know when to be quiet, sit back, listen to others, and learn from them.
- Avoid interrupting others in midsentence. Let them finish and truly hear them out.
- Have a pen handy so that you can make note of your thoughts while listening attentively to other points of view.
- With the notion that "yes, but" works as a verbal eraser, avoid forming your rebuttals too fast.
- Help maintain order and decorum.
- Avoid personal attacks and shouting matches.
- Help in celebrating successes by complimenting others on a job well done.
- Help to introduce a light touch, especially when people seem to be taking things too seriously.

Member's Affirmations

I suggest that each member prepare a set of statements affirming how he or she will contribute to the work of the group between and during meetings. These affirmations can be prepared when the member first joins the group and goes through the orientation program. To make such affirmations work, they should be reviewed periodically. How about reading them to yourself every meeting? For example:

> *I pledge to participate constructively in our deliberations and thereby help to improve the quality of our collective decisions. I will raise legitimate questions and concerns about the way our meetings are run and about the quality of the decisions that we make. I will resist finger-pointing and instead will assist the chair and other members in making our meetings efficient, timely, orderly, fair, and inclusive. I pledge to speak my mind, but also to balance my advocacy with listening to others with an open mind. I will respect the confidentiality of issues addressed in in-*

camera meetings and will act with principle and integrity
if I encounter a conflict of interest.

Scripts to Assert Yourself without Getting Angry

If you want to intervene and express a concern during a meeting, make your intervention brief, constructive (solution oriented), principled, and objective (hard on issues but soft on people). The impact of your intervention will be softened if you end it with a question, making you come across as more consultative. You could use these ad-hoc scripts to assert yourself without appearing angry:

- *Off-Mandate Discussions: "May I have a word here? I am having trouble determining how this discussion relates to our group's mandate, which is to _____. Can someone help me out?"*

- *Digressions from the Agenda: "Can someone tell me where we are on the agenda?" Or "I have an unpopular question to ask: How is this discussion related to item 7 on the agenda, which we are supposed to be discussing now?"*

- *Repetition: "Are we ready to make a decision on this issue yet? It seems to me that we said all that needs to be said on it. I am concerned that we might not be able to cover the rest of our agenda unless we reach closure on this issue now."*

- *Chaos: "I am having trouble concentrating. Can we hear from only one person at a time?"*

- *Interruptions: "Can we please let people finish what they're saying?"*

- *A New Idea Being Dismissed Too Fast: "Can we slow down, please? Janet, I'm curious about your idea. What did you mean by . . ."*

- *Dominated Discussions: "May I interject? We've been hearing only two opinions. Could we hear from members who have not spoken, like Judy, who has plenty of experience in this area?"*

- *Lack of Clarity:* *"Just wait a minute. Before we vote on this motion, can someone tell me exactly what we are voting on and what the impact of voting yes or no will be?"*
- *A Lack of Progress:* *"It seems to me that we are not getting very far with this discussion and that important data and significant stakeholders are not here. Can we postpone this item until the next meeting and in the meantime discuss issues on which we can make progress?"*

Inducing a Shift toward Greater Member Empowerment

Members will not become empowered and motivated just because you tell them to be. Attitudes cannot be legislated. True motivation and sustained attitudinal changes have to come from within each individual member. Each member must be on board willingly and enthusiastically so that your entire team can reach the same destination together. Consider these ideas for entrenching shared responsibility and building a team of empowered, proactive, and highly motivated members:

- Make your meetings and collective decision-making processes more engaging and inclusive.
- Have orientation programs and manuals on the roles and responsibilities of members, the principles of due diligence and accountability, and the vision of successful meetings (Chapter 2).
- Have private discussions with members who do not assume their assigned responsibilities.
- Offer encouragement to members who need a boost to assert and express themselves.
- Remind members that suffering is optional. Say this at the beginning of the meeting and reinforce this notion in words and in action as the meeting progresses. Encourage members to raise both substantive and procedural concerns and to share ideas and suggestions.

- Give members lead roles and challenging and interesting assignments in connection with agenda items that are suitable to their skills, potential, and professional development needs.

- Use participatory discussion activities to engage quieter members in the deliberations (e.g., "Work on your own for 3 minutes and jot down your thoughts on the following question. After 3 minutes, members will be polled at random for their thoughts").

- Invite and welcome feedback from members between meetings (an open-door policy).

- Take feedback humbly and nondefensively—that is, examine its merits with an open mind and take action when warranted.

- Express appreciation on an ad-hoc basis, privately or publicly, to a member who shares a valid concern, raises a significant question, or offers a good idea. This should be done especially if the member's contribution enhances the quality of a collective decision or if it helps to make a meeting more productive.

- Structure programs to acknowledge and reward member achievements, contributions, and good ideas and suggestions (e.g., a semiannual awards banquet or a member-of-the-month award). Such programs encourage, legitimize, and perpetuate empowered participation.

5

A Masterful Facilitator

Even with empowered and proactive members (see Chapter 4), the chair is in a position to significantly affect the productivity of a meeting. With an effective chair, the likelihood of entrenching the ten key ingredients of a successful meeting (see Chapter 2) increases dramatically. With an ineffective chair, the task becomes much more difficult, regardless of the good intentions of the members. Even with the best of crews, a ship will likely founder without a good captain.

In this chapter, the following subjects are covered:

- The chair's greatest enemy
- Methods of ascertaining the collective wishes of the members
- General questions about the role of the chair
- Ineffective and effective chairs
- The chair's debating and voting rights
- The chair's overall challenge
- The chair's roles between meetings
- The chair's procedural interventions during meetings
- The chair's substantive interventions during meetings
- Offering challenge and celebrating successes

The Chair's Greatest Enemy

The chair's greatest enemy is the word *I*. The chair's position is seen by many to be one of personal power: leading, taking a lot of initiative, and making many decisions. But this power is hollow if it draws on the chair as an individual. Conversely, this power is legitimate if it reflects a principled and inclusive approach, as well as democratic decision making.

Given that the *I* approach is so entrenched in organizations, many people shy away from leadership, since they believe that the burden of decision making is too heavy, that leadership is a thankless job, and that it gets very lonely at the top.

But it doesn't have to be lonely at the top. As the chair, you can adopt a *we* approach and descend from your self-imposed ivory tower. Be in touch and in tune with the members and you will earn their respect and support. A *we*-oriented chair:

- Facilitates decision making and builds consensus especially when the decisions are significant and affect many parties.
- Knows when and how to let go and share control
- Is always in tune with the members and is in the habit of ascertaining their expressed and unexpressed wishes and responding to them.
- Engages the members in collective decision making not only on substantive issues (e.g., an important expenditure) but also on procedural ones (e.g., the amount of time to set aside for a discussion).

Ascertaining the Collective Wishes of the Members

As an effective chair, you will constantly seek directions from your group. Having ascertained those wishes, you will ensure that they are carried out. Ascertaining the collective wishes of the members does not always have to be via a formal vote. In the case of a routine and noncontroversial decision, seeking direction might be as simple as asking a question (e.g., "Shall we take a 10-minute break?"). A formal vote is only needed to resolve disputes or to make a substantive decision of a significant nature.

Either way, you will be assured that the group is with you for the duration of the journey and that everyone will arrive at the same destination together. The fact that the members are asked what they want instead of being told what to do will help you create a balance of power in the meeting. You will thereby avoid complaints about autocratic management (i.e., "I will allow two more speakers and then we'll close the discussion") or anarchy (i.e., "Whoever has the loudest voice and most persistent manner prevails").

At first, many leaders are uncomfortable with the notion of true and full democratic control, fearing that the risks of empowered members are too great. In fact, the autocratic approach has greater risks, such as low levels of commitment, limited exchanges of ideas, low-quality decisions, and resistance to change. Undemocratic decisions are unlikely to be implemented enthusiastically and may even be undermined or challenged through adversarial processes.

As suggested in Chapter 4, empowering your members and involving them as proactive partners is the smart approach to doing business. Give them their power back even if they seem content to leave it in your hands and even if they seem to defer to the more experienced members. You can ascertain the collective wishes of the members by doing the following:

- Articulate a direction and seek confirmation.
- Seek direction from the group and then ascertain its collective wishes.
- Check if there is an objection to a proposed direction.
- Summarize consensus and seek confirmation.
- Take a formal vote.
- Shift power back from individuals (anarchy) to the group (democracy).

Articulating a Direction and Seeking Confirmation

If you can guess what the members want to do, take the pulse of the group by articulating this direction and then looking for confirmation. Ask a question instead of imposing a decision. This is the soft way of entrenching democracy. Key preambles for such questions are:

- "What is the wish of the members? Shall we _____?"
- "Do the members want to _____?"
- "Would it be fair to limit discussion in the following way: _____?"
- "Would it be productive for us to proceed by _____?"
- "Would it be reasonable to _____?"
- "It seems that a logical way to proceed is by _____. Does it make sense to you?"
- "Are we in general agreement that _____?"
- "What do you think? Shall we _____?"

If there seems to be general agreement, proceed in the confirmed direction. If there seem to be some doubts, you may need to pursue a different direction. In most cases, the regularity of the questions will mean that no formal votes will be needed (except when there is a dispute as to the proposed direction).

EXAMPLES

"We've worked hard for the past 2 hours and it seems to me that we could use a break. Shall we take a 15-minute recess?"

"We're running short on time. Does anyone have something new to add to the discussion or shall we proceed to the vote?"

"It seems to me that the logical approach is to start with a 10-minute presentation, then have 15 minutes for clarifying questions, and then 20 minutes to debate the proposal. Does this sound reasonable to you?"

"Given that the membership committee chair needs to leave soon, is it acceptable to consider her report now instead of 8 o'clock as scheduled?"

"Are we in general agreement that Jack and Ruth should prepare the report?"

"Are we in agreement that the computers should be IBM compatible? Is there any opposition to this?"

"Given this generous offer, shall we hold the awards reception at the Four Seasons Hotel?"

Seeking Direction from the Group

If you are uncertain as to the direction, look for suggestions from the group.

EXAMPLES

''We seem to be making very little progress on this issue and we have many others on the agenda. We are running short on time. What shall we do with this agenda item? Shall we postpone it, or shall we refer it to the Education Committee for study? Any suggestions?''

''Congratulations. We seem to have agreed on the first five components of the budget. Component 6 is contentious, because it involves some new and unusual expenses, such as a proposed lease of a new building. Does anyone have ideas to bridge the gaps between the various interests?''

Checking for an Objection to a Proposed Direction

If you are not sure that there will be broad support for a proposed direction, ascertain the wishes of the group in a more tentative way.

EXAMPLE

''In the interest of time, is there any objection to closing debate on this proposal once the two members at the microphones have spoken?'' (Pause.) ''There being no objection, we will do so. Mr. Jones, go ahead.''

If there is an objection to the proposed action, you may need to propose another possibility, or, if there seems to be some support but it is not unanimous, take a formal vote.

Summarizing Consensus and Seeking Confirmation

If your group operates informally, substantive decisions can be made by consensus, with votes taken only to resolve disagreements. To ascertain the group's collective wishes in such cases, you can summarize or ask the secretary to summarize the areas of agreement and then the areas of disagreement (if any). Afterward, you can look for informal confirmation of the summary and establish the actions to be taken.

EXAMPLE

"Let me see if I can summarize in point form the areas of agreement. We appear to agree that: First, _____. Second, _____. Third, _____. Is this summary an accurate reflection of the group's consensus?" (Pause and make corrections based on the group's input.) "We now need to decide about implementation: Who will do what and by when? Starting with: _____."

Taking a Formal Vote

If a substantive proposal needs to be approved and your group operates formally, you will need to ascertain the wishes of the members by having the proposal presented, debated, and formally voted on. See Chapter 7 for more details.

Similarly, if a procedural decision proves to be controversial, a formal vote on it may be needed. For example: "Those who believe the member should be given a third opportunity to speak, raise your hands. Thank you. Those opposed to this, raise your hands. Thank you." Then announce the result.

Shifting Power Back from Individuals to the Group

Far too often, a decision is made because a few outspoken individuals insist on it, with the silent majority left out of the loop. This is the worst abuse of power and establishes the tyranny of the minority. The members can regain their power if the chair ascertains their wishes by a formal vote. This approach places the desires of the outspoken members in the proper context: One member, one vote.

EXAMPLES

``John, thank you for your opinion. We need to move on and hear from those who have not spoken. Is there anyone who has not spoken with an opinion on this issue?''

``Tammy, with respect, I understand that this is what you want. However, as you know, this is a decision that must be made by the group, and I need to ask the members how they want to proceed. What is the wish of the members? Should we _____, or should we _____? Those in favor of _____ raise your hands.''

``Sir, I understand that you want to speak for longer than 3 minutes. However, the rules that the members approved for this meeting indicate a time limit of 3 minutes each time. In fairness to others, the decisions of the members must be respected.'' If the member persists, take a vote on allowing him to speak longer than 3 minutes.

A Success Story: The Power of a Good Process

While preparing for a contentious membership meeting, a president was urged by his board to show leadership and to defend the board from attacks by "misguided members." In contrast, outside advice was that the president should let go and should avoid trying to control the substantive outcomes of the meeting. It was suggested that he focus instead on guiding the debate in a completely fair and unbiased manner, that he give all sides equal opportunities to be heard, and that he let the members make the decisions they were entitled to make. The president followed the outside recommendations, the meeting went well, and it was much shorter than everyone expected. The warring factions found common ground and all issues were resolved to everyone's satisfaction.

Ineffective and Effective Dialogues

Dialogues A and B are typical of many meetings. They illustrate the tyranny of the minority and what happens in the absence of effective interventions. Refer to the discussion about giving power back to the group to analyze what is wrong with Dialogues A and B. Then review Dialogue C as a more effective alternative.

Dialogue A: Capitulation

Member A: "I think we should consider a phone survey of a selected sample of members to get their feedback on . . ." (can't finish because of an interruption).

Member B (interrupts): "Come on, already. We tried it 5 years ago. The members don't care."

Chair: "Please let member A finish."

Member B: "Enough already. We are wasting our time. Let's move on."

Chair: "Okay. I guess we'd better move on."

Member A: (Shakes his head with disbelief but doesn't say anything.)

Dialogue B: Power Struggle

(Same start as in Dialogue A.)

Chair: "Member B, I must ask you to stop interrupting."

Member B: "But I'm completely fed up with our meetings and how much time is wasted."

Chair: "Member B, stop this or I will ask you to leave."

Member B: "You have no right to do this. I am a voting member of this board." (The meeting deteriorates into a shouting match. Member B leaves a few minutes later, threatens a lawsuit, and slams the door behind him. Other members say: "Good riddance.")

Dialogue C: The Power of Democracy

(Same start as in Dialogue A.)

Chair persists (no capitulation): "Member B, I am sure everyone respects your experience with this organization. At the same time, one of the rules that we agreed to is to allow people to finish what they say, uninterrupted, unless they digress from the agenda or go overtime."

Member B persists: "But this idea is a waste of time."

Chair: "You seem to be opposed to even considering Member A's idea. Let me check what the members want to do. Those who wish to hear Member A's idea, please raise your hands. Thank you. Those opposed, raise your hands. Thank you. Member A, please continue."

General Questions about the Chair

1. Who should chair a meeting?

The determination of who should chair a meeting depends on the circumstances of the group.

A. Elected or Appointed President or Chair

Ordinarily, the chair is an elected or appointed officer (president, chair, moderator, or another title). The bylaws or terms of reference of the group often specify who chairs meetings. This designation should generally be followed.

B. Vice Chair

If the chair is absent or is unable or unwilling to preside, the vice chair ordinarily chairs the meeting. If the chair resigns, the vice chair automatically takes this position, with the vacancy in the office of vice chair filled by the appointing body (unless the bylaws state otherwise).

C. Choosing Another Facilitator

If both the chair and vice chair are unable or unwilling to preside, the members can choose a facilitator for the respective meeting.

D. Rotating the Chair

In some organizations the members take turns, with a different member assigned to plan and chair each meeting. This practice introduces variety to meetings, increases the group's leadership base (good succession planning), reduces the dependency on one person, and enhances shared responsibility. Members gain an appreciation of the challenges that the chair faces and are more likely to help if needed.

E. External Chair

If the issues scheduled to come before the meeting are complex or controversial, or if the chair has strong advocacy positions on issues and wants to fully participate in the discussions, it can be advantageous to invite an outsider to serve as an impartial facilitator. If the bylaws state that the president shall preside over meetings, the external facilitator should only conduct the meeting, with the official chair making procedural rulings.

2. How should the chair be referred to?

Depending on the level of formality of a meeting, persons who facilitate the proceedings are referred to in one of several ways:

- By first name (a small or informal meeting)
- By title and last name, for example, "Mr. Smith" or "Ms. Stewart" (a little more formal)
- By a more formal title such as Madam President, Mr. Chairperson, Madam Moderator, Madam Speaker, and so on

- Mr. Chairman or Madam Chairman, but there is growing opposition to this title for its perceived gender bias

Ineffective and Effective Chairs

An Ineffective Chair

An ineffective chair:

- Does not prepare for meetings.
- Is egotistical and power hungry.
- Finds it hard to delegate power and let go of control.
- Dominates discussions and rebuts every statement made.
- Needlessly interrupts speakers.
- Is disrespectful and condescending.
- Is passive, indecisive, and hesitant to intervene.
- Accommodates dominant individuals at the expense of everyone else.
- Legitimizes tardiness by waiting for latecomers.
- Arrives late or misses the meeting altogether.
- Takes criticism as a personal attack.
- Mumbles, rambles, and wanders from the topic.

A Horror Story: The Condescending Lecture

The president of a large national organization introduced a controversial proposal at a large annual meeting. He then opened the discussion with a 20-minute lecture, the essence of which was: "You would be very stupid to vote against this proposal."

The president's comments were divisive. Given the sensitivity of the proposal, he should have just facilitated a free-flowing discussion on it. If he wanted to speak in favor of the proposal, he should have asked the vice president to facilitate that portion of the meeting (see the next section on the chair's rights in a large meeting). In that case, he should have contained his comments within the same time limit that other members had to observe (3 minutes in that case, not 20), unless permission for a longer presentation was granted by the members.

An Effective Chair

An effective chair:

- Is guided by the group's mandate and the needs of its stakeholders.
- Is dedicated to maximizing the return on investment in a meeting.
- Is able to articulate the principles of fairness, equality, and common sense in a clear and compelling manner.
- Is decisive and purposeful, and is able to inspire a sense of direction among the members.
- Treats members with respect and gives them the benefit of the doubt.
- Balances the right of the majority to rule with the right of the minority to be heard.
- Establishes order and decorum gently but firmly.
- Listens, listens, and then listens some more.
- Is in tune with the members and is able to bring out the best in them.
- Prepares for meetings thoroughly, thereby serving as a good role model.
- Ensures that every known detail receives attention.
- Understands the substantive issues addressed by the group.
- Is resourceful, able to think quickly, able to deal with surprises, and able to elicit helpful ideas from the group.
- Constantly seeks agreement and builds consensus.
- Is able to balance the need for full and open discussion with the need to move forward.
- Is open-minded, flexible, creative, and able to think outside the box.
- Welcomes feedback and takes it as an opportunity to learn.
- Offers corrective feedback regularly.

- Celebrates successes and offers praise generously and regularly.
- Is humble and leaves his or her ego at home.
- Has a good sense of timing.
- Has a healthy but appropriate sense of humor.
- Communicates with confidence, brevity, clarity, and precision.

EXAMPLE: Affirmations of an Effective Chair

``I am here to lead you in a fair, free, and open discussion of issues that relate to our group's mandate. My job is to work with you to ensure that our time is spent wisely and that we make responsible and durable decisions for our organization—decisions that reflect due diligence, creativity, and visionary and proactive thinking. Knowing that God gave us two ears and one mouth, I will work with you to ensure that we use them in that proportion; that is, we should listen at least twice as much as we speak.

``I will facilitate our deliberations in a way that respects our governing documents (the act, the bylaws, and our terms of reference) and in a manner that protects the rights of the majority to rule, and the rights of the minority, the individual, the absentee, and the entire organization to be protected. Notwithstanding the contentious nature of some of the decisions that we need to make, I will work with you to ensure that we conduct ourselves with civility, decorum, and principle, being hard on the issues but soft on the people. As your chair, I intend to take myself lightly and my work seriously.''

Success Story 1: The Never-Ending Speech

A vote was taken at the beginning of an annual meeting on the rules of the order: speaking from the microphone after recognition by the chair, being limited to two comments of up to 3 minutes each on each issue, and first-time speakers being given priority over second-time speakers.

Later in the meeting, a member exceeded the 3-minute time limit and the end did not appear to be near. After a short grace period, the chair intervened and advised the member that his time was up. When the member refused to cooperate, the chair did not capitulate (this would have been anarchy in action), nor did he raise his voice, bang the gavel, or turn off the member's microphone (this would have been monarchy in action). Instead, he said calmly:

> Sir, as you may recall, at the beginning of this meeting the members agreed on a 3-minute time limit per person for every speech. I am here, on behalf of the members, to ensure that their wishes are respected and that everyone is treated the same way and has equal opportunities to participate. With this in mind, I am asking you to stop. Your time is up.

The members responded with a round of applause and the speaker got the message.

Success Story 2: The Amendment

A member's suggested amendment to a proposal was ruled out of order because it was made at the wrong time. The member seemed visibly angered and sat down. She apparently found the process confusing and frustrating. A few minutes later, the amendment was in order, but the member was not pursuing it. The president called the member by name and invited her to introduce the amendment. The president did not have to advise the member, but he was sensitive and wanted to make the rules more user-friendly.

The Chair's Debating and Voting Rights

Myths and Misconceptions

There is a great deal of confusion about the rights of the chair. It is often assumed that the chair, even if she or he is a voting member, virtually loses the rights to speak and vote, and must always show absolute neutrality. Some of these myths are drawn from longstanding practices, many with no basis in principle, and they may not even be documented in the group's bylaws. Here are a few of the common myths:

- *Myth:* The chair must never speak in discussion unless he or she vacates the chair.
- *Myth:* The chair cannot even present a report unless he or she vacates the chair.
- *Myth:* The chair never votes except in the event of a tie.
- *Myth:* A person who has a bias on an issue cannot chair a meeting.

These restrictions are borrowed from different ball games, where the referee must display complete impartiality and have no influence over the outcome. The benefits of such restrictions in meetings are not always evident. In fact, if such limits are to be imposed blindly, without anyone questioning their validity or usefulness, the harm or confusion that they produce are likely to erase the perceived benefits. For example:

- In the case of a small board or committee, the chair is often the most knowledgeable and experienced member, and stifling him or her would be counterproductive. If the chair is able to ensure equality and fairness and does not dominate the debate, what purpose would be served by requiring that he or she vacate the chair to speak in discussion?
- Some organizations follow the puzzling practice of the president vacating the chair when presenting the annual report and then resuming it immediately afterward. What harm would be done by the president continuing to preside while presenting the report?

Distinguishing between Large and Small Meetings

The various books on parliamentary procedure and rules of order treat the chair's rights differently. After analysis, the relevant principles that apply are as follows:

- In large and/or controversial meetings, the need for formality and structure increases. When motions are debated in such meetings, there is a need for the chair to remain neutral and concentrate on facilitating the discussions.

- In small and noncontroversial meetings, only a minimum amount of formality is needed and the only restrictions that apply to the chair are those that apply to other members. Additional restrictions will likely prove to be counterproductive.

As a result of this analysis, a common-sense approach is recommended to govern the chair's participation in a meeting. Please note that it may be necessary to amend your bylaws or terms of reference to reflect this approach.

The Chair's Debating Rights in a Small Meeting

In a small meeting of a board or a committee (no more than about a dozen members present), the debating rights of the chair should be as follows:

1. The chair may speak in debate and should not be required to vacate the chair to do so.
2. The chair's participation in debate should be governed by the same rules that apply to other members and should be done in a way that does not hamper the chair's facilitation duties (i.e., keeping decorum, order, and principled and collaborative discussions). If the chair wants to speak, she or he can say: "I want to speak on this proposal, so I will add my name to the speakers' lineup"; or "I want to speak for the second time and I will wait until first-time speakers have spoken."

The Chair's Debating Rights in a Large Meeting

In a large meeting (substantially more than a dozen members present):

1. The chair is required to primarily concentrate on facilitation duties: recognizing members to speak, monitoring progress and timing, and enforcing the rules of order.

2. The chair is prohibited from speaking in favor or against motions unless:
   - He or she vacates the chair. The vice chair or another person who has not spoken on this issue at the meeting could then preside.
   - The members ask for the chair's opinion on an issue or agree to waive the requirement to vacate the chair (i.e., they consider it too disruptive and unnecessary).
   - The chair's comments are in the nature of clarifications and not advocacy positions. They are given sparingly, only when needed, and without dominating the discussion.
   - The comments are an objective summary of key concerns and issues raised, leading to closure or assisting the members in making progress, for example: "Before we continue, would it help the members if I briefly summarized the key points raised and see where the members want to go from here? (Pause.) The main points in favor of this proposal appear to be . . . The main concerns about it appear to be . . . Does anyone have anything to add to these points, or shall we proceed to the vote?"
3. The requirement to vacate the chair does not apply to the presentation of a report and to the question period that follows (since the chair is not taking an advocacy position on a pending proposal but just presenting information).

The Chair's Voting Rights in a Small Meeting

Assuming that the chair is a voting member of the group, in a small meeting the following guidelines should apply:

1. The chair is free to vote or abstain like other members.
2. Some governing statutes or bylaws preclude the chair from abstaining. For example:
   - Several municipal statutes require all council members (including the mayor) to vote. In such cases, the

mayor has no option of abstaining, except by leaving the room.

- Some bylaws unwisely specify that a majority of the members present is required to adopt a motion. Here again, the only way to truly abstain and have no impact on the outcome is by leaving the room. For example, with twelve members present, six voting in favor, five against, and the chair abstaining, the motion would be defeated, even though a majority of those who voted were in favor of it. The chair's abstention would have the impact of a negative vote in this case.

The Chair's Voting Rights in a Large Meeting

In a large meeting (substantially more than a dozen members present), there is some validity in requiring the chair to remain neutral as much of the time as possible. The chair's voting rights would be as follows:

1. If the vote is by secret ballot, the chair—if a voting member—would be allowed to vote like other members (at the same time), since the voting is private and the perception of his or her impartiality would not be affected.
2. In the case of a counted show of hands or a counted standing vote, the chair would be allowed to vote (but wouldn't have to) only if her or his vote would alter the result. For example:
   - *A Tie Vote.* There are fifty votes in favor and fifty against the motion. A tie vote means that the motion is lost. If the chair is opposed to the motion, he or she does not vote, since his or her negative vote would not affect the outcome. However, if the chair is in favor of the motion, he or she can (but does not have to) vote in favor, causing the proposal to be adopted.
   - *A Close Vote.* There are fifty votes in favor and forty-nine against a motion, meaning that the motion would be adopted. If the chair is in favor of it, he or she does not vote, since that positive vote would not change the outcome. If, however, the chair is against the motion,

she or he can (but does not have to) vote against the motion, creating a tie and causing it to be lost.

- *A Close Vote on a Super-Majority Motion.* Assume that a two-thirds vote is required for adoption and sixty vote in favor and thirty against a proposal (attaining the two-thirds vote requirement, but barely). The chair can vote in the negative, block the attainment of the two-thirds vote, and cause the motion to be defeated. Or, with fifty-nine in favor and thirty against, a two-thirds vote is not attained. The chair can (but does not have to) vote in favor and change the outcome (i.e., cause the motion that would otherwise be defeated to be adopted).

3. The chair may be prevented by the bylaws or governing statute from abstaining and taking a neutral position. In such cases, the preceding examples would not apply.

A Trick Question

"The debate on a proposal to change the name of our organization was heated. The vote was close: seventy-eight in favor and seventy-eight against. The chair voted in favor of the motion and we now have a new name. Did the chair do the right thing?"

The common but incorrect answer given by many people is: "No, the chair should not have taken a position on such a sensitive issue." Others have argued that the chair was simply exercising her right and there was nothing procedurally wrong in what she did. Technically speaking, the former answer is right, but the reason given for it is wrong!

The difficulty with this question is the underlying premise that a simple majority was sufficient to change the organization's name. In most cases, the organization's name is in its bylaws or other governing document and typically requires a super-majority (a two-thirds or three-fourths vote) to change. In this case, the chair's vote made no difference: Seventy-nine in favor to seventy-eight against is nowhere near a two-thirds or three-fourths vote. The chair should have stayed out of voting and should have declared that the motion was defeated.

The Chair's Overall Challenge

The chair's overall challenge is to create the appropriate balance between efficiency and structure on the one hand, and creativity and inclusion on the other. The chair's overall task is to manage three main entities: issues, people, and time:

- *Issues.* The chair needs to monitor progress and assess whether issues have been covered sufficiently. If so, it is time to say it and facilitate a decision about closure. Conversely, if members appear to be rushing to closure, the chair needs to slow things down and ensure that issues receive the attention and due diligence that they deserve.
- *People.* The chair needs to facilitate the inclusion of members in discussion and decision making, and should be guided by the principles of fairness, equality, and common sense. Treating people with respect will bring the best out of them and will likely induce them to work together as a coherent and cohesive team. As a result, the group will advance its mandate and serve its stakeholders. With good leadership and with due process in place, members will likely accept the group's decisions as legitimate, even if they do not match all of their personal expectations.
- *Time.* Time is money. The chair needs to ensure that this precious resource is invested wisely so that the return on the investment in the meeting is maximized. The chair should always have an eye on the clock, make periodic progress reports on time, and take action to expedite discussions and initiate closure as needed.

The chair should constantly monitor the progress and mood of the meeting and ensure that each of the preceding three entities receives due attention, but not at the expense of another. For example, if too much emphasis is placed on time, the members may feel frustrated and constrained. Conversely, if every person is always accommodated, progress on issues would be slowed down and the quality of decisions might suffer.

The Chair's Roles between Meetings

Between meetings, the chair should be involved in all planning activities (see Chapter 3):

- Designing agendas in consultation with the members and with senior staff members
- Interfacing with staff, officers, directors, stakeholders, meeting planners, hotel staff, guest speakers and others, and ensuring that all planning activities are carried out
- Making routine and administrative decisions that do not require the involvement of the group
- Facilitating consensus building on urgent issues that cannot wait until the next meeting
- Reviewing minutes for accuracy
- Being available to give support, guidance, and feedback to members
- Receiving feedback, concerns, and suggestions, and taking appropriate actions

The Chair's Procedural Interventions during Meetings

The chair's procedural roles at a meeting include:

- Establishing order and decorum
- Ensuring balanced participation
- Keeping the meeting on track
- Keeping the meeting on time

This section elaborates on the above roles and includes ad-hoc scripts for principled and constructive interventions. You'll note that many intervention scripts end with a question mark, making them more consultative and softening their impact. Asking instead of telling will make you a more democratic leader.

Establishing Order and Decorum

The chair should ensure that members speak only after being recognized, generally going by whoever raises his or her hand first (or is first in line at a microphone) and not by whoever raises his or her voice first. The chair should also ensure that members are courteous, use proper language, avoid personal criticisms, stay on track, and avoid speculating on the motives of others. Here are some intervention scripts for common scenarios:

- *A member barges in and speaks without permission.*
"Could you please raise your hand if you want to speak?"
Or:
"Hands up, please!"
Or:
"In fairness to others, and so you can be heard, could you please approach the microphone and wait in line? Thank you."

- *Several members speak at the same time (chaos).*
"Can we stop for a moment, please?" (Pause until they are quiet, or blow a whistle to get their attention.) "Can we have only one person speaking at a time, please? Let me take a speakers' lineup. Who wants to speak? Please raise your hand and I'll take your name down in order."

- *Many members want to speak on the next issue.*
"I believe that many of you will want to speak on this important issue. Before we begin the discussion, how about establishing a speakers' lineup? Who would like to speak on this issue? Jack, Rose, Eleanor, and Jim. Thank you. I have one more request: If you are farther down on the speakers' lineup and your point has been made, please avoid repeating it. We have a busy agenda and travel schedules dictate that we end the meeting by 4 PM. Thank you."
Or:
"We will hear from the speaker at microphone number 4, then 1, and then 3. Speaker at microphone number 4, go ahead."

Notes

- If you find it difficult to keep track of the speakers, you can assign someone to do it for you.

- Make sure that first-time speakers are given priority over second-time speakers.

- *A member raises his or her hand and does not put it down.*

"I've seen your hand, Gerry, and added your name to the list. Could you please put your hand down? It may be distracting for other members."

Or:

"Gerry, whatever you're thinking about, can I ask you to please write it down, and focus on what Barb is saying right now? I will add your name to the speakers' lineup."

Note

- If you do not intervene in this way, the member will be more focused on his or her rebuttal than on listening to what's being said. The hanging hand will also distract others.

- *There are distracting side conversations.*

"Rose and Emily, can we have only one meeting at a time? It is difficult to concentrate otherwise."

Or:

"May I have everyone's attention please? Can the members please give the person who is speaking the same attention and respect that you want when you are speaking?"

Or:

Ask the current speaker to pause, and then wait quietly, subtly looking in the direction of the side talkers. The silence will likely bring an end to the conversation.

Or:

"Jill and David. Is there a problem?" If there is a problem, it may be productive to address it, or to allow the side conversation or activity to reach its natural end.

Intervention to avoid.

"Rose and Emily, if you can't participate productively, I will have to ask you to leave." Threats should be left as a last resort. Assume that people are reasonable and want to participate constructively, and this will become a self-fulfilling prophecy.

Intervention to avoid.

"Rose and Emily, is there something you want to add to the discussion?" This remark would give them priority over those who are lining up to speak. Avoid legitimizing and rewarding disruptive behavior.

- *A member is being heckled and booed.*

"John (heckled member), please wait a moment. Can the members please wait for their turn to speak? You have the right to disagree with someone else, but each one of us deserves the opportunity to speak without disruption, as long as we keep our comments to the issues, and as long as we observe time limits."

- *Members interrupt one another.*

"Can we please have only one person speaking at a time, and could we please let people finish what they are saying? It seems to me that we would all benefit if we listen to one another with an open mind before we form a judgment or a rebuttal to a statement."

- *A member speculates on another member's motives.*

"Can we please limit our comments to what people are actually saying and avoid speculation?"

- *A member discusses personalities or insults another member.*

"Rudy, can you please stay focused on the issue, which is _____ ?"

- *A member uses profanities.*

"May I ask you to please soften your language? It may be hard for some members to take."

Or:

"Can you pause for a moment, please? I need to ask you to use proper language. We want to hear what you want to say, but your choice of words is distracting."

Ensuring Balanced Participation

The chair should do what is needed to prevent domination and to ensure fairness and equality of opportunity to participate in discussions. Here are a few intervention scripts:

``Derek, you want to speak for the second time. Is there anyone who wishes to speak on this motion for the first time?''

``We've heard from Joan and Peter. Are there any first-time speakers on this issue?'' (Pause long enough. This will emphasize the importance of balanced participation.)

``Joanne, you have a great deal of experience in this area. Can you help us out?''

``We've heard several opinions so far and I was just wondering: Would it be productive for us to take the round-table format, go around the room, and give each member an opportunity to say briefly where they stand on this issue? Would a 1-minute comment per person be enough? Okay then, let's do it. Keep in mind: If you have nothing to add, you don't have to speak. Just say: 'pass.' How about starting with you, Joe . . .''

Keeping the Meeting on Track

The chair should monitor the discussion and the agenda, and intervene to keep the meeting on track. Here are examples of intervention scripts:

``Can we stay on track, please? Right now we are on agenda item 9, and the topic under discussion is _____.''

``Just a reminder: We have two proposals before us: a proposal to purchase a new computer and an amendment to add the 'words provided that the costs be kept below $5000, including all taxes.' Right now, discussion is on the amendment regarding keeping the costs below $5000. Is there any discussion on the amendment?''

``Rebecca, your point relates to the financial aspect of the proposal, and right now we're trying to resolve the ethical issue. Can you save your comment for later? You're a bit ahead of us.''

Keeping the Meeting on Time

At the start of a meeting, the chair should introduce time limits and facilitate a decision on them. Depending on the needs of the group, it can be asked to approve:

- A tentative closing time for the meeting
- Major milestones, (e.g., 10 AM: New computer system, 11 AM: Hiring new staff)
- Time per issue (e.g., each resolution will be allocated a grand total of 15 minutes)
- Time per comment (e.g., 3 minutes per speech)

Here are a few practical points to consider:

- To make these time limits compelling, the group should be asked whether they are acceptable. In a formal meeting, it is often wise to take a formal vote on such limits.
- The chair (or a designated timekeeper) should monitor the clock and alert members in advance of time running out: "Fifteen minutes left before we break for lunch"; or: "You have 1 minute left to speak."

Establishing the Overall Time Frame for the Meeting

''The proposed timing for the meeting is as shown on the agenda. You'll note that we have scheduled the new hiring discussion for 10 AM. At 10:45 we will have a 15-minute refreshment break, and coffee, juice, and pastries will be available. The proposal regarding furniture is scheduled for 11:30, and we're scheduled to adjourn at noon. Is the proposed time frame acceptable? (Pause, address concerns.) Thank you. The agenda and the proposed time frame have been approved. We will need to work together to keep the meeting on track and on time.''

Reminders of Agreed Time Limits on an Issue

''It is now 11:30 AM. We have 30 minutes left before our lunch break, and we are scheduled to complete the following tasks by then: _____.''

"We have 10 more minutes left in the discussion on next year's budget."

Facilitating a Time Extension on an Issue

"Before we go any further, we need to discuss the time available for discussing this proposal. It appears unlikely that we will be able to reach a logical closure on this issue by the scheduled time of 3 PM. What shall we do? Shall we extend the time by, say, 15 minutes? Is there any objection to such an extension? (Pause.) There being no objection, discussion on this proposal will end by 3:15 PM. Let's keep the discussion focused. We do not want to take more time away from the remaining issues on our agenda."

Reminders of an Agreed Time Limit per Speaker

Say with a soft voice: "You have 1 more minute to speak." Then: "30 seconds left." Then: "Time is up."
Or:
"Jocelyn, we have established a time limit, and your 3 minutes are up. We need to move to other speakers. Rudy, you're next. Go ahead." (You don't have to wait for Jocelyn's approval before giving the floor to Rudy.)

Facilitating a Time Extension for a Speaker

If a member needs an extra 2 minutes beyond the agreed time limit and you sense that there would be support for this request (i.e., the comments appear to be a good use of the group's time), say: "Jim, before you continue, I need to ask the members for an extension of your time. Would 2 more minutes be enough? Is it acceptable to grant Jim an extra 2 minutes? (Pause.) Any objection? (Pause.) Jim, go ahead."

Avoid inducing the extension decision if the comments are repetitive or if time is tight.

If there is an objection to a requested extension, or if the need for it appears questionable, facilitate a vote on it: "Those in favor of granting Jim an extra 2 minutes, please raise your hand. Thank you. Those opposed, raise your hand. Thank you. Two more minutes have been granted. Jim, after the 2 minutes, we will need to move on. Go ahead.''

Discouraging Rambling and Repetition

''In the interests of clarity, focus, and efficiency, I suggest that the members open by stating whether they support or oppose the proposal, and then give us the reasons why. To enable us to hear from as many members as possible within our limited time, I suggest that you keep your comments brief and to the point, and that if your argument has already been made, there is no need to repeat it.''

''In the interest of saving time and given our busy agenda, does anyone have anything to add to the discussion, and, if not, shall we proceed to the vote?''

''We've been hearing from the affirmative. Does anyone want to speak against this proposal, and, if not, shall we proceed to the vote?''

To a ''rambler'' (if no speaker time limit has been agreed to): ''Bob, in the interest of time, we need to move on. Your point about _____ has been made. Thank you. Our next speaker is Shawn.''

Nonverbal Interventions to Establish Respect for Time

Have a buzzer, a whistle, a light timer, or an hourglass at hand. Use these devices to inform individuals that their time is about to run out (e.g., a 30-second warning) and that time is up. With this approach, they will be able to conclude gradually rather than abruptly.
Or:
If the discussion goes in circles, or if an individual makes a long-winded statement, you can gently point to a watch or give another visual indication that time is running short.

The Chair's Substantive Interventions during Meetings

In addition to the chair's procedural roles in a meeting, there are several important roles that relate to consensus building on the substantive issues:

- Establishing the parameters for each agenda item
- Clarifying issues
- Summarizing issues
- Facilitating the decision-making process
- Introducing variety and creative problem-solving techniques

Establishing the Parameters for Each Agenda Item

Before discussion on an agenda item begins, it is helpful if the chair maps it out and clarifies some or all of the following:

- The nature and significance of the item
- The precirculated documents or background information that relate to it
- The key issues and questions to be addressed in the ensuing discussion
- The decisions that need to be made by the group
- Options that are available for decision making (if any are known)
- How much time has been allocated to the agenda item

Sample Intervention

''The next item on our agenda is the proposed upgrades to our computer system. A report that includes three options for us to consider has been circulated to you. Today we will need to choose between the three options or create a new one. There is urgency to this decision, since management wants to get this project completed by May 1. We have allocated 1 hour for this discussion, so it should end at 11:30. Derek

Cheung, our systems analyst, will lead the discussion. Are there any questions before we proceed? If not, Derek, go ahead. . . .''

Clarifying Issues

The chair should listen for ambiguities, missing data, generalizations, and misunderstandings, and ensure that issues are clarified and that people are heard and understood. In clarifying points, the chair should be precise, clear, and brief. A concise point format should be used, and lecturing or dominating the discussion should be avoided.

Sample Interventions

''Joan, I must say that I am having difficulty following your argument. What specifically are you proposing and how will it solve the problem at hand, namely that customers are complaining about poor service?''
Or:
If someone has made two significant points that were drowned in a convoluted statement: ''Richard, let me just clarify. I think I heard you make two main points. They are: 1 . . . , and 2 . . . . Am I right?'' (Make your intervention concise and brief. Don't cure rambling with rambling of your own. And never twist what the member is saying to suit your own agenda.)
Or:
If two members are too busy arguing and are not listening to each other:
''Tom and Monica, can I ask the two of you to pause for a moment? Listening to both of you, it seems to me that—yes—there are some areas where you disagree. But I can't help but hear some areas where you do agree. Both of you appear to say that _____. Where you seem to disagree is _____.''
Or:
If a member's comment indicates that he or she misunderstood a point:
''Timothy, am I correct in understanding that you believe that _____? If so, you may want to know that _____.''

Or:

If a member's comments or questions indicate that he or she has not read a precirculated report and this lack of preparation (a consistent occurrence) is consuming too much time at the meeting:

- The report's author should answer the question and should indicate that the information is in the precirculated report. Before the meeting ends, request that members review their packages in preparation for the next meeting so that time can be saved.
- To avoid embarrassing delinquent members in front of their peers, follow up with them after the meeting (i.e., a phone call, memo, or discussion over coffee, whereby you can learn more about how they work and then share your feedback). Also consider how your pre-meeting communications can reinforce the value of preparation.

Summarizing Issues

Summary statements that are accurate, objective, and concise are a very helpful tool in a meeting. They capture the essence of the consensus reached. They add a sense of purpose and direction and refocus the deliberations and the decision-making process. It is truly amazing how a good listener can convert rambling statements and discussions into concise point-form summaries. Summary statements can be made:

- After significant progress on an issue
- When an important milestone has been reached
- Just before closure and decision making

EXAMPLE: Sample Intervention

``Before we continue, let me see if I can briefly summarize the main issues that we have covered so far, the areas where we appear to agree, and the areas where we still need to do some work. The areas that we have covered so far are: _____. (Count them off, 1, 2, 3.) We seem to agree that _____. (Count: first, second, ...) Where we seem to disagree is _____. (Count again.) Did I get it right? If so, shall we record the areas of agreement in the minutes and then continue with the remaining areas?''

Facilitating the Decision-Making Process

The chair should listen to the discussion and guide the group toward closure. The flow of the discussion on each substantive agenda item generally consists of:

- *Lateral Movement:* a free-flowing discussion on specific questions
- *Forward Movement:* closure and decision making, followed by the next issue being introduced for lateral movement

The chair should listen carefully to the discussion on each issue, sense whether there has been enough lateral movement, and then facilitate a shift to closure and forward movement—that is, determine what should be done, by whom and by when, and how progress will be measured. Closure can be on a per issue basis, or, if an issue is complex or controversial, it can be divided into more manageable components, with separate closure reached on each item.

EXAMPLE: Decision and Implementation

''The time allocated for this issue has ended and it appears that we have covered it sufficiently. The apparent consensus is that we do the following: _____. Is that correct? If so, let's take a vote. Those in favor of _____ raise your hand. Thank you. Those opposed, raise your hand. Thank you. The affirmative has it and we will _____. The remaining question is how to implement this decision. Who should do _____? By when? Thank you. Are those suggestions on implementing the decision acceptable to the members? Any objection? (Pause.)

There being no objection, the decision and its implementation will be recorded in the minutes. Would those who are involved in implementation please contact me if you have trouble meeting your deadlines so that we can arrange for someone to help you out?''

Note: This example does not show that any motion was made and seconded. These formalities of parliamentary procedure are not as essential as the general principles of collective decision making, which are clearly articulating a proposal, an opportunity to discuss it, and determining whether the group is in agreement with it (with an opportunity to dissent). All of these components are present in the preceding script.

EXAMPLE: Preventing Premature Closure or an Unwise Decision

Members are rushing a decision through, but you are aware of some gaps and deficiencies in the document or proposal. You are concerned that an unwise decision could be made.

"It really is laudable that the members want to make progress and proceed to the next agenda item. But just before we take a vote on this proposal, I would like to bring to your attention a few concerns about it. You can tell me whether you still want to vote on it now, or whether you want to address these concerns before a vote.''

EXAMPLE: A Multicomponent Issue

A proposal contains various parts, but only one of them is contentious. The discussion is not going anywhere.

"It seems to me that the only contentious segment of this proposal is part 2. Shall we take it out for a separate vote? Is there any objection to doing that? (Pause. If there is an objection, you may need to take a formal vote on whether the proposal will be divided.) There being no objection, we will deal first with parts 1, 3, and 4. Is there any further discussion on these parts? (Pause.) If not, those in favor of parts 1, 3, and 4, raise your hand. Thank you. Those opposed, raise your hand. Thank you. Parts 1, 3, and 4 are approved. We will now focus on part 2. Is there any discussion on it?''

Note: Given the controversy, part 2 may end up being amended, postponed, or referred to a committee for study.

EXAMPLE: Avoiding the Tyranny of the Minority

The scenario: An assertive individual insists that the language of the proposal be changed, or that the vote on it be postponed. If the group capitulates to the individual, the risks are:

- The proposal could become so diluted that it is meaningless. Quality may suffer.
- Time is taken away from other issues because a persistent member just wouldn't give up.
- Resentment and acrimony could develop among the members of the silent majority.
- A precedent could be set whereby the group is governed by the minority.

With these risks in mind, it is important that you give the majority back its power. There are times to listen and accommodate the minority (it may have valid points that could improve the quality of a decision). But once there has been sufficient debate and amendment, there is a need to ascertain the wishes of the majority regarding closure. At this point of closure, disputes on how to proceed should be settled by a formal vote.

Intervention: ''Jack, I appreciate the fact that the wording of the proposal is not acceptable to you. I need to check what the other members want. Those who believe that the wording of the amended proposal is acceptable, raise your hand. Thank you. Those who believe that it isn't acceptable and that the alternative word choice is preferable, please raise your hand. Thank you. The original proposal has been approved.''

Intervention: ''Warren, I understand that you prefer to delay the decision and to have the matter referred to the Education Committee for more study, but other members seem to feel differently. I will therefore take a vote. Those who prefer to vote on this proposal today, please raise your hand. Thank you. Those who prefer to delay the vote and refer the proposal to the Education Committee, please raise your hand. Thank you. It appears that the majority prefer to deal with the issue today."

Intervention (if an assertive member persists even after a vote has been taken): "Thank you, Mike. I am sure everyone realizes how important this issue is to you. However, as you may recall, we already voted on it, and we must be governed by the wishes of the majority. We have several additional issues to consider today and our time is precious. We need to move on. The next item is _____."

Introducing Variety and Creative Problem-Solving Techniques

The chair can propose varied and creative discussion activities to lead to greater inclusion and to enhance the quality of the discussions and of the decisions made.

EXAMPLE: Involving Quieter Members in Discussions

To involve quieter members in the discussion of an issue, define a key question that needs to be addressed by the group and then use one of these approaches:

"For the next 3 minutes, I would ask you to consider a key question on your own and jot down a few notes about it. After the 3 minutes, I will poll you at random and see what you came up with. The question is as follows: _____. You have 3 minutes on your own. Jot down your thoughts."

Or:

"For the next 5 minutes, I would ask you to discuss a key question with the person sitting next to you. After 5 minutes, I will poll the various groups for their answers. Here is the question: _____. You have 5 minutes."

Or:

"The next issue is _____. This is a complex issue that consists of several subissues. I thought that it would be productive to address it in this way: I have prepared four questions that we need to address. They are: 1, 2, 3, 4. We can divide ourselves into four task forces and each task force can consider one of the questions for 10 minutes. At the end of 10 minutes, we will regroup, each task force will report, and we'll carry on with the discussion in the full group. Does this approach sound reasonable?''

If this approach is acceptable, create the four task forces (consider the composition of each task force: Are the views and expertise diverse enough? Do the members of each group know enough about the question?) and distribute the four questions. Circulate among the groups, monitor progress, and give specific time warnings (e.g., 3 minutes left).

EXAMPLE: Resolving Deadlocks

There are three distinct and seemingly opposing views on an issue. The discussion is going nowhere.

''We've been discussing this agenda item for a while and I am concerned that other agenda items could suffer if we don't reach closure by the designated closing time of 2 PM. Given that there seem to be three distinct views on this issue, may I suggest that we take a 15-minute break and that Jim, Joan, and Jill (the three opinion leaders) gather separately and come up with common ground. Does it sound like this approach would be productive?''

Other Alternatives That Could Be Proposed to Resolve a Deadlock

- Suggest that the committee of three report back at the next meeting.
- If the decision must be made expeditiously, ask if the members want to vote on each of the three proposals and see which one has the most support.
- Ask the advocates of the views that are furthest apart to go for a walk and try articulating the opposing view for a

change. This way they will know how well they have been listening, may be challenged to think outside the box, and may arrive at creative solutions that are better than their own.

Offering Challenge and Celebrating Successes

In addition to the procedural and substantive interventions in the preceding sections, the chair should offer leadership to the group. Two key leadership functions that are often ignored are:

- Offering challenge
- Celebrating successes and offering recognition

Offering Challenge

Far too often, groups rely on the eternal volunteers to perform tasks, thereby depriving themselves of the talents of others. You may say: "But the others never volunteer." The question is: "Why not?" Could it be that no one ever asked them, or maybe they were not given enough time to consider the assignment, or maybe they do not know enough about the task and the commitment it would take, or possibly they are a little nervous or new to the group and could use some encouragement?

Task assignments should not be handed out randomly. The question: "Who would like to do this?" should be avoided. An effective leader draws on the many talents within the group, and spreads the work around. The chair should offer challenges to every member without them needing to ask: "How can I help?" or "How can I make a difference?"

As an effective chair, you should get to know the members and their unique strengths, talents, and skills. Find out what makes them perform to their potential. If you don't know, ask them. With this knowledge, you can customize the assignment of tasks without waiting for volunteers. This approach can:

- Empower the members and increase the levels of commitment to the work of the group.

- Increase the group's leadership base and make for good succession planning.
- Distribute the work of the group more evenly and reduce the likelihood of burnout.
- Shift negative energies into constructive channels.
- Raise the quality of the group's work and its decisions.
- Put the group in a stronger position to move beyond what it has to do and direct its attention to proactive work.

EXAMPLES:

``Rebecca, you have special expertise in the area of _____, and we need this job done well. Would it be okay if I put your name forward to do it? I know that this may seem like a big job, but I promise to give you my support and advice if you need it.''

Or:

``Melanie, thank you for volunteering for this assignment, but I am wondering if we might involve some of our newer members in the work of the group. Dawn, what do you think? Would you consider it? Do you want to think about it, call me with your questions, and let us know your decision at our next meeting?''

Celebrating Successes and Offering Recognition

Most people tend to be sparing with recognition and positive feedback. The chair should lead the efforts to celebrate successes by noting special events, achievements, and contributions. Recognition can be done publicly and privately. Be generous but genuine. Reward positive efforts with tangible means (gifts, awards) and intangible means (a compliment, a personal memo, or public recognition). Among its other benefits, positive feedback will:

- Reinforce positive contributions and perpetuate them.
- Boost morale and commitment levels among members.
- Make meetings more varied and engaging.

- Make it easier to give corrective feedback and soften its impact.
- Make for a kinder and gentler meeting and soften the impact of controversies.

EXAMPLES

''Rick, on behalf of the committee, I would like to thank you for the efforts that you put into preparing this report. It is a clear and complete document, and it has helped us resolve a very challenging and complex issue. How about giving Rick a round of applause?''

Or:

''Susan, you are the winner of the award for the most consistent attendee. You did not miss even one meeting this year. Moreover, you've been a constructive and active participant in our discussions, and we have appreciated your insights and creative thoughts. You challenged us to think outside the box. For your contribution to the work of the committee, we have this special award for you.''

Or:

''Before we go any further, we have a special event today. Happy birthday to . . . .'' (Or celebrate family events or a promotion, etc.)

6

Surviving the Contentious Meeting

In this chapter the challenge of chairing contentious meetings and dealing with divisive issues and difficult members is confronted. The information and intervention scripts should be particularly useful when such meetings are preceded by nasty infighting and power struggles. Specific questions addressed are:

- What are the wrong questions to ask about a contentious meeting?
- What assumptions should be made about contentious meetings?
- What questions should be asked about contentious meetings?
- What other notions should you consider about organizational controversies?
- How will you prepare for a contentious meeting?
- How will you chair a contentious meeting?
- What are some useful remarks to make at a contentious meeting?

Wrong Questions to Ask about a Contentious Meeting

Your mission, should you choose to accept it, is to prepare for and chair a highly contentious meeting, such as:

- A church membership meeting, with a proposal to remove the pastor.

- A staff meeting, called to discuss a proposal to become unionized, with the proposal not sitting well with the board of directors, and with much infighting taking place right now.

- A shareholder meeting, with a proxy fight developing to take over the board of directors.

- A meeting of a club scheduled to vote on a proposal to borrow a substantial sum of money for the purchase of a new building. There is a loud and aggressive majority in favor of the proposal, but the two-thirds vote required in the bylaws would be tough to get. You are concerned about the possibility of physical violence directed at the minority if the proposal is defeated.

- A public meeting, organized by a mining company, to discuss a new mine proposed for a pristine and ecologically sensitive area. Environmental groups have mobilized their members to attend the meeting. There may be demonstrations outside and disruptions at the meeting.

How do you respond? Instinctively, you panic. Next, you look for the quickest way out of this assignment. Finding none, you may find yourself asking questions such as:

- How will I survive this meeting?
- How will I control the members and stop them from fighting with each other?
- How will I overpower disruptive members or aggressive minorities?
- How will I avoid chaos and confusion?
- How will I prevent the meeting from taking 5 hours and achieving nothing, as it did last year?
- Will I need to hire security guards?

The answers to some of these questions become evident when you read previous chapters of this book: With preventive and visionary planning (Chapter 3), and with effective and principled facilitation (Chapter 5), you will be well equipped to address most, if not all, of the preceding challenges. But there is more.

The problem with the preceding questions is that they provide the wrong focus for your efforts and preclude other more important questions from being asked. These questions are negatively and defensively driven, and therefore limit the potential of the contentious meeting to achieve positive results. They seek to prevent something from happening instead of making something happen. They assume that some people are unreasonable, childish, and misguided enemies of the organization.

With these adversarial notions in mind (``It's them against us''), one of two outcomes can be predicted: either ``we win and they lose,'' or ``we capitulate.'' In order to win, the typical strategy is to stifle, control, dominate, manipulate, or placate. What you need is a different set of assumptions and a different approach as outlined in the following sections.

Right Assumptions to Make about a Contentious Meeting

Here are two rarely made assumptions that are suggested for a contentious meeting:

- Assume that people are reasonable and you will likely get reasonable people.
- Assume that the majority of the members want a principled and productive discussion.

Assuming Reasonable People

As you prepare for the contentious meeting, your departure point should be that you are working with reasonable people, who, being treated as such (notwithstanding their seemingly disruptive behavior), will likely respond in kind, if not immediately, then eventually.

Success Story 1: The Man Next to Microphone 3

Susan, an outside consultant, was asked to chair a meeting for a national association. At the outset, she was warned about ''the man next to microphone 3,'' who had been very disruptive at past meetings. Susan expressed her appreciation for the caution, but then proceeded to treat the man at microphone 3 with the same respect as she treated everyone else, giving him the benefit of the doubt. At the same time, she demanded that he adhere to the same guidelines that others were, that is: Speak by lining up at a microphone or by raising his hand, observe the established time limits, and yield to first-time speakers after he made his point.

The man at microphone 3 was initially disruptive. He was suspicious and skeptical about this new attitude, and even threw barbs to test Susan. However, with persistence and with consistency in our approach, he changed his behavior.

Success Story 2: A Critical Board Member

A president was about to chair a contentious board meeting, with one member who, in the past, had been very critical, negative, and disruptive. On outside advice, the president wrote her a letter, pledging that he would listen to her feedback with an open mind, and would treat her criticism as though she was giving him flowers and chocolates. Much to his amazement, she approached him at the board meeting with a bouquet of flowers and a box of expensive chocolates! She said: ''No one has ever written me a letter like this.''

Treating disruptive members as reasonable people does not mean being 100% nice, and giving them everything that they want. This would amount to anarchy. Yes, there are individual rights, but they must be weighed against collective rights. The minority does have the right to be heard (within established limits), but it is the majority that governs. Which leads to our next assumption.

Assuming a Collective Desire for Principled and Productive Discussions

Most members appreciate a meeting with a clear focus on issues, conducted with order, decorum, fairness, and common sense. Their views on issues may be sharply divided, but the members will likely accept that compromises need to be made. *Note:* With a clearly focused discussion, it has often been found that perceived differences are much larger than real differences, and that common ground is much broader than initially thought. This has often led groups to creative solutions outside the adversarial box that everyone was trapped in before the meeting. Such solutions are hard to reach when the real issues are clouded by rumors, innuendos, and animosities built over a long time.

Building on the assumption that most members are interested in a principled and well-focused discussion, you can define the agenda and rules of order for the meeting (some refer to those as the "rules of engagement"), and present them for approval at the start of the meeting. Once this process-related work is done, you can lead the group to focus on the substantive issues.

Having the rules of engagement approved by the members is a powerful tool. Once this is done, it is not your personal wishes that you are enforcing, but the collective wishes of the group. When faced with a disruptive minority, it will not be you against them. You will have the power of democracy behind you, making your interventions compelling. You could say: "As you may recall, *the members* approved a rule that first-time speakers receive priority. This rule is intended to ensure fairness and equality, and we must respect the decisions of the members."

Democratically based interventions are powerful. They will be your most effective tool in convincing a disruptive minority to cooperate. Such interventions will also help you to convert eternal critics into constructive participants and possibly to turn them into visionary creators.

Right Questions to Ask about a Contentious Meeting

Ask the following questions about a contentious meeting:

- What are the bottom-line issues at the core of this dispute? What are the side issues that may be clouding the real ones?

- What are the principles on which everyone seems to agree and where do people truly differ?
- How can the meeting be focused on the things that matter and shift away from those that do not matter (e.g., personality conflicts, meaningless technicalities)?
- How can the meeting be focused on the organization's mandate and the stakeholders that it is intended to serve?
- What needs to be done and what decisions need to be made to bring closure to this dispute and to start an internal healing and reconciliation process? How can the organization get back on track and refocus on its mandate and purposes?
- What positive returns can be obtained on the investment in this meeting?

These questions will lead you away from the goal of trying to prevent something bad from happening (e.g., disruptions, chaos) and lead you toward making something good happen (e.g., closure, healing and reconciliation, organizational realignment). With the majority being committed to a principled and constructive approach, with the minority joining in, and with your effective planning and leadership, what may seem to be an ambitious goal is definitely attainable. The meeting may or may not be enough to reach full and final closure on this dispute, but the healing process can at least begin.

General Points to Consider about Controversy

This section addresses the following questions:

- What are some of the fundamental notions to consider about controversy?
- What are the legitimate causes of controversy?
- What makes controversy worse than it needs to be?
- What can be done to prevent controversy or to reduce its negative impacts?

Fundamental Notions about Controversy

Division of opinions is only natural and should not in itself be a problem. Indeed, if controversy is well managed, it can become an opportunity for growth and learning, as well as a catalyst for making long-needed organizational changes.

It has been said that diversity of opinions makes a strong organization. If all organizational decisions were made with everyone voting exactly the same way, there would be a major lack of healthy questioning, due diligence, individual initiative, and independent thought. At the same time, organizations cannot be governed by the personal wishes of every individual, because this situation could result in anarchy, or the rule of the minority. Collective decision making should take into account individual views but should eventually reach the destination that the majority finds most compelling and logical.

Consider this quote: "If two of us have different opinions, it means that each one of us has a different piece of the truth." If we listen to each other, we will discover the bigger truth, learn about other perspectives and interests, and be able to make more intelligent and informed decisions. At the end of such a process, there may remain disagreements, but we may also discover that we have a lot more in common than we first thought.

Therefore, discussions must shift away from the adversarial mode and into the collaborative mode. The approach must be hard on the issues but soft on the people, and must continually seek the broader truth on which wise and responsible decisions should be based.

One more notion about controversy is: "Never attribute to malice what can reasonably be attributed to a misunderstanding, or a lack of knowledge or skill." Don't ask questions that imply the offensive or unproductive behavior is deliberate (e.g., "Why is John being so unreasonable?"). Give others the benefit of the doubt and check your assumptions about them.

Remember that the other side is not responsible for *all* the problems. If you find yourself justifying and rationalizing how right you are, proving how wrong your adversaries are, and denying the validity of criticism of your leadership style, chances are that you are equally wrong, or even more guilty than the other parties.

You need to stop defending your actions and take an honest and truly open-minded look at what you may be doing to worsen the situation. Remember that whenever you point a finger at someone, there are three fingers pointing right back at you. The fact that you may perceive other parties as acting in bad faith or with a hidden agenda does not mean that you are right. No one has a monopoly on virtue, and, incidentally, the hidden agenda may have merit.

Legitimate Causes of Controversy

A meeting can become controversial due to legitimate reasons, such as fundamental differences of opinion on substantive issues. For example:

- Should a major purchase or initiative, whose benefits are disputed, be made?
- Are proposed cutbacks in staffing or service levels justified?
- Should the organization change its name?
- Is the organization poorly managed? Is the leadership fiscally responsible?
- Should the services of a key staff member or elected officer be terminated?

What Makes Controversy Worse Than It Needs to Be

Differences of opinion on issues are natural. By themselves, such differences can be settled through open discussions and appropriate compromises, and without chaotic and disorderly meetings. However, conflict can be unnecessarily worsened and become increasingly difficult to manage due to process-related factors. Watch for the following systemic vulnerabilities and gaps within your organization:

- A lack of clarity of the organization's mandate, or a lack of commitment to it

- Poorly written, poorly conceived, or nonexistent organizational policies and procedures
- Mandates, policies, or procedures that are outdated, unrealistic, and unenforceable
- Misunderstandings, misconceptions, and unfounded assumptions
- A corporate tendency to generalize, categorize, compare, and speculate
- A tendency to take criticism and dissenting opinions as personal attacks
- A tendency to search for guilty persons rather than identify systemic problems
- A tendency for people to take themselves too seriously
- A communications breakdown, resulting in rumors, innuendos, fear, lack of trust, personal animosities, and nasty power struggles
- Leaders losing touch with followers and refusing to listen to them
- Leaders becoming obsessed with a desire to control, refusing to let go and engage followers in meaningful consultation and share decision making (a top-down approach)
- A lack of logical and principled processes to address significant differences of opinion
- A lack of clarity of roles and responsibilities, and confusion about the division of decision-making powers among the organization's various bodies

How to Prevent Conflict or Reduce Its Negative Impacts

Organizational conflict and its negative impacts can be reduced by:

- A clear organizational mandate, widely understood, accepted, and supported by all
- Leaders who are open, honest, humble, ethical, principled, entrenched in the organization's mandate, and dedicated to delivering quality service to the various stakeholders
- A commitment to keep members and stakeholders in-

formed, in addition to ensuring that they are consulted, especially when decisions that affect them in a significant way are about to be made (early involvement rather than involvement after the decisions have been finalized)

- Clear definitions of roles and responsibilities (of staff members, board members, and appointed and elected officers) that are widely understood and accepted
- Open channels of communications (two-way, i.e., leaders who communicate and listen)
- Channels for exchanging feedback on a regularly scheduled basis and on an ad-hoc basis
- Early detection systems to anticipate conflict and proactively address it in its early stages
- Respect for individuality and diverging views, while seeking to uphold overall mandates

EXAMPLE: Two Ways of Addressing an Organizational Dispute

The Situation

The president of a church and its pastor are not getting along. In addition, some members are dissatisfied with the spiritual leadership that they are receiving. The president believes that the pastor should be removed. Many members of the church object to this idea and communicate their concerns to the board.

Note the differences between the two routes of addressing this organizational dispute:

Route 1

The president introduces a proposal at the next board meeting to remove the pastor. He speaks passionately and dominates the discussion. By a majority vote, the board decides to remove the pastor. Members vote in favor partly because they are intimidated by the president and partly because the minority did not have a real opportunity to explain its views.

The pastor decides to sue the church and the board. In addition, several members organize a special general meeting to remove the entire board and reinstate the pastor. The board (under the guidance of its president) becomes entrenched in its position and refers to the dissidents as enemies of the church. The ensuing membership meeting is adversarial and chaotic, and the motion to remove the directors is dismissed on a technicality.

In the meantime, the court action continues and becomes nastier by the day. The church pays substantial legal fees. The focus on the church's spiritual direction is lost. Several members leave the church. Some decide to start their own church, hire the dismissed pastor, and sue the original church and every member of its board for damages.

Route 2

The president brings the issues to a board meeting, explains them, and then stops talking and starts listening for feedback. The board directs the president to meet the pastor, with the assistance of a mediator, to discuss and resolve the issues. The president and the pastor fully explore and resolve the issues. Both agree that from now on they will meet twice a month to exchange feedback (positive and negative) and resolve outstanding concerns.

The Differences between the Two Routes

- Route 1 is adversarial, hard on people, and soft on issues. Route 2 is collaborative, soft on people, and hard on issues.
- Route 1 is expensive and destructive. Route 2 is simple, logical, inexpensive, and yields constructive results.
- Route 1 is dictatorial (the president effectively makes all the decisions). Route 2 is democratic and inclusive.
- Route 1 finds the board in a reactive position, showing leadership that divides the church. Route 2 finds the board in a proactive position, showing leadership that unites the church.

Preparing for a Contentious Meeting

Leaders who prepare for a contentious meeting are often in denial mode, pretending that no problem exists, or just hoping that it will somehow go away. By preparing, you can lessen the likelihood of a chaotic meeting. More important, you can increase the likelihood of a constructive and profitable outcome. In preparation for a controversial meeting, follow the planning steps outlined in Chapter 3. The information that follows offers planning suggestions specific to contentious meetings.

Reinforcing the Group's Mandate

In preparing for the contentious meeting, reinforce the group's mandate as articulated in your governing documents (constitution, mission statement). With a focus on this mandate, hard positions can be softened and common ground becomes easier to find. You can reinforce the mandate in these ways:

- Build it into any premeeting discussions with members.
- Use it to determine the bottom-line issues and the side issues in this controversy.
- Build it into the opening of the chair's script (see example at the end of this chapter) and include it as an ad-hoc script to be used if and when needed (e.g., when things become heated, the chair could say: "It might be useful to remind ourselves what our mandate is . . .").

Defining an Affirmative Purpose for the Meeting

Define the purpose of the meeting in affirmative terms. Don't hesitate to be ambitious, even when faced with skepticism: "It seems to me that a worthwhile goal for this meeting would be to bring closure to divisive issues, resolve areas of disagreement, and put the organization on a path of healing and reconciliation. In the end, we need to get back on track and work together to achieve our mandate, serve our stakeholders, and get ready for the future. It may sound like a tall order right now, but we need to articulate it nonetheless."

Negotiating the Agenda for the Meeting

Involve all sides of the controversy in designing the agenda, so as to develop a sense of joint ownership and commitment to it before the meeting begins. Consider these steps:

- Work with proponents of adversarial proposals and see if they can be converted into ones that might facilitate healing.
- Contact leaders of various factions and obtain their feedback on the agenda.
- If there is opposition to a proposed agenda item, indicate that this dispute will be settled by a vote at the meeting.
- If a faction presses you to make a unilateral change to the agenda, say: "I understand what you want. At the same time, my task is not to impose decisions but to facilitate decision making. Just like you wouldn't want me to impose a decision on you, it wouldn't be fair for me to impose a decision on other parties."

EXAMPLE: Premeeting Discussions of Procedural Concerns

Prior to a meeting, it became clear that one group would be disruptive and ruin all the planning efforts. The facilitator met the group separately, explained how he proposed to run the meeting, and asked for feedback. The group made a few suggestions and requested time to make a presentation. The facilitator indicated that changes to the agenda would require agreement by those present at the meeting. With these issues settled, the group arrived the next day ready to work instead of coming to do battle.

Engaging and Broad-Based Discussion Activities

Structure the discussion to involve as many members as possible. This will likely reduce the impact of vocal minorities (who tend to dominate the microphones), make the outcomes more representative of the silent majority, soften the debate, and make it more principled and focused on bottom-line issues. Explain your approach and the principles behind it to the different factions prior to the meeting. Here are examples of discussion activities to create balanced discussions and level the playing field in a contentious meeting:

■ Hold breakout group discussions, with specific assignments given to different groups, and with each group reporting its findings later to the full group. Frame the questions in a way that will lead to resolution rather than deepen the conflict. For example: Instead of asking: "Is our organization really falling apart?" ask: "What are the fundamental issues that divide us right now, and what key decisions do we need to make to get back on track?"

■ Include a box for written questions or comments to induce the participation of those who prefer not to speak in public. The chair should alternate between questions from the microphones and questions from the box. Ask everyone to write legibly.

Avoiding the Risks of Excluding Certain Stakeholders

Who you invite to a contentious meeting sends a message. Who you exclude also sends a message. Ensure that all parties who have a legitimate stake in the outcome are invited to the meeting or that they are at least involved in the consultative process in some way (e.g., by making a written submission, or by being interviewed by phone prior to the meeting). Include adversarial parties because they can undermine the process or the implementation of decisions if they are excluded, and, more important, because their views are important pieces of the truth. Past disruptive behaviors should not be a factor in your decision of whom to include.

EXAMPLE: The Impact of Excluding a Stakeholder

A mining company decided to exclude an environmental group (known to be aggressive and vocal) from a public consultation meeting. The story made damaging news headlines for several days, raising questions such as: "What are you afraid of? Can't you handle the heat?" The company eventually bowed to the pressure. To everyone's surprise, with a professionally facilitated meeting, the environmental group participated constructively.

Facilitating a Contentious Meeting

The role of the chair in a meeting is discussed in detail in Chapter 5. This section includes examples of procedural and substantive interventions to deal with situations that typically occur in contentious meetings.

EXAMPLE: A Speaker Is Being Heckled

"Can we have only one person speaking at a time please?"
Or:
"Ladies and gentlemen, I would ask that you give the person speaking the same respect and attention that you want when you are speaking."
Or:
"May I have your attention please? (Pause until they are quiet.) I am sure everyone recognizes that the issues before this meeting are difficult. But to get them resolved and to get this organization back on track, we need to listen to members with an open mind and let them speak without interruption."
Avoid threats such as: "Stop heckling or I will have to ask you to leave the room." Do not reinforce the adversarial sentiment. With most people, the principled approach works, and penalties and threats are not necessary.

EXAMPLE: There Is Excessive Applause

Excessive and enthusiastic applause for one side makes it intimidating for those with opposing views to speak. You could say: "Before we go any further, I appreciate the fact that there is support for certain views, as shown by your applause. However, I am concerned that this applause may make it intimidating for members with opposing views to express them. We need to hear all sides of the issue fully if we are to make wise decisions. This discussion is not about one side winning and another side losing but about making the best decisions for the organization. With this in mind, I would ask you to avoid applause altogether.''

Minority members will feel protected, safe, and freer to express themselves. Majority members will hopefully be more sensitive to others. Eventually they may even listen more carefully and soften their positions.

EXAMPLE: Someone Is Resorting to Abusive Language and Personal Attacks

''Can we please speak on the issues and avoid personal criticism?''

Or:

''Mrs. Yates, I am sure everyone recognizes how strongly you feel about this issue. But I must ask you to tone down your choice of words, because some members may find them hard to take.''

EXAMPLE: Shifting from Criticism to Affirmative Suggestions

A board of directors held a meeting with twenty irate members to listen to their complaints and concerns. Each member was given 3 minutes to make a statement. The facilitator focused at first on managing the group and keeping each member within the time limit. The discussion was lively and passionate, and consisted mainly of harsh accusations: ''You are not listening to us . . . You never let us know what's coming . . . You make decisions without consulting us . . .''

Throughout this discussion, the facilitator did very little speaking, except to say: ''Thank you. The next speaker is . . .'' Or: ''You have 30 seconds left.'' Or (with a louder voice): ''Time's up.'' Or: ''Can we have only one person speaking at a time, please?'' He kept his involvement purely at the procedural level and avoided the substantive issues.

The facilitator's leadership earned the members' trust and respect—so much so that when all prepared statements were read, the time was right for him to say:

''Thank you for your presentations and for the order and civility. While you were speaking, I couldn't help but make note of the main points that you raised. Would you like me to give you a brief summary?'' They said: ''Yes, of course.'' He proceeded, but in his summary he converted negatively and harshly worded remarks (''You are not doing this . . .''; ''You are guilty of that . . .'') into affirmative solution-oriented statements:

''The main issues that I heard you raise are: First, you appear to want your board to listen to you and to be more sensitive to your concerns. Second, you want your board to involve you in some way in decision making, and you indicate that a more inclusive approach would increase your support and respect for its decisions. Finally, you want your board to communicate with you on a more regular basis. Is this an accurate summary of what you want?''

Although that was not at all what they said, it was an accurate summary of what they wanted. The tone of the meeting softened considerably. The members were now talking about constructive solutions, and about healing and reconciliation. They were turned from critics into creators.

Partial Chair's Script for a Contentious Meeting

Sample opening and closing remarks for the chair of a contentious meeting are supplied next. For an example of a full script, see Chapter 4.

Opening Remarks

''I have brief opening remarks to make. As your president, I fully recognize that the issues scheduled to come before this meeting have been difficult. Our organization has changed and we are undergoing growing pains.

''While the issues to come before us are challenging, I am confident that we can work together and deal with them tonight with openness and integrity, and with order, civility, and respect. With your support, I know that we can create a climate whereby passionate advocacy is balanced by careful listening, and where the debate is hard on the issues but soft on the people.

''We will need to work together to uphold the principles of equality, fairness, and common sense, and to serve the best interests of the organization and its stakeholders. We need to resolve and bring closure to divisive issues so that we can move forward toward fulfilling our collective mandate.

''Our mission statement articulates our mandate and purposes, and it is always useful to review it, especially when times are tough, to remind us of who we are, who we serve, and what we are trying to accomplish. I would like to read our mission statement to you now.''

Closing Remarks

''Before we adjourn, I would like to thank you for your support and for working together to maintain a civil and respectful tone throughout this meeting. The issues that we faced today were not easy, but, as you proved so well, rational discussions can lead to positive outcomes for our organization.

''As your president, I will remember this meeting as a pivotal point in the development of our organization. I am looking forward to working with your governing board to ensure that the concerns expressed in this meeting are properly addressed, so that we can move ahead, as a coherent and cohesive team, and fulfill the mandate of this organization.''

7

Rules of Order That Make Sense

In this chapter rules of order or parliamentary procedure and their use in meetings is addressed. This chapter demystifies and humanizes the rules and makes them more user-friendly. It also dispels common myths and misconceptions.

This approach is sensible and practical, but it is likely to represent significant departures from what you may be used to. Some consider this approach unorthodox, whereas others find it to be refreshingly relevant to today's realities. In any event, you will discover some new options that you didn't know you had. Here are two qualifiers and one reassurance:

- *A Qualifier:* The information contained herein is not a comprehensive guide to rules of order. Only the essential rules that you are most likely to encounter in your meetings are covered. If you require a complete guide on rules of order, refer to your favorite parliamentary manual.

- *A Qualifier:* The information given herein is not legal advice. It is only advice on rules of order, offered by the author, who holds the designations of PRP (professional registered parliamentarian) and CPP (certified professional parliamentarian), and has practiced in the field for more than 15 years.

- *A Reassurance:* Based on my professional assessment, none of the advice given in this chapter violates the fundamental principles of parliamentary procedure. The fact that the approach is flexible and customized to today's realities does not make it incorrect or flawed in any way. In fact, in many respects, this approach is more likely to uphold the fundamental principles of democratic decision making than the prevailing practices.

The subjects addressed in this chapter are:

- Governing principles and general concepts of parliamentary procedure
- Parliamentary procedure and the real world
- How to determine voting results
- Voting without the formality of a motion
- Main motions: definitions followed by scripts to prevent counterproductive motions from consuming time
- The six steps of handling a main motion and their significance or lack thereof
- Amending a motion—the traditional approach
- An informal approach to main motions and amendments
- Delaying or avoiding a vote on a proposal: the tabling dilemma
- Revisiting a past decision: reconsideration, rescission, amendment, renewal
- Points of order and appeals
- Determining the significance (or lack thereof) of procedural violations
- Tools and intervention scripts to combat procedural nonsense and to reposition common sense and principle in the forefront

Governing Principles and Concepts of Parliamentary Procedure

This section addresses the following subjects:

- The purposes and fundamental principles of parliamentary procedure
- Adjusting the level of formality to the needs of your group

- The governing documents of an organization
- The types of meetings when collective decisions can be made
- The quorum requirement

The Purposes of Parliamentary Procedure

Parliamentary procedure is the set of rules and customs that govern the conduct of formal business meetings. The rules of order are intended to achieve certain results and uphold fundamental principles. Specifically, the rules are intended:

- To facilitate progress, that is, to enable the group to make collective decisions within a reasonable amount of time
- To involve the members in discussion and decision making on an even playing field, whereby each member has the same opportunity to affect the outcome
- To entrench the principles of equality, fairness, and common sense
- To ensure that order, decorum, and clarity are preserved, regardless of the size of the meeting, and regardless of the complexity and divisiveness of the issues at hand
- To protect certain rights within the organization, namely:
  —The right of the majority to rule, avoiding monarchy, whereby the chair imposes his or her will on the group, and avoiding the tyranny of the minority, whereby the most knowledgeable or outspoken members prevail
  —The right of the minority to be heard within established limits before decisions are made (preventing a steamroller effect, whereby a majority pushes decisions through)
  —The right of individuals to be treated with fairness, dignity, and respect
  —The rights of the absentees and the entire organization to be protected from abuse

If the rules of order are used in a way that undermines the preceding principles or achieves opposite results (e.g., frustrating progress, wasting time, tilting the scales in favor of a minority, or using them for obstructive or adversarial purposes), something must be done to get back to the basics. Raise the appropriate questions with your group and reentrench the preceding goals and principles.

Adjusting the Level of Formality to the Needs of Your Group

Rules of order tend to introduce formality and structure to a meeting: Proposals are introduced formally as motions, changes in wording are presented and debated as amendments, and so on. The level of formality can be adjusted to suit the needs of the group as long as the fundamental principles are upheld. The formality and the precise terminology are less significant than the principles. The needed level of formality differs from group to group and usually increases with:

- *The Size of the Group.* A small staff or committee meeting can be run casually and with no formal rules. A large meeting of shareholders or members requires tighter control and hence a greater level of formality. A governing board will likely need a medium level of formality.

- *The Complexity and Sensitivity of the Issues.* Noncontentious or routine decisions require very little formality and can be made without motions. In contrast, discussions of contentious or complex issues may become chaotic without a high degree of structure.

Determining the necessary level of formality is more like an art than a science. The amount of needed structure may even vary within the same meeting. For example:

- Even in a large meeting it is possible to conduct some discussions less formally (e.g., breaking a large meeting into small group discussions, thereby making it easier for the microphone-shy members to participate in a meaningful way). It is also possible to make some collective decisions without the formality of a motion (e.g., making changes to the agenda or adopting noncontentious amendments).

- Even in a small meeting discussions of contentious issues can become heated and in those instances the members will likely need a greater degree of formality than normal (e.g., if there is no common ground and a decision must be made now, a formal vote may be needed to resolve the dispute).

In groups that operate informally and make decisions by consensus, motions and votes may indeed become oppressive and constrain the free and creative flow of ideas. However, caution should be taken in such groups to ensure that the informality does not compromise fundamental principles. For example:

- The casual conduct of the meeting may lead to proposals not being clearly articulated, and it is often left to the secretary to interpret the decisions of the group. This practice is risky.
- In casually run meetings, the wishes of the majority are often not ascertained. A statement by the chair or a dominant member is often mistakenly recorded as a decision of the group.
- A lack of structure often brings with it hesitancy to enforce rules. Intervening to prevent interruptions, domination, digressions, or rambling is not a popular thing to do. The meeting becomes a free-for-all. Anarchy—not democracy—reigns, because no one has the courage to introduce a basic structure to the meeting.

The Governing Documents of an Organization

Governing documents establish the formal framework within which an organization operates. Among other things, they define how the organization's membership is structured, how it is governed, and how its meetings are run. The number of governing documents depends on your group and how it is organized.

A Committee's Governing Document: Terms of Reference

Committees and task forces are typically appointed by a higher authority (usually a board of directors or a senior officer).

A committee is typically subject to one governing document, which is often referred to as terms of reference. This governing document is established and can be modified by the body that establishes and appoints the committee.

In order to avoid confusion and disputes, terms of reference should be in writing and should include all the essential parameters that govern the committee and its work. Questions to address in the terms of reference may include:

- What is the mandate of the committee? What exactly is it supposed to achieve?
- What is the scope of its work? What products are to be delivered to the appointing body?
- What deadlines does the committee have to meet?
- Is it a permanent committee (finance, personnel, education), or is it established for a limited time?
- Is the committee only investigative and advisory in nature, or does it also have powers to act on behalf of the appointing body? Does it have spending powers, and, if so, what are its budgets and how is its accountability maintained?
- What is the membership of the committee? Who chairs it? How are vacancies filled?
- How often does the committee meet? What is its quorum (typically a majority of the members holding office)? Are there policies, rules, or procedures that it must follow?

Formally Established Organizations: Hierarchy of Rules

Unlike a committee, a formally established organization (board, council, credit union, public company, nonprofit society, labor union) is usually subject to a set of governing documents. Typically, these documents fit within the following hierarchy:

- *First, the Laws of the Land.* This category includes the statute under which the organization is incorporated, as well as any laws that apply (national and state or provincial laws, and municipal bylaws). Your organization has no control over these documents (except by lobbying your favorite elected representative). The laws of the land have precedence over all internal governing documents and supersede them in the event of conflict. Suppose a statute stipulates that an abstention is counted as a vote in the affirmative. A municipal council incorporated under this statute cannot adopt a bylaw stating that an abstention is counted any differently.

- *Second, the Constitution, Bylaws, Rules, or Articles of Incorporation.* For the sake of simplicity, this document is referred to as "bylaws." Your organization has control over bylaws but will likely be required to undergo a special process to amend them, for example, a previous notice, a super-majority (e.g., three-fourths or 75% vote), and acceptance by a government agency. The bylaws are the highest-ranking internal document and have precedence over other internal documents.

Bylaws for an incorporated organization may cover some or all of the following areas:

- Membership categories, application and approval process, voting and other rights
- The governance structure: board, officers, committees, staff
- The nomination and election process for directors and officers
- The frequency and conduct of meetings, and quorum requirements
- The applicable guide on parliamentary procedure
- How the bylaws can be amended
- Other fundamental provisions that should not be easy to change

Common weaknesses in bylaws include:

- Provisions that are too detailed or unnecessarily restrictive
- Provisions that are unrealistic and unenforceable (leading to frequent violations)
- Outdated provisions

- Internal contradictions, ambiguities, repetitions, and re-dundancies
- Provisions that should be addressed outside the bylaws, in policy documents (which are easier to amend)
- "Legalese" instead of plain language
- Cumbersome structure, poor organization, fragmenta-tion, and poor flow
- Reader-hostile (as opposed to reader-friendly) style
- Provisions written to prevent a one-time human dynamics problem from reoccurring

---

EXAMPLE: An Excessively Restrictive Bylaw Amendment

An attempt to take over a board of directors was made by a dissenting group of members. In response, the board intro-duced a bylaw amendment that stated: "To be eligible to serve on the board, a member shall be required to have been in good standing for at least 3 years." The proposal was soundly defeated. Had it been adopted, it would have de-prived the organization of the talents and fresh ideas of new-comers.

More sensible alternatives to address the preceding situa-tion might have been:

- Having a 1-month (instead of a 3-year) membership re-quirement, with the ability to suspend the requirement by a two-thirds vote on a case-by-case basis.
- Presenting all slates of nominees, allowing each candi-date to explain why he or she is running for the board and then letting the members decide.
- Asking a few simple questions: What caused the at-tempted takeover? What can the board do to improve its governance and maintain better relationships with stakeholders?

- *Third, Internal Policy and Procedure Documents.* Exam-ples of internal policy documents include a code of ethics, conflict-of-interest guidelines, personnel policies, finance poli-cies, and confidentiality guidelines. Such documents should be referred to in the bylaws, for example: "The board shall be authorized to establish policies, not inconsistent with these by-laws, to govern the day-to-day operation of the company."

- *Fourth, a Parliamentary Guide.* In order to avoid rein-venting the wheel, your organization can rely on a recognized manual on meeting procedures and rules of order, with a state-ment to this effect in the bylaws: "In all cases not covered in these bylaws, *The Complete Handbook of Business Meetings* shall apply to meetings of the board, the committees, and the general membership."

Types of Meetings

Under parliamentary procedure, collective decisions can be made in duly called meetings in which a quorum is present. This section covers:

- The types of meetings recognized by traditional parlia-mentary procedure
- What needs to be done to allow decision making in virtual meetings, for example, by teleconferencing, videoconfer-encing, e-mail, fax, or mail (see Chapter 9)

Regular and Special Meetings (Boards, Councils, etc.)

Formally organized groups typically hold two types of meet-ings:

1. Regular meetings (monthly, weekly, or otherwise)
2. Special meetings, scheduled on an ad-hoc basis, to ad-dress issues that cannot wait until the next regular meeting

General Meetings (Members and Shareholders)

Public companies and member-based organizations typi-cally hold:

- Annual general meetings to elect directors and officers, receive reports and financial statements, and conduct other business within the jurisdiction of such meetings
- Special general meetings to address urgent issues that cannot wait until the next annual general meeting

Closed or Open Meetings

Issues of a sensitive or confidential nature should be addressed in a closed or in-camera meeting. Only the voting members of the respective body are entitled to attend a closed meeting, and they can invite advisers or other individuals to attend such meetings or portions thereof. The minutes of a closed meeting should be approved in another closed meeting (see Chapter 8).

Reconvened Meetings

If it is impossible or impractical to conclude the agenda for a meeting (e.g., it is late, or there is no quorum, or the room is too small to accommodate an overflow crowd), the members can schedule a reconvened meeting (referred to sometimes as an adjourned meeting or a continued meeting). At the reconvened meeting, the agenda is resumed where it was interrupted.

Virtual Meetings

Under traditional parliamentary procedure, collective decisions can only be made in face-to-face meetings, with members present in one room where they can see and hear one another. However, given the costs and disruptions caused by meetings, and given technological advances and the advent of telecommuting, decisions are often made in virtual meetings (meetings in writing, meetings by phone, teleconferencing, and videoconferences; see Chapter 9).

To give your group the flexibility that it needs and to ensure that the validity of your collective decisions is not questioned, you will need to legitimize virtual meetings. To do so, check what needs to be done to amend the applicable governing document (bylaws, or terms of reference) so that a statement like this can be included: "The board's decisions may be made by teleconferencing, videoconferencing, fax, mail, or e-mail consultations, or such other means that the board deems appropriate, provided that each board member has been so notified, and provided that a quorum participates in the proceedings."

This approach still leaves you with one dilemma: What will you do about the decisions that have been made in virtual meetings until your bylaws are amended? Bring all such decisions to an actual meeting for ratification.

The Quorum Requirement

A quorum is the number of voting members who must be present so that business can be validly transacted. The quorum requirement is intended to protect the absentees and the organization from abuse by ensuring that a representative number of members is present when collective decisions are made.

A quorum should be specified in your bylaws or other governing document. It can be a number (e.g., six board members) or a percentage (e.g., a majority of the board members holding office). If the quorum is too large or is difficult to obtain, consider the following suggestions:

- Introduce a bylaw amendment to make the number more realistic (but you will need a quorum at the existing level to approve the change).
- Find out why members are absent from meetings. Their feedback might suggest that your meetings need to be scheduled at a more convenient time, or that you need to make your meetings more engaging and productive. Treat the root cause to achieve better results.

The quorum requirement cannot be suspended even by a unanimous vote. A quorum must be present throughout the meeting unless the bylaws allow otherwise (which they should not). The quorum requirement is designed to protect the organization, including the absentees, from abuse. In the absence of a quorum, you have a few options:

- Adjourn the meeting.

- Recess, and see if some absent members can be brought back to the meeting (look for them in the hallways, the hospitality suite, etc.).

- Establish the date, time, and place for a reconvened meeting, and see what you can do to attract more members to it.

- If a decision must be made now (e.g., the special discount on the furniture to be purchased will expire before the next meeting), you can take your chances and make the decision. However, to make it valid, you will need to bring it for ratification at the next meeting when a quorum is present.

Parliamentary Procedure and the Real World

This chapter explains the difficulties presented by the way parliamentary procedure and rules of order are typically used. Methods are suggested to soften the impact of the procedural formality.

Why Do Many People Dislike Parliamentary Procedure?

Often the formal rules of order (motions, amendments, points of order) overtake common sense and are used in a mechanical way. Little or no thought is given to what these rules are intended to achieve (see discussion on governing principles at the beginning of this chapter). Sometimes arguments about rules of order consume inordinate amounts of expensive prime time in a meeting—time on which the returns are minimal, nonexistent, or even negative.

Many people are cynical about adopting a book on rules of order for their meetings. They believe the rules stifle the free flow of ideas and make everyone uncomfortable. They think their decisions will be better if they operate informally. Often, the formal rules of order are described as:

- Confusing, useless, senseless, unnecessary, artificial
- An oppressive constraint on the creative, flexible, and free flow of ideas
- An abnormal and unnatural way of communicating
- Onerous and voluminous
- An impediment to progress
- A manipulative tool in the hands of members who know them ("closet parliamentarians")
- A tool used for adversarial, obstructive, manipulative, and disruptive purposes

Typically, certain procedures are followed "because the rule book says so," or "because we've always done it this way," or "because Ernie, our closet parliamentarian, says so." Minor departures from the rules, having absolutely no negative impact, are treated as breaking the law, and cause panic and anxiety. Worse yet, members are afraid to let go of formality even when it would yield positive results. Without a principle-driven approach, rules of order achieve all of the wrong results and none of the legitimate purposes for which they have been designed.

How Can You Soften the Impact of the Rules?

To address the preceding concerns and still benefit from the rules of order, you need to soften their negative impact and make them more sensible and relevant to your group. To make the rules more user-friendly, consider the following options:

- Adjust the level of formality to the needs of your group.
- Use unanimous consent to facilitate voting without the formality of a motion in the case of routine and noncontroversial decisions (see later in this chapter).
- Learn to determine the significance (or lack thereof) of perceived and real procedural violations so that you can deal effectively with nitpicking points of order (see later in this chapter).

- Feel free to suggest an informal approach to problem solving and discourage the premature introduction of motions.

- Educate members on their rights and privileges (rather than withholding this knowledge for fear of having empowered members). To do so, arrange for a training program, or circulate a brief summary of the procedures that members will likely need during a meeting. You could include suggested scripts to cover specific procedures.

- Advise members on the procedure needed to achieve a certain goal. For example:
  —If a member says: "I am really not ready to vote on this proposal," ask if he or she wants to propose to delay the decision or refer the proposal to a committee for study.
  —If a member states legitimate objections to a proposal, ask what modifications or amendments would address his or her concerns.
  —If a member is complaining about something, help her or him in preparing an affirmative solution-oriented proposal or motion that the members can debate and vote on.

- Use plain language and place greater importance on intent than on precise terminology. For example: Teach members to say: "I propose to close debate," instead of "I call the question"; or "I suggest that we refer this proposal to the finance committee for further study," or "I propose that we postpone this decision until the next meeting," instead of "I move to table."

- Establish with the members that nitpicking, insisting on procedural accuracy, and using obscure procedures for adversarial or strategic means are not acceptable.

- Look for common-sense solutions before you pursue procedural ones.

Below is an example of how short-sighted the procedural approach can be, and how a common-sense approach can offer more wholistic and long-lasting solutions to an organizational problem.

EXAMPLE: What Should We Do with Bob?

"We have a problem on our board. The name of our problem is Bob. He is our proverbial nitpicker, always proposing amendments and raising nuisance points of order. One day Bob missed a meeting and it was shortened by half. How do we expel Bob from our board?"

The procedural answer to this question (relying on the governing statute, bylaws, and parliamentary manual) may be perfectly accurate but also completely useless. It may generate a short-term gain (the removal of Bob from the board) with potential long-term pain (an adversarial climate, the possibility of legal action, etc.).

A common-sense approach is suggested instead. Arrange to meet Bob for coffee after the meeting. Give him honest and direct feedback on his participation in the meeting and its impact on progress, and find out what can make him a more constructive participant.

Determining Voting Results

To become binding, a proposal requires a decision by the members. The general rule is that a proposal requires a majority vote in favor of it to be adopted. Exceptions to this rule are when governing documents require a super-majority (e.g., a two-thirds or three-fourths vote). This section discusses the following topics:

- A definition of a majority
- Tie votes and what they mean
- Abstentions and their impact
- The use of proxies
- Super-majorities
- The significance (or lack thereof) of having a vote

How Is a Majority or Simple Majority Defined?

A majority or simple majority is ordinarily defined as more than half of the votes cast, excluding abstentions. However, your governing documents may specify or imply a different definition. Definitions of a majority as "50% plus 1" or "51%" are common but incorrect. Under the correct definition of "more than half," a majority of 1001 votes is 501 votes (more than 500.5, which is half the votes). However, under "50% plus 1" it would be 501.5 (How do you count the 0.5?), and under the "51%" it would be 510.

What Is the Impact of a Tie Vote?

If the number of votes on a proposal is equal (e.g., six in favor and six against), the required majority is not obtained and the proposal is defeated. This outcome is no different than a situation when one member voted in favor and eleven against the motion. In an election, if the votes for candidates for the same position are equal, no candidate is elected and an action is needed to conclude the election.

Common Mistakes Concerning Tie Votes

When faced with a tie vote, organizations often make the following mistakes:

- *Mistake 1:* Stipulating that the chair only votes to break a tie, or even forcing the chair to vote in the event of a tie. Clearly, in the case of a motion, there is no benefit for this practice, since there is no dead-lock, and the motion is defeated. If the chair is against it, how would his or her vote make any difference?
- *Mistake 2:* Giving the chair a second vote to be exercised only in the case of a tie. Such a practice gives one member an unfair advantage over others. In some instances, such a practice may even be in contravention of a statute (e.g., a statute that gives each member only one vote).
- *Mistake 3:* In an election, forcing the chair to cast a vote in a sealed envelope, to be opened and counted only in the case of a tie vote. Such a practice deprives the chair of the privacy of a secret ballot. A better

alternative for resolving a tie in the election is by a second ballot, or, if there isn't enough time for a second ballot, by drawing lots to determine the winner (e.g., flip a coin).

- *Mistake 4:* Insisting on an odd number of members on a board or a committee to prevent a tie vote from occurring. This practice is based on a misunderstanding and provides no benefit whatsoever. First, as explained earlier, a tie vote means a deadlock only in the case of an election. Second, if there is a vacancy on a board with an odd number of members, or if a member misses a meeting, or if a member abstains, you are back to an even number of voters and the possibility of a tie still exists.

What Is the Impact of an Abstention?

How should an abstention be counted? Is it a vote in the affirmative? Is it a vote in the negative? Is it a vote in support of the majority (whatever that may mean)? The answer is: *It depends.*

Under parliamentary procedure (which applies in the absence of any provision to the contrary in your governing documents), an abstention is not counted as anything. The chair only calls for the affirmative and negative votes and does not check who abstains. An abstention in such cases indicates a desire to "sit on the fence" and not take a favorable or a contrary position. Members should always have this option without having to leave the meeting.

Notwithstanding the above, your governing documents may preclude abstentions. Sometimes this preclusion is deliberate, and other times it is the result of carelessness. Here are two examples:

- *Example 1:* Some municipal statutes stipulate that all members present must vote, and an abstention is counted as a vote in the affirmative. This is apparently done with the intention of forcing members to maintain accountability to the public. However, this provision is unfair, since it deprives a member from making an honest choice by taking a neutral position. The only way for a member to truly abstain under such a stipulation is by being absent, in which case the meeting could be left without a quorum, with its decision-making process paralyzed.

- *Example 2:* Some statutes or bylaws—usually by mistake and not by design—stipulate that for a motion to be adopted, an affirmative vote of a majority of the members present is required. In such cases, an abstention has the effect of a negative vote. If you have such a provision in your bylaws, seek to replace "members present" with "votes cast." If, on the other hand, this provision is in the statute (which your organization has no control over), you'll need some concentrated advocacy with your favorite elected official to change it.

Numerical Comparison of the Different Provisions

Out of twelve members present, five vote in favor, three against, and four abstain. The result is:

- Under the principled approach (i.e., members have the right to remain neutral), the vote is five in favor and three against, and the motion is carried. The abstentions don't count.
- Under Example 1, the four abstentions are counted in the affirmative and added to the five votes in favor. The result is nine in favor and three against. Here too the motion is carried.
- Under Example 2, a majority of those present (twelve) is seven. The number of votes in the affirmative is five, or less than seven. Therefore, the motion is defeated.

Commonly Asked Questions about Abstentions

- *Question 1:* Should the chair abstain and vote only in the event of a close vote (e.g., to make or break a tie)? *Answer:* It depends. In Examples 1 and 2, the chair, like other voting members, does not have the true option to abstain (unless the governing statute or bylaws make an exception for the chair, or unless he or she is absent from the meeting). In other cases, the chair is free to decide whether or not to vote, and should not be limited to voting only when the vote is close.

- *Question 2:* If several members who are present abstain, and, as a result, less than a quorum participates in voting, is the vote valid? *Answer:* Yes. A quorum is the number of members who must be present to conduct business. As long as a quorum is present, the result is valid.

- *Question 3:* Should a member with a conflict of interest abstain from voting? *Answer:* Yes. If a member is affected by a proposal in a way that no other member is (e.g., a member is bidding on a project to be approved by a board), his or her ability to make an independent decision on such a proposal can be impaired. This member should be outside the meeting while the proposal is discussed, so as to avoid influencing the outcome in any way.

- *Question 4:* What should be done if there are many abstentions? *Answer:* Find out why. If members abstain because they do not have enough information on the issue, suggest that the decision be postponed to another meeting or referred to a committee for study or research.

Should Proxy Voting Be Allowed?

A proxy is a written assignment of a vote by one member to another. Although proxy voting is normally provided for in shareholder meetings, it is not automatic for other organizations and is only allowed if the governing documents (statute and/or bylaws) authorize it. In such cases, the provisions in the governing documents should be followed.

Generally, proxies in a nonprofit organization are not advisable, since they tend to tilt the balance of power in a meeting in favor of those who hold proxies. Members should attend the meeting, hear the debate, and then make informed decisions.

EXAMPLE: Proxies Tilting the Balance of Power

A nonprofit organization held a meeting to approve a significant document following several years of work and substantial expenses. The motion required a two-thirds vote for approval. Under the bylaws there was no limit on the number of proxies that a member could hold. One member was able to solicit a substantial number of proxies, amounting to more than one-third of the votes, and was able to unilaterally block the proposal. The unlimited number of proxies gave one member substantial power and "tilted the scale" in favor of those who were absent and did not hear the discussion.

Is It Advisable to Legislate Super-Majorities or Consensus Requirements?

Sometimes organizations impose a requirement of a two-thirds vote, a 75% vote, or even a unanimous vote for certain decisions, for example, amending the bylaws, spending or borrowing a large sum of money, or selling property. The purposes for imposing such a requirement are typically:

- To guarantee that significant decisions cannot be made without a broad level of support
- To prevent an aggressive majority from pushing through important decisions, thereby creating winners and losers
- To force the group to more fully debate issues and to seek compromises that would address more fundamental needs, interests, and principles

A common mistake is to assume that a governing board or the members have the power to force a super-majority requirement for making a seemingly significant decision. However, a super-majority requirement cannot be validly imposed without amending the organization's governing documents. If a super-majority requirement is arbitrarily imposed and causes a motion to be defeated (e.g., 55% vote in favor, when someone decides that a 75% vote should be required), the losing majority could validly claim that it was deprived of its right to govern.

The main difficulty with a super-majority requirement is that it makes it hard to move ahead on controversial decisions. The organization can then effectively be governed by the minority and not the majority. For example:

- In the case of a two-thirds vote, all the opposition needs to do to defeat a proposal is mobilize more than one-third of the votes.
- In the case of a three-fourths vote, all the opposition needs to do is mobilize more than 25% of the votes to defeat a proposal.
- In the unfortunate cases where unanimity is required (or forced), a single member can block a proposal and leave an organization in a state of paralysis.
- Efforts to accommodate the minority may lead to modifying a proposal so much that its effect is diluted, making it meaningless and irrelevant to the needs of the organization.

With these difficulties in mind, you need to strike the right balance between the organization's need to move forward and be governed by the majority, and the need to build a broad internal consensus and ensure that the minority is heard and protected. Here are a few suggestions:

- Limit super-majorities to significant decisions, for example, amending the bylaws or dissolving the organization. Avoid legislating a super-majority unless it is absolutely essential.
- Prevent rules from being used for adversarial purposes (e.g., to enable an aggressive majority to push through a decision quickly) and work to avoid the sense of winners and losers.
- Work informally to broaden the level of support for significant decisions (even if you don't have to). Soften your decision-making processes and make them inclusive, fair, and principled. Your members will likely accept and respect majority-based decisions and will be less likely to undermine them. Even if a decision is not perfect, it will be accepted as a fair compromise, and very few, if any, will complain about the decision-making process itself.

Is Having a Vote Really All That Significant?

Intense arguments often ensue over who should have the right to vote and how that right should be exercised. Typical issues that arise include:

- Should senior staff officers (e.g., chief executive officer) have a vote on a board?
- How long should you be a member before being eligible to vote?
- In the case of corporations being members of a larger umbrella organization, should larger members have more than one vote? Should there be weighted voting?
- Should committee membership be opened to individuals from outside the organization, and, if so, should outsiders have the right to vote on committees?

It is up to your organization to determine who should have voting power. However, having a vote is not always as significant as it is made out to be. Here are a few examples:

- A chief executive officer, having no vote, but having been with the organization for many years, has far more influence on decisions than an inexperienced board member who has a vote. Is the entitlement to vote really that significant in this case?

- An outspoken, persistent, and assertive member dominates the discussions and takes up plenty of time. This member has a large impact on a meeting—far more than the voting power that she has. How significant is a vote when a level playing field has not been established?

- In an umbrella organization with weighted voting, a representative with less votes speaks with passion, confidence, and conviction, and knows how to use rules of order to achieve certain goals. Is the amount of influence proportionate to the voting power?

- In many organizations, after all the arguments about voting power, formal votes are rarely taken and decisions are made informally (by consensus).

A vote enables you to definitively exercise your share of the decision making. But the level of influence and clout that you truly have will depend on more than just your vote. Your clout increases substantially by:

- Being knowledgeable, prepared, and having researched the issues
- Having respect, stature, and credibility within the organization
- Showing long-term commitment, loyal service, and a successful track record
- Being persistent, assertive, and having a strong belief in your ideas
- Being a team player and a consensus builder
- Being a listener and being in tune with other members
- Being guided by the organization's best interests
- Having a basic knowledge of parliamentary procedure

Taking Votes without Motions

Must motions be used to validate every collective decision? Even under traditional parliamentary procedure, the answer is no. A collective decision, especially a noncontentious or procedural one, can be validly made without a motion or a formal vote. This section outlines the general principles that should guide you as you ascertain the wishes of the group. The unanimous consent procedure for taking votes informally is then described.

Significant Principles in Collective Decision Making

How a proposal is introduced (moved and seconded, or introduced informally without a motion) is less significant than the following key principles:

- The proposal must be articulated in a concise, complete, and unambiguous manner before the collective decision is made.
- Members must be given opportunities to debate and amend the proposal, and may also decide that the decision-making process be delayed.
- The collective wishes of the group (regarding substantive or procedural decisions) must be ascertained by a vote. This vote can be formal (by a show of hands, by voice, by

standing, or by a secret ballot) or informal (by acquiescence, or unanimous consent).

Informal Votes: Unanimous Consent

As long as the preceding principles are observed, collective decisions can be made without a motion or a formal vote. The vote on routine and noncontroversial decisions can be taken via unanimous consent. The procedure is as follows:

- On a member's request or at the chair's initiative (no motion is necessary), the members are asked whether they object to a certain action (usually such an action is purely procedural, or of a routine and noncontroversial nature).
- The chair asks if there is any objection to the proposed action and pauses to see if there is a response.
- If there are no objections, the chair directs that the action be taken. (The group has voted in favor of it by acquiescing to it.)
- If there are objections, the chair ascertains the nature of the objection and may need to take a more formal route (e.g., a vote by voice or by a show of hands).

EXAMPLE: Approval of the Agenda

''The agenda has been circulated. It includes several routine items, scheduled to take until 2 PM, then a proposal to purchase furniture, scheduled to take until 2:45 PM, then a 15-minute break, then a special presentation on proposed computer upgrades, and then new business. We are due to end the meeting no later than 4 PM. Is the agenda as circulated acceptable? Are there any objections to it? (Pause.) There being no objections, the agenda is approved.''

Notes

- This decision, by acquiescence, is just as valid and as binding as one that is made by a formal vote on a motion to approve the agenda.
- If there are objections to the proposed agenda, address them by ascertaining the wishes of the members. You can do so by unanimous consent (''Is there any

objection to allocating 10 more minutes to item 7?'') or by a formal vote (''Those in favor of switching items 3 and 10, raise your hand''). After these decisions are made, ask if the amended agenda is acceptable and proceed accordingly.

EXAMPLE: Approval of the Minutes

''The minutes of the last meeting were circulated. Are there any corrections to those minutes? (Pause.) There being no corrections, the minutes are approved. The next item of business is . . .''

Notes

- If there are corrections to the minutes, they are usually approved by unanimous consent: ''If there is no objection, the correction will be made.'' If there are objections, check the collective memory by a formal vote: ''Those who believe the correction reflects what took place at the last meeting, raise your hand. Thank you. Those who believe the correction should not be made, raise your hand. The negative has it and the correction will not be made.''
- It is a mistake to ask: ''Is there any discussion on the minutes?'' Members will waste time rediscussing previous decisions at the expense of new ones scheduled on the current agenda. Ask only about corrections, not discussion, of the minutes.

EXAMPLE: Recess

''Is there any objection to a 10-minute recess? (Pause.) There being no objection, we will take a recess and resume at 2:45 PM.''

EXAMPLE: Adjournment

''Is there any other business to come before the meeting? (Pause.) There being no further business, the meeting is adjourned.''

Note

- A formal motion to adjourn is not needed. However, some chairs declare a meeting adjourned on such a motion being made and don't bother asking the members whether they agree. If a motion to adjourn is made, the members still need to be asked whether they wish to adjourn—by unanimous consent or by a formal vote. It is a majority that governs and not the member who moved to adjourn. The wishes of the majority must be ascertained.

EXAMPLE: A Noncontroversial Amendment

''Is there any objection to amending the motion by adding the words 'including all taxes and delivery charges'? (Pause.) There being no objection, the words are added, and the motion now reads: 'To purchase five new personal computers at a cost not exceeding $2500 each, including all taxes and delivery charges.' Is there any discussion on the amended motion?''

Notes

- If the amendment is contentious, you will need a more formal route of action—that is, open it for debate and take a formal vote on it.
- It is a mistake to ask the mover of the motion whether he or she agrees to this ''friendly'' amendment. Once debate on a motion begins, it belongs to the assembly, and the personal wishes of the mover on amending it are irrelevant.

Main Motions: Clarity and Screening

A main motion (sometimes referred to as a resolution) is a proposal on which the members take certain action, or go on record as holding a certain opinion.

- *Example 1* (substantive action): "I move that we donate $100 to the United Way Campaign."
- *Example 2* (expressing a collective opinion): "Resolved, that the committee go on record as believing that the City Council should have no tax increases for the next 3 years."

How Can You Avoid the Confusion over the Wording of a Motion?

Members deserve to know precisely what they are discussing and voting on. Here are a few ideas that will help you make the process for handling a main motion clearer, more logical and efficient, and more user-friendly:

- As a chair, ensure that the proposal is concise, complete, and unambiguous. Prior to a vote, ascertain that members know what they are voting on and that they understand the impact of voting yes or voting no. Don't assume anything, especially if the wording is complex. Members should give themselves permission to say: "Excuse me, what exactly are we voting on?"
- Check if the proposal fits within your group's mandate and does not violate your governing documents. If there is a problem, advise the proponent and see if it can be addressed.
- Ideally, the proposal should be submitted in writing. If an audiovisual aid (flip chart or overhead projector) is available, you could have the motion displayed on a transparency. Even better, preliminary wording of all known or potential proposals should be circulated to members before the meeting.
- If someone says "I so move" or "I move what she said," confirm the precise wording of the motion. Say: "What exactly is your motion?" or "Are you proposing to _____?" or "Would the secretary please read the motion before we continue?"
- If, in a large meeting, a member is struggling to formulate a motion at a microphone, say: "Would you be amenable to just stating it as a request to the board?" Or: "In the interests of efficiency, would you please write the motion down and then pass it to the secretary? While you are doing that, we'll continue with other business."

▪ Members can take the initiative to ensure clarity if the chair is not doing his or her job.

Must Every Motion That Was Made and Seconded Be Discussed and Voted On?

It is a misconception that if a member makes a motion and another member seconds it, then the motion has "legal status" and the meeting has no option except to debate and vote on it. If you have held this opinion, remember that the meeting is not a free-for-all. The general principle is that the majority rules and the members have a say on how their time will be spent (after all, time is money, and you need to ensure a good return on investment). Here are a few scenarios that illustrate the difficulties with the above misconception:

▪ *Scenario 1:* A member blurts out a motion without being given permission to speak at the same time that another member is speaking or is about to be recognized. If the chair processes this motion, basic justice and fairness will be sacrificed. Instead of dealing with the motion, the chair should say: "Would the members please speak by raising hands and waiting for permission to speak? Jack has the floor. Jack, please continue."

▪ *Scenario 2:* A member makes a motion that violates the bylaws and it is promptly seconded. The motion cannot be pursued and should instead be ruled out of order.

▪ *Scenario 3:* A member makes a motion that is confusing and poorly worded. If the motion is pursued, precious time will likely be wasted on nitpicking amendments (not a good return on investment). The member should instead be asked to improve the wording of the motion before introducing it.

▪ *Scenario 4:* A member makes a motion, but a better researched alternative (which the member does not know about) is already scheduled for consideration. The member should be advised of this, and, even if he or she refuses to withdraw it, his or her motion should not be allowed.

What Are Some of the Questions to Ask When Screening Motions?

There are some legitimate questions to ask about a motion before allowing discussion on it:

- Is this motion within the mandate and jurisdiction of the group (e.g., a shareholder introduces a motion in an area that the statute places exclusively under the governing board's control)?
- Can this motion be classified as micromanaging—i.e., the type of action that is routinely delegated to the staff to free the board for broad policy setting for the organization?
- Is this proposal a premature move to solution mode? Will its discussion create a structure that would constrain the creativity needed for a complex subject? Would it be more productive to explore the problem first before rushing to solution mode?
- Will the investment of time and efforts in discussing this proposal yield sufficient returns?
- Is enough time available to give the proposal the full consideration that it deserves?
- Should this motion be handled now (i.e., if it is urgent) or later, under "new business" (once all prescheduled items have been dealt with)?
- Do the members have enough information to make a wise decision?
- Is the motion catching the members by complete surprise? Are they mentally and physically ready to deal with it (e.g., at midnight, when they are tired and ready to go home), or is it better to give them more time to think about it?
- Are you hearing murmurs or sighs? Are you observing facial expressions that suggest some members are frustrated by this motion? If so, is it a good idea to check what elicited this reaction?

These questions can be raised by the chair or by a member, and the fact that the motion was made and seconded does not preclude this questioning. The answers to the preceding questions may cause the group to address the motion in one of the following ways:

- Deal with it (now).
- Delay it (postpone it until later in the same meeting or to a future meeting).
- Delegate it (refer it to another body, e.g., staff, committee).
- Drop it (refuse to deal with it).

What Is the Procedure to Prevent or Delay Discussion of a Motion?

The following procedure can be used to drop, delay, or delegate a motion:

1. The chair or another member raises a concern about the motion.
2. If the motion is inappropriate, the chair advises that it will not be allowed.
3. If it is not clear whether the motion is appropriate, the chair asks the mover to address the concern. If the explanation is satisfactory, the motion is allowed. If not, it is disallowed.
4. If, after the mover's explanation, the chair is unsure about the appropriateness of the motion, he or she can shift the decision on whether it will be allowed to the group for a vote: "The question is: Should we consider this motion now? Those who believe that we should, please raise your hand. Thank you. Those who believe that we shouldn't, please raise your hand. Thank you. The motion will not be considered."
5. If the chair makes a unilateral ruling and the proponent disagrees with it, the group will be asked to vote on how the disagreement will be settled.

EXAMPLE 1: Board or Staff Decision?

``Rebecca, your concern about staff schedules is noted. However, our policy indicates that these decisions are made by the chief executive officer and not by the board. We will pass your concern to the CEO.''

EXAMPLE 2: Topic Already Scheduled?

''Graham, this topic is already covered under agenda item number 6, and we have included a motion on it with the pre-circulated material. Please wait until item number 6.''

EXAMPLE 3: Members Not Quite Ready for This Motion?

''Thank you, Mike. Your motion brings forward an important issue. At the same time, it seems to me that the members don't have enough information to make an informed decision on it. Would you be prepared to wait for the next meeting and prepare background information for the discussion?''

EXAMPLE 4: A Surprise Motion? Late at Night?

''Darlene, thank you for your motion. I am wondering, though: Given that it is late in the meeting and given that this is an unscheduled topic, would your proposal be better discussed at the next meeting?''

EXAMPLE 5: Moving Too Fast to Solution Mode?

''Charlie, I am wondering if you could please wait with your motion until we have spent some time defining what the problem is. It seems too soon to go to solution mode.''

EXAMPLE 6: Motion outside the Group's Jurisdiction?

In an annual meeting: ''Thank you, sir. The motion deals with our lending policy, which the Articles of Incorporation place within the exclusive jurisdiction of the board. Therefore, it is out of order for this meeting. However, you can submit it as a personal suggestion to the board.''

The Six Steps of Handling Main Motions

Under traditional parliamentary procedure, a main motion requires six steps:

Two Steps to Initiate the Motion

1. A member makes the motion.
2. Another member seconds the motion.

One Step to Screen the Motion

3. The chair determines whether the motion is in order, and, if it is, places it before the members (see screening scripts in the previous section).

Three Steps to Process the Motion

4. The motion is debated and amended.
5. The motion is put to a vote.
6. The chair announces the result and action required, and then proceeds to the next agenda item.

Which Steps Are Significant and Which Ones Are Not?

■ Steps 1 and 2 are not significant. Yes, the formality of making a motion and seconding it add a sense of clarity and direction. But these steps are not absolutely essential and there is absolutely nothing wrong with introducing a proposal in the following ways:

—Chair: "The next item on our agenda is a proposal to approve the budget. A proposed budget has been circulated, and we will now open it for debate and possible amendment" (no motion formally made or seconded).

—Chair: "Based on our discussion so far, it appears to me that one way to solve this problem is by hiring an executive assistant. Is my assessment correct? If so, is there any discussion on this idea?" (Without anyone moving or seconding anything.) If the proposal is approved, the minutes of the meeting will state: 'A proposal to initiate a search for an executive assistant was approved,' without a reference to a mover or a seconder.

- Step 3 (screening) is significant, since screening motions mean a better use of time at the meeting (see previous section).

- Step 4 (debate and amendment) is significant. Sufficient debate and opportunities to improve the wording of proposals are essential parts of good decision making.

- Steps 5 and 6 (putting the motion to a vote and announcing the result) are significant. The collective wishes of the members must be ascertained if the decisions are to be representative, and the voting result must be announced.

A script for the six-step process is as follows:

Member (after being recognized to speak): ``I move to hold an awards reception on June 11.''

Another member: ``I second the motion.''

Chair (after having determined that the motion is appropriate): ``It is moved and seconded that we hold an awards reception on June 11. Is there any discussion on this motion?''

Members discuss the motion. Amendments may be introduced, debated, and voted on.

Chair: ``Is there any further discussion on the motion? (Pause.) If not, we will proceed to the vote on the motion to hold an awards reception on June 11. Those in favor of this motion, please raise your hand. (Pause.) Thank you. Those against the motion, please raise your hand. (Pause.) Thank you.''

Chair: ``The motion is carried'' or ``The motion is defeated.''

Pertinent Details on Each of the Six Steps

Steps 1 and 2 (Making and Seconding a Motion)

Steps 1 and 2 are procedural formalities relating to the introduction of a motion and are not as significant as they are often made out to be. As indicated earlier, it is possible and proper to have the motion introduced in some other, possibly less formal, way. The way a motion is introduced is less significant than the facts that:

- It was clearly stated.
- The members were given an opportunity to discuss and amend it.
- The collective wishes of the group were ascertained.

Question: "In our general membership meeting, a motion was made by someone who, as we later found out, did not pay his dues and was not eligible to vote. The motion was debated and adopted. Was our process valid?"

Answer: "Generally speaking, only voting members can make motions. However, this violation is of a purely technical character and appears to have had no impact on progress. The motion was clear, it was debated, and the wishes of the members were ascertained. The process was valid."

Step 1 (Making a Motion)

To make a motion, a member must wait for permission to speak and then open by saying: "I move that we _____." Be definitive and avoid tentative language, such as: "I think I would like to move," or "I think I would like to suggest that perhaps we should consider the possibility of _____." The nitpickers will have a heyday arguing that you never made a motion.

Parliamentary procedure requires that a motion propose a departure from the status quo—that is, a motion to refrain from doing something (a negative motion) or to reaffirm an existing position should generally be avoided. In both cases, the motion would have no impact on the status quo and the same result would be achieved by having no motion at all. The purpose of this rule is to ensure a meaningful expenditure of time and to avoid confusion. For example:

- If a motion to not hold a banquet is defeated, does the double negative mean that a banquet will be held? Of course not, but some members might disagree.

- If a motion to reaffirm the opposition to a construction project is defeated, does it mean that there is no longer opposition? No, but again confusion could reign.

The maker of a motion is not entitled to speak against it, but he or she can vote against it. This rule is intended to ensure that members make motions consistent with their wishes. For example, instead of moving "that we donate $100 to the Red Cross" only "to get the issue on the floor and then speak against it," move "that we refuse the request to donate $100 to the Red Cross," or don't move anything at all.

Notwithstanding the preceding rules, there is a risk of being too precise and rigid. At times it would be productive to vote to reaffirm an existing policy. Other times it would take less time to debate and vote on a negative motion than to argue that it is incorrect to do so. Finally, what harm would be done if the mover speaks against his or her motion, if he or she has had a change of heart, or if it was substantially amended and he or she no longer supports it?

Step 2 (Seconding a Motion)

The seconding of a motion is a relatively meaningless procedural step designed to ensure that motions do not consume time if only one person is interested in the discussion. To second a motion, a member does not need to be recognized by the chair. All that he or she needs to do is say: "Second," or "I second the motion."

There are several myths and misconceptions about seconding a motion, and it is often given far more significance than it deserves. Here are some of the myths:

- *Myth 1: Seconding a motion signifies agreement with it.* In fact, by seconding a motion, all that you say is "I agree that it should be discussed." You might even second a motion because you are opposed to it and want the group to go on record as rejecting it.

- *Myth 2: It is rude not to second a motion.* That's interesting. Does this mean that you should be dishonest and second a motion even though you don't think it should be discussed?

■ *Myth 3: The name of the seconder must be recorded in the minutes, since it proves that things were done correctly.* In fact, the name of the seconder should not be recorded in the minutes. Why would you want your name next to the mover's name if you seconded the motion for the purpose of having it defeated?

■ *Myth 4: If a motion was not seconded and is subsequently debated and adopted, the entire procedure is invalid.* A point of order that a motion was not seconded must be made at the time of the violation. If the members discussed a motion that was never seconded, then by their action they indicated that they wanted it discussed. The lack of a seconder becomes immaterial once discussion begins.

■ *Myth 5: A seconder is always required, even in small meetings of committees.* In fact, seconding is required only in large meetings, and this requirement is waived in small boards and committees (i.e., no more than about a dozen members present).

In light of these myths, you should seriously question the need to have motions seconded. You could formally adopt a rule to eliminate the requirement of a second altogether. Relying on the seconding requirement to block motions does not work well, especially when members second motions out of courtesy and because they want to avoid hurting someone's feelings. A much more effective way of screening motions is explained earlier in this chapter (see also Step 3 below).

Step 3 (Screening a Motion and Placing It before the Members)

After a motion is introduced, it is the chair's duty to screen it. As indicated previously, the fact that a motion was made and seconded does not mean that the group must deal with it. The chair (or the members) may prevent a motion from coming before the meeting if it is inappropriate, or delay it if it is poorly worded or poorly timed.

Far too often, it is assumed that the mover of a motion owns it forever. The fact is that the mover loses ownership of the motion as soon as debate on it begins. Here is how it works:

- During steps 1 and 2, the mover (not the seconder) owns the motion.
- After the motion has been screened and opened for debate, it becomes the property of the group. From this point onward, the mover's wishes regarding the motion are irrelevant—that is:
  —It is incorrect to ask the mover for permission to withdraw the motion. The decision to withdraw the motion after debate begins is made by the members. If this decision is noncontroversial, it can be made informally, by unanimous consent ("Is there any objection to having the motion withdrawn?" Pause, then say: "There being no objection, the motion is withdrawn). But it is the members' permission that is needed, not the mover's. It's a democracy, not anarchy.
  —It is incorrect to ask for the mover's permission to make a "friendly amendment." Actually, this vague term should be avoided. Instead, the members must be asked whether they agree to the amendment. A noncontroversial amendment can be adopted by unanimous consent.

Step 4 (Debate and Amendment)

After the motion has been screened and placed before the members, it is opened for debate and amendment. Members will likely speak in favor or against the proposal, or they will try to improve the wording and make it more acceptable to more interests.

Members should be encouraged to communicate clearly and concisely and avoid repetition so that as many areas as possible can be covered. They can be encouraged to use structured communications. For example: "I speak in favor of this proposal for two reasons: First, . . . Second, . . . Therefore, I am in favor of this proposal."

To ensure clarity and to keep the meeting on track, repeat

the motion from time to time: "As a reminder, we are now discussing the motion to _____. Is there any further discussion on it?" Discussion of the motion should be orderly, with members having equal opportunities to be heard. It may be useful to review the basic rules of order at the start of a meeting, or have them printed and precirculated to the members. Here are the main guidelines to consider:

- Members speak only after being recognized by the chair ("Please approach the microphone if you want to speak").
- Recognition of speakers is generally on a first-come, first-served basis. The chair can establish a speakers' lineup, but members further in the lineup should be encouraged to avoid repetition if their views have already been expressed.
- Exceptions to the first-come, first-served rule are as follows:
  —The maker of the motion, when speaking for the first time, is entitled to be recognized before others. However, it is a mistake to allow the mover to speak last and thereby close the debate (unless your bylaws state otherwise): What if, after the mover speaks for the second time, another member has a new point that will improve the quality of the decision? Why should the group be deprived of this new piece of information?
  —To speak a second time on the same issue, a member must wait for those who wish to speak on it for the first time.
  —The chair may alternate between proponents and opponents of a motion: "We've heard several members speaking in favor of the proposal. Is there anyone who wishes to speak against it, and, if not, shall we proceed to the vote?"
- Members must speak courteously and maintain respect for other members. They must use proper language, keep their comments to the issues, avoid personal attacks and avoid speculating on the motives of other members.
- On each debatable proposal, each member is allowed to

speak up to two times (unless the rules adopted by the group allow more or fewer times), each time for no longer than _____ minutes (the time limit can be formally established by the group to ensure efficiency).

Step 5 (Closing Debate and Taking a Vote)

At some point in the debate on a motion, there is a need to reach closure and move on to the next issue on the agenda. The decision to close debate should be made by the members, not unilaterally by the chair or by one member.

Discussion can be closed informally by unanimous consent (see earlier in this chapter): "Is there any further discussion on the motion? (Pause.) There being none, we will proceed to the vote." Discussion can also be closed by previously adopted time limits: "The 20 minutes that we allocated to this discussion has ended and we will proceed to the vote. The motion is _____, etc."

If no time limit on a motion was established and some members just keep on talking, with no end in sight, a formal vote on closing debate can be taken. A member may initiate such a vote by moving that debate be closed. The motion to close debate cannot interrupt a speaker. It is often referred to as "calling the question." "Moving that debate be closed" is the preferable plain-English phrase for clarity.

EXAMPLE: Voting on Closure

"Those in favor of closing debate, please raise your hand. Thank you. Those opposed to closing debate, raise your hand. Thank you. Debate is closed. We will now vote on the main motion, to hold an awards ceremony on June 11."

Consider these tips on closure:

- Instead of "I will close the debate after two more speakers" (an autocratic decision), say: "Is there any objection to closing debate after hearing from two more speakers?" (democracy).

- If debate appears to have ended, there is no need to wait for someone to call "Question." Just say: "There appears to be no one who wants to speak. We will therefore proceed to the vote."

- If someone blurts out the word "Question" while others are lining up to speak, say: "I would advise the members that calling the question cannot interrupt a speaker"; or: "I would advise the members who are calling 'Question' that, in fairness to others who are lining up to speak, a motion to close debate must be made from a microphone."

Consider these tips on taking the vote:

1. Before the vote, repeat the motion, to ensure that members know what they are voting on. Any member should feel free to request that a motion be clarified before the vote.
2. Call for both the affirmative and the negative votes, even if the number of those voting affirmatively appears overwhelming. The minority still has the right to be heard.
3. You can take the vote by voice (ayes and no's), by a show of hands, or by a standing vote.
4. There is no need to count the vote if the result is obvious and conclusive.
5. If the vote appears close, retake it and arrange to have it counted. Alternatively, a member can move that the vote be counted, and the members, by a majority vote and without debate, can decide whether the time should be taken to count the vote.
6. If members are more likely to vote their true sentiments privately, they can, by a majority vote, decide that the vote be taken by a secret ballot. If there is a possibility that this may be needed, get ready for it with enough sets of blank ballots (small pieces of paper for each count). To reduce the likelihood of vote-tampering, try an obscure-color paper.
7. Avoid the mistake of asking those who abstain to raise their hands, since the result is usually determined by a majority of the votes cast, excluding abstentions.

8. If you are unfortunate to have a bylaw or a statute that requires a majority of the members present to adopt a motion and the vote appears close, you will need to follow two steps: First, determine how many members are present. Second, count the votes in the affirmative. Then determine whether a majority of those present has been achieved.

Step 6 (Announcing the Result)

After all the number crunching, you will have a result. Examples of announcing the result are as follows:

- "The motion is carried."
- "The motion is defeated."
- "There are seventeen votes in favor and fifteen against the motion. The motion is adopted."
- "There are fifteen votes in favor and fourteen against the motion. The chair votes against the motion, making fifteen in favor and fifteen against the motion. The motion is defeated."
- "There are fifteen votes in favor and fifteen against the motion. The chair votes in favor of the motion, making sixteen in favor and fifteen against the motion. The motion is carried."
- "The motion requires a 75% vote. There are seventy-five votes in favor and twenty-five against the motion. The chair votes against the motion, making seventy-five in favor and twenty-six against the motion. The motion is defeated."

The Traditional Approach to Amending a Motion

An amendment is defined as a proposal to change the wording of another motion. This section examines the traditional approach that parliamentary books offer for amendments.

For precision and clarity, an amendment should be presented in one of the following forms:

- "I move that the motion be amended by adding the following words: _____."
- "I move that the motion be amended by inserting the words _____ between _____ and _____."
- "I move that the motion be amended by deleting the words _____."
- "I move that the words _____ be replaced by _____."

The traditional approach, whereby the amendment is debated and voted on before the main motion, is often not the most sensible use of time. You can logically ask: Why should we debate the amendment, before we figure out whether we want to adopt the main motion at all? Following a detailed explanation of the traditional approach to amendments, the next section introduces a simpler and more logical approach.

Sample Amendments

> *Main Motion:* "To purchase three personal computers and four desks."
> *Amendment:* "I move to delete the words 'and four desks.'"
> *Amendment:* "I move to add 'at a total cost not exceeding $7000.'"

Primary and Secondary Amendments

Parliamentary procedure permits up to one main motion, one primary amendment, and one secondary amendment to be pending at the same time. A third-level amendment is not permitted. A primary amendment is a proposed change to the main motion (see preceding examples). A secondary amendment is a proposed change to the wording of a primary amendment (e.g., the last amendment can be amended by adding "including taxes and delivery costs").

Sequence of Debate and Voting

"Pending" means introduced for discussion but not voted on yet. "Immediately pending" means the most recently introduced proposal. When multiple proposals are pending, the sequence of debate and voting is last in, first out, or, stated formally, the immediately pending proposal is debated and voted on first— that is:

1. Debate and vote on the secondary amendment.
2. Debate and vote on the primary amendment.
3. Debate and vote on the main motion (as amended or in its original form).

Amending the Motion in More Than One Place

As soon as a primary amendment has been voted on, another primary amendment can be introduced (following the principle that only one primary amendment can be pending at a time). Similarly, as soon as a secondary amendment is voted on, another secondary amendment can be introduced.

EXAMPLE: An Awards Banquet

Main motion: ''I move that we hold an awards banquet on July 19.''

Chair: ''The motion is that we hold an awards banquet on July 19. Is there any discussion on this motion?'' (Discussion on the banquet idea ensues.)

A member moves a primary amendment: ''I move that we replace the word 'banquet' with 'reception.'''

Chair: ''The proposed amendment is that we replace 'banquet' with 'reception.' Is there any discussion on the amendment to replace 'banquet' with 'reception'?'' (Discussion of the amendment ensues.)

Another primary amendment is made (not allowed now): ''I move that we add the words 'with spouses included' to the main motion.''

Chair: ''We can only have one primary amendment pending at a time. Please wait until the primary amendment to replace 'banquet' with 'reception' has been voted on. Is there any further discussion on the amendment to replace 'banquet' with 'reception'? (Pause.) There being no further discussion, we will vote on the amendment to replace 'banquet' with 'reception.' Those in favor of this amendment, raise your hand. Thank you. Those opposed, raise your hand. The amendment is carried and the main motion now reads: 'To hold an awards reception on July 19.' Is there any further discussion on the amended motion?''

A member moves another primary amendment (now permitted): ''I move that we add the words 'with spouses included.' ''

Chair: ''The proposed amendment is that we add the words 'with spouses included.' Is there any discussion on the primary amendment to add the words 'with spouses included'?'' (Discussion of the amendment ensues.)

A member makes a secondary amendment: ''I move that we amend the amendment by inserting 'or significant others' between 'spouses' and 'included.' ''

Chair: ''The proposed amendment to the amendment is that we insert 'or significant others' between 'spouses' and 'included.' Is there any discussion?'' (Discussion ensues.)

Chair: ''I will now review the parliamentary situation. We have before us three proposals: a main motion to hold an awards reception on July 19, a primary amendment to add 'with spouses included,' and a secondary amendment to insert 'or significant others' between 'spouses' and 'included.' Right now we are discussing the secondary amendment to insert 'or significant others' between 'spouses' and 'included.' Are you ready for the vote on the secondary amendment?''

When debate on the secondary amendment ends: ''Those in favor of the secondary amendment to insert 'or significant others' between 'spouses' and 'included,' raise your hand. Those opposed, raise your hand. The secondary amendment is carried. The primary amendment now proposes to add the words 'with spouses or significant others included' to the main motion.'' When debate on the amended primary amendment ends:

''We will now vote on the primary amendment to add the words 'with spouses or significant others included.' Those in favor of this amendment, raise your hand. Those opposed, raise your hand. The primary amendment is defeated.

> "We are now back to the main motion, which reads 'To hold an awards reception on July 19.' Are you ready for the vote on this motion? (Pause.) Those in favor of holding an awards reception on July 19, raise your hand. Those opposed, raise your hand. The motion is carried."

General Comments on Amendments

What Goes in the Minutes?

In the latter example, the minutes will need to show only the final wording of the motion and the fact that it was adopted—that is, "After discussion and amendment, the following motion was adopted: 'To hold an awards reception on July 19.'" There is no need to record all the amendments separately.

Ensuring Clarity

The chair and the members should insist on clarity: The amendment should be articulated in a precise form. If a visual aid is available (flip chart, overhead projector), show motions and amendments in different colors, and clarify what is being debated and voted on at any given time. For example: "We are now debating the amendment to add the words 'and payroll software.' Is there any discussion on adding these words?"

Can an Amendment Change the Intent of a Motion?

Under parliamentary procedure an amendment can change the spirit of the original motion. The main restriction on an amendment is that it must be germane, or closely related, or have some impact on the motion at hand. An amendment cannot introduce an independent subject, but an amendment can even be hostile to the spirit of the motion and still be germane. For example: If the motion is to purchase five copies of the *Guide to Meetings,* an amendment to replace *Guide to Meetings* with *Negotiating: Getting to Yes* may at first seem unrelated and out of order. But if there is a limited budget for books, the money spent on the *Guide to Meetings* could mean that no money would be available for other books. With this argument, the amendment would be germane and in order.

Adopting Amendments by Unanimous Consent

The amending process can be made simpler and more user-friendly by using unanimous consent to approve noncontroversial amendments. For example: "Is there any objection to adding the words 'effective January 1, 2002?' (Pause.) There being no objections, the words are added and the motion now reads _____, effective January 1, 2002."

The Gordian Knot

The formal procedure for amendments, as previously described, can be cumbersome, confusing, and counterproductive (investing the time in it may not yield good returns). At times it may be more productive to withdraw all the pending amendments and the main motion and start from scratch: "Is there any objection to having the main motion and all amendments withdrawn and introducing in their place the following main motion: _____?" Remember that suffering is optional. The purpose of the rules is to facilitate progress, and, if they have the opposite effect, a different approach may be needed. Time is a precious commodity and you need to ensure that it is invested wisely and prudently. See the next section for a different approach to amendments.

Is the Mover's Consent Required before a Motion Can Be Amended?

The mover's consent is not required before a motion can be amended. As stated earlier in this chapter, once a motion has been screened and placed before the members, the mover has lost control over it. From this point on, it is up to the members to decide whether to amend or withdraw it, and the mover's wishes are irrelevant (It's a democracy, not anarchy . . .). Turning to see if the mover agrees to "a friendly amendment" makes no sense.

How Can You Prevent Amendments from Preempting Debate on the Main Motion?

Under parliamentary procedure, amendments can be introduced anytime after the main motion has been opened for debate. If an amendment is introduced too quickly, the focus of the discussion shifts away from the main motion, with members subsequently agonizing over precise wording and failing to focus on underlying principles and overall intent. The procedures used in such cases are not incorrect, but the way they are used make no sense. Here are suggested scripts to prevent this problem from happening:

"In the interests of clarity, proper focus, and a logical discussion, I would suggest that the members hold back any amendments until we have had some discussion of the main motion and the principles behind it.''

"Feedback from members has suggested that our time would be spent more wisely if we discussed the principles and overall intent of proposals, and that we should leave it to the board to interpret the precise meaning and the implementation details. With this in mind, I would encourage the members to avoid making amendments of a purely housekeeping nature so that we can spend our time discussing substantive issues.''

The Informal Approach to Motions and Amendments

Deformalizing the decision-making process can yield substantial benefits: a smoother and more logical and productive discussion, a more user-friendly and less intimidating process, and better decisions. As indicated at the beginning of this chapter, the rules are intended to facilitate progress. As long as basic rights are respected and fundamental principles are followed, there is no one right way to get there. Just ensure that:

- Proposals are clearly articulated and understood.
- The members have an opportunity to debate and amend proposals.
- The wishes of the majority are ascertained (by a formal vote or by unanimous consent).

EXAMPLE: The Awards Ceremony

Referring back to the awards reception on July 19 (see previous section), here is a less formal way to reach the decision:

Member: "I suggest that we hold an awards banquet. July 19 is a good day for it. My reasons for it are as follows: _____."

Chair (not too worried about looking for a seconder): "Thank you. It's been proposed that we hold an awards banquet on July 19. Does anyone else have a comment on this proposal?"

Member: "Recognizing our members in an awards ceremony is a great idea. I wonder though, given our financial constraints, whether it would be more prudent for us to have only a reception and not a full-fledged formal banquet."

Chair: "Thank you for your suggestion. We'll put it on our list of ideas to consider. Are there any other comments on the proposal to hold an awards banquet on July 19?"

Member: "I too am in full support of recognizing our achievers in an awards ceremony. I would, however, like to see our spouses invited as well. It would add a social aspect and make the event more enjoyable."

Member: "I too support the idea of an awards ceremony. But if we are going to include spouses, we should also include significant others."

Member: "I don't like the idea of having outsiders at our awards ceremony. Plus our meeting hall is too small to accommodate our members alone, and we would need to rent a bigger hall. That's expensive. We also don't have enough time to organize it. Why don't we try it without our spouses this year and see whether we miss them . . ."

Chair (after some additional discussion but no formal motions or amendments): ''It seems to me that there are several decisions for us to make: First, whether we want to hold some kind of an award ceremony; second, whether July 19 is a good date for it; third, whether we want it to be a banquet or a reception; and fourth, whether we want to invite our spouses or significant others. Let's make one decision at a time.

''First, do we want to have some kind of an awards ceremony? Is there any further discussion on that? I see no one wanting to speak, so we will take a vote. Those in favor of holding an awards ceremony, raise your hand. Anyone opposed? Then we will have an awards ceremony.

''Second, is July 19 an acceptable date? Is there any objection to it? (Pause.) There being no objection, the awards ceremony will be held on July 19.

''Third, we need to decide whether it should be a banquet or a reception. Is there any discussion on this decision? (Members speak.) Is there any further discussion on 'banquet' versus 'reception'? There being no further discussion, we will take a vote. Those in favor of the banquet option, raise your hand. Thank you. Those in favor of the reception idea, raise your hand. Thank you. It looks like it will be a reception.

''Finally, we need to decide whether to invite our spouses or significant others. Is there any further discussion on this decision? (Members speak.) We will now vote. Those who believe that we should invite our spouses or significant others, please raise your hand. Thank you. Those opposed, please raise your hand. Thank you. It looks like our spouses and significant others will have to make other plans for July 19.''

In analysis, the preceding process appears to be:

- Simpler, more flexible, less confusing, and more user-friendly than the traditional parliamentary process.
- Leading to the same destination but probably faster.
- Facilitating a logical progression, whereby one decision is made at a time, starting with the one that needs to be

made first: Do you want to hold an awards ceremony at all?

- Avoiding an unnecessary waste of time. If the first decision (to have an awards ceremony) were negative, no time would have been wasted on the next three decisions.
- Progressing from less contentious decisions to more contentious ones.
- Involving fewer formal votes (three instead of four).
- Using plain English and avoiding parliamentary terms.
- Preserving all the fundamental principles of parliamentary procedure: articulating proposals clearly, allowing members to debate and amend them, and ascertaining the wishes of the group.

EXAMPLE: "Let's Put the Horse before the Cart"

This example illustrates how rushing to make a motion (or offer a solution to a problem) constrains the discussion and leads to a shortsighted decision, especially when the issues are more complex than is readily obvious.

Route 1 (The Traditional Parliamentary Approach)

Member (anxious to move on with the agenda and reach closure on issues): ''I move that the board authorize the hiring of five additional computer programmers and the purchase of five computer workstations.'' The motion is seconded, stated by the chair, and opened for debate. (The chair feels trapped by the motion and believes that there is no option but to debate and vote on it.)

Reasons Given for the Proposal
Programmers are behind in their work. Customers are complaining about lateness and poor service. There is a need to expand the scope of the company's services and serve the customers for longer hours.

Proposed Amendments to the Motion
''To replace 'five' with 'six.' ''
''To add 'at a grand total of annual budgetary increase

(salary, equipment, furniture, and maintenance costs) not exceeding $450,000.' ''
Proposed secondary amendment to the latter: "To add 'including all taxes.' ''

Progression
Board members are not sure about the large expense, but the structured discussion does not give them the flexibility to discuss other options. Discussion on the secondary amendment consumes a lot of time, at the end of which members are truly exhausted. Tired and ready to go home, they approve an amended motion: "To authorize the hiring of six additional computer programmers and the purchase of six computer workstations, at a grand total of annual budgetary increase (salary, equipment, furniture, and maintenance costs) not exceeding $450,000, including all taxes."
It is midnight and the meeting is adjourned without addressing the five additional items remaining on the agenda.

Route 2 (A Common-Sense Approach)

Board member: "I move that the board authorize the hiring of five additional computer programmers and the purchase of five computer workstations" (same starting point . . .).
Chair: "John, it's great that you want to help us move forward and reach closure on issues. But may I ask you to please wait with this motion? There are several issues to be addressed in our computer department. But it seems to me that we need to explore the full scope of the problem first, and only then look at ways of solving it. A motion would constrain us too much right now."
The board then shifts to an informal and semistructured discussion exploring the issues and challenges that the computer department faces. A few new and highly relevant facts emerge:

- Tensions among programmers and the department manager are reducing staff's efficiency.

- Some programmers operate in isolation (``loose can-ons''), not as team members.
- There may indeed be a need for more staff, but the shortage is not in the computer department; it's in the customer service department.
- Customers complain more about how they are treated on the phone than about lateness.
- The competition serves its customers on an expanded schedule, from 7 AM to 7 PM. Some customers have been lost to the competition because of this.

After this informal discussion of the problem, a few op-tions for solutions emerge. The discussion is concluded with the adoption of the following motion: ``That the chief execu-tive officer be instructed to work with the head of the com-puter department and initiate the following processes:

- Analyze all tasks currently being performed by the com-puter department, followed by a realignment of prior-ities, so that all essential work can be completed expeditiously and so that nonessential work is dropped or rescheduled.
- Revise the mandate and work practices of the com-puter department to make it more customer respon-sive.
- Initiate a mediated team-building effort within the computer department.
- Explore the need to serve customers on an expanded basis and present a proposed new schedule, required staffing and equipment, and associated costs to the board for approval.''

Comparison between Routes 1 and 2

In both routes 1 and 2, the departure point is the same: A mem-ber makes a motion. But, as you can see, the end result is very different. Route 1 delivers a shortsighted result that addresses the symptoms but does not solve the real problem. Route 2 delivers a solution that reflects more creativity, due diligence, and visionary and holistic thinking.

When considering the time invested in the meeting, route 1 delivers a bad decision, and the return on investment is negative: $450,000 is a lot of money to spend without solving anything. Route 2 delivers a more substantial return on a smaller investment.

In route 1, the chair felt duty bound and believed that there was no option but to deal with the motion that was made. As a result, the discussion was constrained by the parameters of the proposal, and the freedom to consider the full scope of the problem was curtailed. The board (and the organization) fell victim to the formality of the traditional parliamentary approach.

In route 2, the chair dared to question being formal and entering solution mode prematurely. He used common sense to gently persuade the member to put the brakes on the motion (a solution), and allow a free-flowing and unstructured discussion of the problem first. He was more concerned about doing the right thing than about doing things exactly right. In fact, even from a parliamentary procedure perspective, there is nothing wrong with route 2, since fundamental principles are upheld: The motion is clearly articulated, the members are free to debate and amend it, and the wishes of the majority are indeed ascertained.

What can a member do if, as happened in route 1, the chair did not dare to question the wisdom of taking the procedural route prematurely? In this case, any member could intervene, rescue the group from slavery to procedures and formality, and prompt it to place common sense in the forefront.

And what can be done if, as happened in route 1, members become frustrated by the process when it is already well under way (i.e., the motion and the amendments are on the floor)? It is acceptable to withdraw everything and switch over to the informal route 2. It is never too late to cut your losses and invest the rest of your time more wisely. Here is a script for you:

``May I make an observation here? It seems to me that we have become entangled in formalities, lost sight of the real issues, spent a lot of time, and achieved very little. I am wondering if it would be more productive for us to have the motion and the amendments withdrawn for now so that we can have a free and unconstrained discussion of the problem that we are trying to solve, and only then start with motions.''

Delaying or Avoiding a Vote on a Motion

A motion was made, seconded, and debated. Now the chair wants to put it to a vote. But somehow you feel constrained by the number of options with which you are presented:

- To vote in favor of it
- To vote against it
- To abstain (assuming that you truly have an option to do so; see earlier in this chapter)

You need and deserve additional options that will enable the group to look beyond dealing with the motion and instead choose to delay it, delegate it, or drop it. Here are your potential dilemmas and the procedural options to address them:

- Though you are generally in favor of the proposal, it has not been debated sufficiently. However, it is late, and members are tired and want to go home. You want to avoid making a decision when you are not thinking clearly, fearing that it may come back to haunt you later. Move that the motion be postponed to a future time (delaying it).

- Though you were initially against the proposal, you are intrigued by the points that you heard during the discussion. You can see that the proposal has some merits and may work well for the organization. However, you need more details to convince you to support the proposal. Move that the motion be referred to a designated committee for study (i.e., another way of delaying the decision).

- You support the proposal but don't want to spend your group's time defining the details. You can move that it be referred to a designated committee for action, with instructions to define the specifics, address any lingering concerns, and implement it (delegating the motion).

- You are uncomfortable voting on a motion, or you doubt that it fits within the group's mandate, or you think the group should not be forced to take a direct yes or no position on it. You would like to get rid of the motion in some way without a direct vote on it. Suggest that the motion be withdrawn (i.e., drop it).

The remainder of this section explains the procedures to postpone, to refer, and to withdraw a proposal. The more obscure and less useful procedure of tabling is then explained. Note that the treatment of these procedures differs (in small technical details but not in the principles) from commonly used books on parliamentary procedure.

The Motion to Postpone

"Postpone to a certain time" is a proposal that decision making on a main motion (and any pending amendments) be postponed to a future time. The motion to postpone should be opened for debate on its merits and requires a majority vote to adopt.

EXAMPLE: Postponement to a Certain Time

Main motion: ''To establish a policy whereby latecomers to meetings pay a $1 fine each time, except in the case of illness or family emergency.''

A primary amendment: ''To replace '$1' with '$5.''''

Member: ''I believe we are moving too fast on this decision and that we need more time to consider other ways of causing our members to come to meetings on time. I move that the motion and the pending amendment be postponed until the October 5 meeting.''

Chair: ''Is there any discussion on the motion to postpone?'' (Take comments in favor and against postponement.) There being no further discussion, we will vote on whether the main motion and the amendment will be postponed until the October 5 meeting. Those in favor of post-ponement, please raise your hand. Thank you. Those opposed to postponement, please raise your hand. Thank you. The motion to postpone is defeated. We are now back to the amendment to replace '$1' with '$5.' Is there any further discussion on the amendment?''

Or, conversely: ''The motion to postpone is adopted. The main motion and the amendment will be the first item of unfinished business for the October 5 meeting.''

EXAMPLE: An Informal Approach to Postponement

Member: ''It is really late, and I am concerned that we might make a bad decision when we're tired and not thinking clearly. Given that there is no urgency to making the decision today, can we postpone it until the next meeting?''

Chair: ''Is it acceptable to postpone this discussion until the next meeting? (Pause.) Your enthusiasm for postponement is overwhelming and so we will postpone decision making on this proposal. It also sounds like you want to end this meeting. But before we do this, we need to briefly summarize our progress and any follow-up actions. Then we have a few announcements to make, and then we can adjourn this meeting.''

The Motion to Refer

"Refer" or "commit" is a proposal that a main motion and any pending amendments be referred to a committee, to staff, or to another body for study or for action. The motion to refer should be opened for debate (of its merits) and requires a majority vote to adopt.

EXAMPLE: Referral

Main motion: ''To authorize a paint job of our premises at a total cost not exceeding $5000.''

Primary amendment: "To add the words 'to be completed by June 15, 2003.'"

Member: "It is not clear to me how well we are doing with our budget this year, and, based on our discussion, I doubt that we'll be able to get the right job done for under $5000. I move that we refer the motion and the amendment to the Finance Committee and the Facilities Committee for assessment, with instructions to report back to us at our meeting next Tuesday."

Chair: "It is proposed that the main motion and the amendment be referred to the Finance and Facilities Committees for assessment, with instructions to report back to us next Tuesday. Is there any discussion on the motion to refer? (Allow comments on the wisdom of referral.) There being no further discussion, we will now vote on the motion that the main motion and the amendment be referred to the Finance and Facilities Committees for assessment, with instructions to report back to us next Tuesday. Those in favor of the motion to refer, please raise your hand. Thank you. Those opposed to referral, please raise your hand. Thank you. The motion and the amendment have been referred."

EXAMPLE: An Informal Approach to Referral

Member: "I generally support this proposal, but I need more information on financial feasibility. I am not sure whether we can afford it and how it fits within our overall organizational priorities."

Another member: "I feel the same way. We should probably get some information from the Finance and Facilities Committees before we spend any more time discussing this proposal."

Chair: "Is it agreeable to delay this decision until we receive some answers on priorities from the Finance and Facilities Committees? (Pause.) It looks like there is general agreement on this, so it will be done."

Some Notes on the Motion to Refer

The motion to refer can specify:

- The committee to which the motion is to be referred
- The members who will sit on the committee (for a new committee)
- The person who will chair the committee
- The issues and questions to be addressed by the committee
- Any reporting requirements or deadlines for the committee
- Whether the committee has the authority to take action, and, if so, specifically what action
- Whether the committee has any spending powers

The Motion to Withdraw

The decision to withdraw a motion on which debate has begun is made by the members (a collective decision), and the consent of the mover to withdrawal is irrelevant. The motion to withdraw should be opened for debate and requires a majority vote to adopt.

EXAMPLE: Withdrawal

Scenario: A Meeting Convened to Remove Two Directors

Member (after some discussion): "I really don't think it is appropriate for us as members to vote on this motion. It is too adversarial and divisive and could potentially land us before a judge in court, cost us a lot of money, and distract us from the mandate of our organization. Moreover, I believe the board has not tried hard enough to resolve its differences and that a mediator should be hired to help the board get back on track. With this in mind, I suggest that the motion to remove the two directors be withdrawn."

Chair: "It has been suggested that the main motion to remove the two directors be withdrawn. Is there any discussion on this suggestion? (Members discuss the merits of withdrawal.) There being no further discussion, we will vote on the suggestion that the main motion be withdrawn. Those in favor of withdrawal, raise your hand. Thank you. Those opposed to withdrawal, raise your hand. Thank you. The motion is withdrawn.''

Use of the Motion to Table

There is more confusion regarding the motion "to table" and its effect than the last three procedures combined. People mistakenly use tabling to postpone definitely ("table until the next meeting"), to refer ("table to the Education Committee"), or to withdraw ("Let's just get rid of this thing. Why don't we just table it?"). There would be no harm in tabling if it were used correctly and if everyone had the same understanding of the outcome. But, in reality, there are a few potential difficulties:

- Some members prefer to use tabling because, according to some rule books, this motion is not debatable, and can bring a quick end to a bothersome motion. This is not a legitimate reason for the nondebatable status of tabling, as shown below.

- Uncertainty is created over questions such as: Can the tabled motion be brought back, and, if so, until when? What happens after this deadline? Does it die? Is it a terminal death or a temporary death? This confusion and uncertainty is a recipe for chaos and pandemonium in your meetings. So much for a good return on the time invested.

So what exactly is the motion to table? A definition accepted by many parliamentary experts is: Tabling is a motion to set aside the main motion temporarily, to accommodate another matter that requires immediate attention. The motion to table is not debatable and requires a majority vote to adopt. The reason for the motion's nondebatable status is the urgent matter requiring immediate attention.

EXAMPLE: A Legitimate Use of Tabling

Main motion: "To sponsor five members to attend the winter Olympics in the North Pole." Given the contentious nature of this proposal, it appears likely that another hour will be needed to debate it.

An unexpected event: The plane carrying the president of Russia has stopped in town for refueling. She and her entourage heard some strange noises and walk into your meeting to find out what your members are doing.

Some members have long wanted to hear from this president. This is a once-in-a-lifetime opportunity to do so. However, the president has only 15 minutes left before her plane finishes refueling and leaves.

Member: "I see that a long-awaited and distinguished visitor from Russia has just walked in. I move that we table the motion so that we can hear from her and ask her some questions."

Chair: "It has been proposed that the main motion be tabled. The motion to table is not debatable. Those in favor of tabling, raise your hand. Those opposed, raise your hand. Thank you. The motion to table is defeated. Sorry, Ms. President, but the members apparently don't want to hear you now. Try again in 10 years."

Or:

"The motion to table is adopted. Ms. President, would you please come and speak to us? You don't want to? That's too bad. This is the first time ever we had a legitimate reason to use the motion to table. We will carry on then with the motion to sponsor five members to attend the winter Olympics at the North Pole. Is there any further discussion on this motion?"

Consider the following suggestions regarding the motion to table:

1. The first option is to avoid tabling and the confusion that comes with it altogether, especially since the likelihood of it being used correctly is minimal. Instead, teach your members the plain-language alternatives (postpone to

a specific time, refer to a committee, or withdraw the main motion). Those options are likely to be less confusing, more user-friendly, and more procedurally correct.

2. The second option is to explain what the motion to table achieves (according to your favorite parliamentary manual) and make sure that everyone knows what they are voting on.

Revisiting a Past Decision

Several situations are considered in this section:

- A proposal is adopted. Later new information emerges that makes it necessary to give the proposal a second thought. How can it be modified? How can it be rescinded?

- A proposal is defeated. Later new information emerges that may cause it to be adopted. How can it be reintroduced for discussion and a new vote?

The various books on parliamentary procedure cover revisiting in different levels of detail. Some contain far more rules than are ever likely to be used. Put in the wrong hands, this myriad of rules is a recipe for chaos and pandemonium, and a waste of precious time and efforts.

The proposed alternative is to focus on the essential principles and give you the basic rules that you are most likely to need. If this is not enough, you can do one of two things: Go to your favorite parliamentary book or (the preferred option) use plain old common sense. Just ask the members to define, in plain language, what they want to propose, and then facilitate a collective decision on their proposal.

Four Fundamental Principles

The four fundamental principles to consider when revisiting a motion are:

1. At the same meeting, the same, or substantially the same, motion that was adopted or defeated cannot be allowed to consume the group's time again, unless the group decides to reconsider it.
2. At a future meeting, a motion that was defeated and is still applicable can be reintroduced as new business. Changed circumstances can yield a different outcome, and the group retains the capacity to respond to such changes (new information, new products, changed group composition, changed organizational dynamics, etc.).
3. A proposal that was adopted can only be revisited if no irreversible action was taken to implement it. If the proposal was partly implemented, only the unexecuted portions can be amended or rescinded.
4. Each group needs to strike its own balance between the right of individuals to be persistent and try to revisit a decision, and the right of the majority to be protected from abuse of its time.

With these principles in mind, procedures for revisiting a previously made decision are suggested.

Revisiting Defeated Motions

At the Same Meeting (Principle 1)

Member: ''I propose that the motion regarding new staff that was defeated earlier in this meeting be reconsidered. I have new information that may lead to a different result.''

Chair: ''It is proposed that the motion regarding new staff be reconsidered. Is there any discussion on whether it will be reconsidered?'' (Brief discussion takes place.)

Chair: ''We will now vote on whether the motion regarding new staff will be reconsidered. Those in favor of reconsideration, please raise your hand. Thank you. Those opposed, please raise your hand. Thank you. The motion will now be reconsidered. Is there any discussion on the motion that we hire a secretary and a personnel assistant?''

At a Future Meeting (Principle 2)

At a future meeting, a motion that was defeated and is still applicable can be reintroduced by any member as new business and there is no need to propose that it be reconsidered.

Preventing Abuse of the Renewal Privilege (Principle 4)

To prevent abuse of the individual's right to reintroduce defeated motions again and again in subsequent meetings, a formal and an informal approach can be considered:

- *A Documented Approach.* Adopt a rule to prevent abuse. For example: ``The same or substantially the same motion that was defeated twice during a 3-month period shall only be allowed to be reintroduced if the members agree to its reintroduction by a majority vote.''

- *A Verbal Approach.* Ask the member (preferably outside the meeting) for the reason for reintroducing the motion again and again, or, at the meeting itself, say: ``I am noting that this motion has been before us and was defeated several times recently, and I am not aware of any new circumstances that justify spending more time on it. Given our limited time and busy agenda, the motion will not be allowed.'' If the member disagrees with you, let the members decide (by a majority vote) whether they want to spend the time on this motion again.

Revisiting Adopted Motions

In All Cases (Principle 3)

Revisiting an adopted motion that has been implemented (i.e., action has been taken that is impossible to undo) would be wasteful and futile, and should therefore not be allowed. If a motion has been partly executed, only the unexecuted portions can be revisited. The remainder of this section refers to decisions (or portions thereof) that can be reversed.

At the Same Meeting (Principle 1)

Member: "I propose that the motion regarding the purchase of furniture that was adopted earlier in this meeting be reconsidered. I have new information that may lead to a different result."

Chair: "It is proposed that the motion regarding the purchase of furniture be reconsidered. Is there any discussion on whether it will be reconsidered?" (Brief discussion takes place.)

Chair: "We will now vote on whether the motion regarding the purchase of furniture will be reconsidered. Those in favor of reconsideration, please raise your hand. Thank you. Those opposed, please raise your hand. Thank you. The motion will now be reconsidered. Is there any discussion on the motion to purchase five new desks and five matching chairs?"

Next, the group debates and amends the motion and may vote to adopt it, defeat it, postpone it, refer it to a committee, or withdraw it (see previous sections in this chapter).

At a Future Meeting (Principle 3)

At a future meeting, a motion that was not implemented can be rescinded or amended.

Example 1

Member: "I propose that the motion regarding the purchase of a new computer, which was adopted at the last meeting, be amended by increasing the amount from $2000 to $2500. We checked in many computer stores and we could not find anything suitable for $2000." The group proceeds to debate the motion to amend, and, by a majority vote, the motion is amended.

Example 2

Member: "In light of our current financial situation, I don't believe we can afford to be giving charitable donations right now. In light of this, and given that no check was sent, I move that we rescind our decision to donate $350 to the Red Cross.''

The group proceeds to debate the motion to rescind, and, by a majority vote, the motion is rescinded.

Preventing Abuse of the Privilege to Revisit Adopted Motions (Principle 4)

To prevent abuse of the right to introduce motions to rescind or amend adopted motions (or their unexecuted portions) again and again in subsequent meetings, a formal and an informal approach can be considered.

- *A Documented Approach.* Adopt a rule to prevent abuse. For example: ''The same or substantially the same motion to rescind or amend a previously adopted motion that was defeated twice during a 3-month period shall only be allowed to be reintroduced if the members, by a majority vote, agree to its reintroduction.''
- *A Verbal Approach.* ''The motion to rescind the smoking ban was defeated last month, and no new information that would lead to a different outcome has emerged. Therefore, the motion to rescind will not be allowed.'' If the proponent persists, take a vote on whether the chair's decision will be upheld.

Points of Order and Appeals

This section addresses two formal procedures to handle procedural violations:

1. A point of order
2. An appeal of the chair's decision

The information given in this section should be considered in the context of the broader discussion of informal ways of handling procedural difficulties in meetings, included in the next section.

A Point of Order

A point of order is a complaint that a rule of order has been violated. A point of order should be raised if fundamental rights are infringed upon (e.g., a member was allowed to speak a second time when another was waiting to speak for the first time). A point of order should not be raised on violations of a purely technical nature, when fundamental rights are not adversely affected, or when there is clearly no harm done to the integrity of the decision-making process (see the next section for an in-depth discussion and examples of procedural violations). When a point of order is raised, the chair should:

- Clarify which rule is believed to have been violated. If the member has no definitive answer, the chair should clarify that a point of order (which is one of very few procedures that can interrupt a speaker) can only be used to complain about procedural violations and not to offer a rebuttal. The statement: "I have a point of order . . . I disagree with the speaker, and here is why . . ." is a speech, and the member wanting to make it must wait in the speakers' lineup.
- If the member is indeed raising a point of order, determine its validity or impact.
- If the point of order is deemed to be valid and significant, direct that the appropriate corrective action be taken.
- If the point of order is deemed invalid or insignificant, advise the members of this and move on.
- If you are unsure about the validity or significance of the point of order, or if the issue is contentious, submit the decision on the validity or significance of the point of order to the members and take action as directed by them.

In assessing the validity or significance of the point of order, the chair and the members should consider the following questions:

- Has a violation indeed occurred?
- Is it a ceremonial infraction (nitpicking) or a truly harmful violation?
- What, if any, corrective action is necessary?

Review the next section for a detailed analysis of procedural violations.

EXAMPLE: Organization's Mandate

Member: "I have a point of order. The proposal has nothing to do with the mandate of our organization and should therefore not be considered."

Chair: "The point of order is well taken (or not well taken). The motion is not related (or is related) to our mandate and will not be (or will be) allowed."

Or:

Chair: "What is the sense of the members? Those who believe this proposal is within our mandate, please raise your hand. Thank you. Those who believe that it is outside our mandate, please raise your hand. Thank you. The proposal will (or will not) be considered."

EXAMPLE: Nitpicking

Member: "I have a point of order. The motion was not formally moved and seconded."

Chair: "The point of order does indeed indicate a technical violation, but this violation has no negative impact on our business. Therefore, no action is needed. All we need to do is to ensure that the wording of the proposal is clear, that it is opened to debate and amendment, and that the wishes of the members are ascertained."

An Appeal

The chair has decided that your motion is inappropriate, or that your point of order is not well taken. What can you do? You can demand that the chair's decision be submitted to the members for determination. The procedure to facilitate a vote on the chair's decision is called an appeal.

EXAMPLE

Member (informally): "I disagree with the decision of the Chair."
Or:
Member (formally): "I appeal the decision of the chair."
Chair: "The chair's decision has been appealed and will be put to a vote. The decision was that the point of order was not well taken, and that the main motion is in order. Those who believe that the chair's decision is correct, raise your hand. Thank you. Those who believe the decision is not correct, raise your hand. Thank you. The decision has been sustained (or the decision has been overturned)."

Notes on the Appeal Procedure

- A majority against the chair's decision is needed to reverse it. A tie vote means that the decision has been upheld. The chair, if a voting member, can (if she or he wants) vote in favor of the decision, create a tie, and cause it to be upheld.
- The person presiding over the meeting is not required to vacate the chair while taking the vote on the appeal.
- If the chair's decision is overturned, it is not a "vote of nonconfidence," and he or she can continue to preside.
- Appeals can be avoided if the chair submits contentious procedural decisions to the members (the decision of the members cannot be appealed).

Assessing the Impact of Procedural Violations

The chair's worst nightmare is when a member raises a point of order and claims that an obscure rule of order was violated. Procedural arguments ensue and no one has an authoritative way of determining whether the member is right (your favorite parliamentarian is on vacation). Often, the chair capitulates ("Okay, we'll do it this way. You sound like you know what you're talking about"). Prime time is lost, and chaos and confusion reign.

This section gives you tools to prevent procedural arguments from becoming the focus of the meeting. Ways are offered to determine the significance (or lack thereof) of a procedural violation: Is it a ceremonial infraction that should be ignored? Or is it a harmful breach that must be addressed? This discussion continues in the next section, where tools and scripts are offered to combat procedural nonsense and to shift the focus to principles and common sense.

There is one very significant notion about parliamentary procedure that receives little or no attention in meetings:

> In a meeting, it is counterproductive to complain about minor technical violations of rules of order, if such violations have no adverse effect on fundamental rights, and if such violations do not compromise the quality of the decision-making process.

This statement is at the core of this book's approach to rules of order. It is more important to know and uphold fundamental principles (fairness, equality, common sense, and protection for the majority, minority, individual, absentees, and the entire organization) than to know the precise meaning of every procedural step and enforce it with scientific accuracy. Common sense and principles should always be in the forefront.

Questions Concerning Procedural Violations

So here we go again: Your closet parliamentarian raises a point of order and claims that a rule has just been violated. You are not sure whether there has been a violation and have no time to research a 600-page rule book to find out. What questions should guide you in assessing the significance of this violation (regardless of whether it is a real violation or only a perceived one)?

Here are the *wrong questions* to ask about a procedural violation:

- Did we follow our rule book with scientific accuracy?
- Is our closet parliamentarian in support of how we did things?
- Did we violate our past traditions by doing things differently?

Here are the *right questions* to ask about a procedural violation:

- Was it indeed a violation? (Even if the answer is yes, it may not be significant.)
- Were any rights violated?
- Was there any negative impact on the decision-making process?
- What is the purpose of the violated rule? What principle is it intended to uphold?
- Does this rule make any sense or does it appear to be purely mechanical?
- Is more harm being caused by arguing about the violation than by the violation itself?

Having asked these questions, you will likely be able to place the violation in one of four categories:

1. *Harmful Violations.* They undermine a principle or infringe on basic rights.
2. *Ceremonial Infractions.* They are purely technical and harmless.
3. *Beneficial Suspensions.* They are helpful, not harmful.
4. *Nonviolations.* They are undocumented and nonsensical procedures emerging from past traditions that no

one has dared to question, or from someone's active imagination.

Harmful Violations

There are certain procedures that are intended to protect fundamental rights and that should not be violated. The following three examples illustrate the harm done by common violations. In such cases, raising a point of order would be helpful, prudent, and advisable:

- *The playing field is uneven.* A member raises his hand, politely waiting to speak for the first time on a proposal, when someone else who has already spoken interjects. The principle of equality has been breached and a member has been robbed of his right to speak. In addition, the quality of the decisions can suffer if discussions are dominated by outspoken members.
- *The collective wishes of the group are not ascertained.* At the insistence of one outspoken member, the chair directs that certain action be taken. Conversely, faced with strong and persistent opposition from a minority, the group capitulates and declines to pursue an important initiative. The right of the majority to govern is trampled upon, and the organization succumbs to the tyranny of the minority.
- *The bylaws are violated.* Suppose the bylaws require a special notice and a super-majority to authorize a large expense. Such a requirement forces the organization to move cautiously and exercise fiscal prudence. Violating the bylaw could place the organization at financial risk. The rights of the absentees would be violated if the proposal were presented without notice.

Ceremonial Infractions

There are many procedures that are purely technical. They are often violated for lack of knowledge and cause no harm. Raising a point of order when such procedures are violated would be correct but also counterproductive. The following are examples of harmless procedural violations that should be ignored:

- *A motion is not seconded.* Requiring a second is a way of preventing a motion from being discussed if only one person is interested in it, but if the group goes ahead and discusses the motion without it being seconded, then this action indicates that the group wants the motion discussed. In any event, many times motions are seconded out of pure courtesy and the requirement of a second serves no purpose.

- *The chair introduces or solicits a motion.* You should thank the chair for facilitating progress. The normal practice is that the chair avoids making motions. But this practice is often stretched to absurdity, whereby no one makes a necessary motion and the chair is afraid of being criticized for introducing it. Gridlock prevails. No possible harm would be done if the chair said: "The next item of business is the hiring of a systems manager. The proposal is that we hire Kathy Chen for this position. Is there any discussion on this proposal?" Or: "Is there a motion that Kathy Chen be hired for the position of systems manager?"

- *A member speaks against his or her own motion.* The rule of decorum is that, although members may vote against motions that they introduce, they cannot speak against them. But no harm would be caused if, in the course of the discussion, the mover realized that he or she made a mistake and wanted to let the members know that by speaking against the motion. Such a violation would clearly be a minor one. It would be far worse to waste time arguing about it.

- *Inaccurate parliamentary terminology.* Why not use plain language instead of precise parliamentary terms, especially when the intent is clear (or even clearer)? For example: Instead of "I move the previous question," why not say "I propose that debate be closed"? The plain language is clearer, less awkward, and more user-friendly. This wording makes the proceedings less confusing and intimidating. Insisting on precision would definitely be counterproductive.

Beneficial Suspensions of Formal Rules

There are times when the established procedures are confusing. Other times, formal procedures are rigid and oppressive and stifle the free and creative flow of ideas. In those cases, procedural violations lead to substantial benefits. Consider the following examples:

- *Having a discussion before a motion is introduced.* An assumption commonly made is that no discussion can take place unless there is a motion on the floor. This approach is appropriate for a large meeting, or when there are many proposals to debate and vote on. However, in a small board or committee, this approach, applied rigidly and indiscriminately, robs the members of the benefits of informal discussion of complex issues. Going informal and exploring the problem first is advisable and beneficial. It will likely yield greater returns on the investment in a meeting.

- *Having an external or impartial facilitator.* Ordinarily, it is the elected or appointed chair (or president) who facilitates a meeting. But when a meeting deals with highly divisive or complex issues, or when the president wants to actively participate in the discussions, everyone stands to benefit from an impartial outside person facilitating the meeting. Such a person should be skilled as a facilitator and should have no vested interest in the substantive outcomes. Some will argue that the bylaws say that the president will chair meetings or that using an outside person is an admission that the chair is weak. Regarding the first argument, you can say that the president will remain the official chair and will make procedural rulings, but the facilitator will conduct the proceedings. Regarding the second argument, you can say that knowing when and how to let go of control is not a sign of weakness but a sign of strength.

- *Preventing amendments until the motion has been discussed.* Parliamentary procedure does not preclude amendments from being introduced too quickly, even before any discussion of the main proposal has taken place. This can lead to absurd wastes of time. Other times, when the excruciating amending process is finished, the members can't wait to get rid of the motion. The fact that the rules are used correctly does not change the fact that the situation is ridiculous. The returns on the wasted time are often negligible, nonexistent, or even negative. The chair can ask that amendments be held back until there has been some discussion of the main motion.

Undocumented and Nonsensical Procedures

Undocumented and nonsensical procedures are often used because of the force of habit ("We've always done it this way"), or because an outspoken member says that they must be followed. Consider the following examples:

- *A motion to receive a report or letter after it has been presented.* A report or letter that contains no recommendations is presented for information only. A member then moves that it be received. What does this mean? Hasn't it been received already? If so, why waste precious time on this motion? What would happen if the members voted down this motion? This procedure is meaningless and should be avoided. Instead, the chair can simply invite questions on the document and then say: "Thank you. The report will be placed on file."

- *Calling for nominations three times.* During an election of officers, the chair, at the insistence of "knowledgeable" members, asks three times: "Are there any nominations from the floor?" Why three? Why not ten? All that should be required is for the chair to give the members enough time to make nominations. Asking once or twice and pausing for a few seconds should be long enough. This is an election, not an auction.

- *A motion to appoint a chair and a secretary.* At the beginning of a shareholder meeting, a motion is made to appoint a chair and a secretary, whereas those officers were previously elected to their positions. Do the members really have the power to defeat this motion? What exactly is the benefit of this silly procedure?

- *A motion to ratify the actions of the directors.* Many organizations present a motion to ratify the actions of the directors during the annual membership or shareholder meeting. If the directors acted within the authority vested in them by the bylaws, why would an act of ratification be required? And what would be the impact of having the motion to ratify defeated, when funds were spent and contracts were signed? This procedure should be eliminated.

Interventions for Combating Procedural Nonsense

This section contains sample interventions and scripts to combat procedural nonsense and to reinstate common sense and principle.

Precluding Premature Amendments

''I know there are some amendments that members want to propose. However, it seems more logical and productive to discuss the main ideas in the motion first. Is there any objection to dedicating 15 minutes to a discussion of the main motion before allowing any amendments? (Pause.) There being no objection, we will now have a 15-minute discussion only on the main motion.''

Preventing Nitpicking Amendments

''In the interests of saving time and in order to have a clear focus in the discussion, may I suggest that members avoid trying to make the motion perfect by proposing housekeeping amendments. Instead, it seems that the best use of our time would be to concentrate on the main ideas behind the proposal and give the board the discretion to interpret your sentiments while implementing it. Does this sound reasonable to you?''

Preventing a Premature Motion to Close Debate

''Thank you for the proposal to close debate. May I ask you to wait a few minutes with it? It seems to me that the discussion on this proposal has not covered quite enough ground, and I sense that several members are waiting to make new and very relevant points. Efficiency is laudable, but we need to also make sure that we make informed decisions. Thank you.''

Dealing with Parliamentary Experts or Nitpickers

Preventive Interventions

Establish a few fundamental principles with the members:

- The purpose of the rules is to facilitate progress and not to obstruct it.
- The focus of the meeting should be on substantive issues, not on procedure.
- Plain and user-friendly language is preferable to "parliamentarese."
- Precise parliamentary terminology is less significant than intent.
- The precise benefit of a procedure should be clear before it is used.
- Points of order should only be raised if a procedural violation causes harm (see previous section).
- If the benefit of a rule is not established or if it is disputed, its relevance should be settled by the members by a majority vote.

In a small group that meets on a regular basis, you can entrench the preceding principles in an orientation session. This will help you set a group culture that softens the impacts of procedures, and relies less on meaningless and obscure formalities and more on common sense.

In a large group (e.g., a large annual meeting), you can address the prospect of procedural uncertainty by the following preventive measures:

- Become familiar with the main procedures that could be used at the meeting.
- Circulate a summary of the principles stated earlier to the members in attendance. Also include a brief explanation

of the main procedures that are likely to be used at the meeting. This will reduce anxiety among the members, even out the playing field, and increase confidence in your leadership.

- Consider hiring a professional parliamentarian who subscribes to the above principles to advise you on procedural matters.
- Incorporate the following text into your opening script:

``As this meeting progresses, we will rely on rules of order to help us conduct our business. A summary of principles and main procedures on which we will rely has been circulated to you. I would like to review the main points that we will need to consider, since some of us are obviously more seasoned in the field of parliamentary procedure than others. We need to make sure that we work on an even playing field as much as possible.

``I would remind the members that the purpose of procedure is to facilitate progress, and not to impede it or constrain us. Our focus should be on substantive decisions, and the rules of order should be unobtrusive and user-friendly. Precise parliamentary terminology is less significant than your intent. I would encourage you *not* to raise points of order if a procedural infraction appears to be minor and harmless, or purely technical. Finally, if you make a motion or use a procedure with which we are unfamiliar, I may need to ask you to explain in plain language what you are trying to accomplish with it.''

Remedial Interventions

``Thank you for raising this point of order. As we suggested earlier, points of order should not be raised if a procedural violation is of a purely technical nature and no real harm is done to the decision-making process. I can't see what harm has been done, nor can I see how any fundamental rights have been violated. Am I missing something?''

``It is not clear to me whether this is indeed a violation and how significant it is. What is the sense of the members? Those

who believe that the violation is of a purely technical character and causes no real harm, please raise your hands . . .''

''I must confess that I am not familiar with this procedure and
what it is intended to accomplish. In fairness to the members,
we should use plain language so that everyone knows what
we are doing. Can you please explain what exactly this procedure is intended to accomplish?''

8

Accurate and Useful Minutes

Often there are protracted arguments about the content of the minutes: What should be recorded? What should be left out? Should something be recorded just because someone insists on it? Or should you follow universally accepted standards? The following topics are addressed in this chapter:

- General questions about minute taking
- Principles for recording minutes
- The recording of discussions in the minutes
- Making the minutes more useful, relevant, and reader-friendly
- Adopting minute-taking standards
- Minutes approval process and its meaning
- Impacts of freedom of information and privacy legislation
- Making the secretary's job easier
- An analysis of really bad minutes

General Questions about Minutes

What Are Minutes?

Minutes, once approved by the members, become the official record of what took place in a meeting. Typically, minutes are recorded by a hired or appointed secretary. Draft minutes are usually precirculated to members before the next meeting, and serve as a reminder of what was agreed to and of specific commitments made by members.

Who Needs Minutes and What For?

Minutes are a useful source of reference for various internal and external parties:

- Members who were present at the meeting are reminded of what took place and of commitments they made. This is a useful way of ensuring follow-up.
- Members who were absent are updated on events that took place.
- Those who will implement decisions receive a clear direction of what is to be done.
- Committees learn about the scope of their work and terms of reference.
- Future members learn about the organization's history and its decision-making processes.
- Outside parties (consultants, lawyers, judges, procedural advisers) receive the information that they need to offer advice or to assess the group's decisions and procedures.
- Prospective members receive the information they need to decide whether to join the organization. For example: A potential buyer of a condominium learns about the history of the building and the shape of repairs, and about the relationship among the owners, the governing council, and the management company.

What Are the Typical Problems with Minutes?

Given that minute readers are often busy people, the minutes should be made clear and concise so that it is easy to determine what took place at a meeting. It shouldn't take rocket science or detective work to figure out that a proposal to renovate the organization's headquarters was approved. But often minutes contain so much useless information that locating what you need is like finding a needle in a haystack! Minutes often suffer from some or all of the following ailments:

- Becoming a verbatim record of what was said at the meeting.
- Being reader hostile—that is, fragmented, repetitive, and unorganized.
- Becoming a free-for-all, with anyone who wants something recorded saying: "I demand that you put this in the minutes," or "I want to go on the record as saying that . . ."
- Using subjective language: "The president complimented everyone for an outstanding job that made a huge difference and was incredibly meaningful for so many people."
- Misrepresenting the facts. For example, recording that: "The board agreed that expanding the personnel department was not a good idea," when, in fact, the idea was raised, dismissed by one member, and the group proceeded to something else.
- Doctoring—that is, the chair edits the minutes not to ensure accuracy but to prevent embarrassment, or to facilitate action that was not formally authorized.
- Grammatical and typographical errors.

Principles for Minute Taking

Objectivity

Minutes should focus primarily on the collective decision-making process and much less on the actions or statements of individuals. With this in mind:

- It is less significant to record what the members said, or who made or seconded motions, or how individuals voted.
- It is more significant to record the precise wording of proposals and the collectively made decisions on them: Were

they adopted, defeated, postponed, or referred to a committee?
- Subjective language and interpretations should be avoided. Just stay with the facts.

Accuracy

Minutes should be an accurate reflection of what took place and not what someone wishes had taken place. Therefore:

- It is a mistake to allow doctoring of the minutes by the chair or another officer for a purpose other than ensuring accuracy.
- It is a mistake to move to amend the minutes and thereby modify a decision that was in fact made and was recorded correctly. The legitimate way of altering an adopted decision is by a proposal to amend the previously adopted proposal. This action has nothing to do with approving the minutes and should be taken later. The minutes should be left alone.

Consistency, Standardization, and Professionalism

What goes in the minutes should not be governed by demands of individual members. Instead, standards should be adopted by the group and should be followed consistently. When faced with demands to record something on an individual's request, the response should be: "Our adopted standards prevent me from recording this in the minutes. If you want to modify our standards, you need to make a proposal to the group to do so."

The minutes should be simple, logically organized, and easy to read and follow. Look for user-friendliness ideas later in this chapter. Minutes should be carefully reviewed to ensure not only that they are factually accurate but also that they are free of typographical and grammatical errors. What was said is less significant than the decisions that were made and the actions that were authorized.

The task of taking minutes should be considered in the broader context of meeting management. In a well-run meeting, minute taking is easy. In contrast, it is difficult to document a chaotic and confusing meeting with a poorly designed agenda (or no agenda at all), with everyone speaking at the same time, with no decisions reached, and with many agenda items started but left unfinished.

Recording Discussions in the Minutes

This section covers the following issues:

- Why you should avoid recording verbatim minutes
- An action-only approach to minute taking
- A blended approach to minute taking

Why You Should Avoid Recording Verbatim Minutes

Do not make the minutes a record of every word uttered at the meeting. Such an approach is likely to have some or all of the following negative impacts:

- The focus will be on individual comments instead of collective decision making.
- The minutes will be unnecessarily long, tedious to read, and of little or no value.
- The preparation will consume plenty of time and effort, with little, if any, return on this investment.
- This format will lead to time-consuming (though possibly entertaining) arguments at the next meeting: "I didn't say this." "Yes, you did, and I can prove it!" "Well, maybe I did, but I didn't mean to . . ."
- Verbatim minutes will become an impediment to spontaneous participation in discussions: "I don't want to get embarrassed by the minutes, so I had better not say anything."

An Action-Only Approach to Minute Taking

The complete opposite to verbatim minutes is recording only the decisions made while excluding the comments made during the discussion. Some organizations subscribe to this approach. Others find it inadequate, since it gives no indication of the thought process that the group went through and how it reached its decisions—that is, what were the main reasons in favor and against a decision, and what issues and principles were considered.

EXAMPLE: Action-Only Approach

A proposal regarding a new staff training program was presented by the Education Committee. After discussion and amendment, the following proposal was approved: "To hold five 1-day training sessions in October 2003 on change management, with up to ten managers attending each session, with the sessions being designed and conducted by Action for Change Inc., and with the total budget for the design and professional fees not exceeding $10,000."

A Blended Approach to Minute Taking

With a blended approach, you will record the action but will also summarize the discussion:

- The summary should be an objective and concise point-format synopsis of the discussion and the collective thought process that led to the decisions.
- The summary should make little or no reference to who said what.
- The summary should capture the essence of the discussion—that is, the main points made.
- Only distinctively different points should be recorded. Points that were made several times should be recorded only once.

EXAMPLE: Blended Approach

A proposed training program on change management was presented and discussed (see attached document prepared by Action for Change Inc.).

The following reasons for change management training were identified:

- Our customers are demanding greater responsiveness and higher service levels.
- Our competitors are changing their market strategies, and these changes have been successful for them.
- Profit margins and budgets are getting tighter.
- Studies show that interdepartmental communications are poor and waste resources.

The following points were made in favor of the proposal by Action for Change Inc.:

- The company has a strong track record, as proven by reference checks.
- The proposed budget is reasonable when compared to other companies.
- The company is locally based and by retaining it we would be supporting our community.

The following concerns were raised about the proposal by Action for Change Inc.:

- It is not clear whether the senior trainer will be available on the dates that are convenient for us.
- It is not feasible to take managers away from their jobs for 2 full days, as proposed.

After discussion and amendment, the following proposal was approved:

To hold five 1-day training sessions in October 2003 on change management, with up to ten managers attending each session, with the sessions being designed and conducted by Action for Change Inc., and with the total budget for the design and professional fees not exceeding $10,000.

Actions to be taken:

- Russell Peckford to contact Action for Change Inc., schedule training dates, and express a strong preference for the senior trainer to be involved
- Joanne Reynolds to contact the various departments, inform them of the training, and identify who should participate
- Rebecca Moore to arrange the training room, audiovisual aids, catering
- All members to report back on progress at the August 15 meeting

Thoughts to Consider

- With the point format, whereby you capture only the essence of the discussion, you will listen less for words and more for distinctively different ideas. Your minute-taking task will become much easier, more logical, and less time-consuming.

- With the blended approach—that is, point format—you can convert a seemingly random and aimless discussion into a concise and perfectly logical summary. Imagine what would happen if, at the end of a 15-minute rambling discussion, you interjected and said: "Let me see if I can highlight the key points that were made so far. First, . . . Second, . . ."

- If you are able to capture the discussion in point form and create accurate and concise summaries, it might compel others to communicate in this way. Not only will your minutes be better but so will your meetings.

- With this approach, you should even be able to chair a meeting and record the minutes at the same time.

Making the Minutes Reader-Friendly

Have mercy on your members and produce minutes that can be easily read and followed. Here are a few ideas on making your minutes more reader-friendly:

- Make your paragraphs short (ideally no more than five lines each).

- Highlight decisions, action items, and key points. Use boldface, underlining, italics, smaller or larger fonts, and so forth—but do so in moderation. Too much of a good thing can be distracting.

- Develop a numbering system for agendas and minutes, and follow it consistently between the documents. The number assigned to each item could reflect the place of the item on the agenda, the date, whether the meeting was open or closed, and other relevant information. Always include an explanation of what the numbering system means. For example: C9909-07 could indicate: Agenda item number 7, September 1999, closed meeting.

- Organize the minutes so that they flow logically, even if the discussion flowed randomly. For example: Suppose the discussion of item 3 began, then the group proceeded to item 7 without concluding item 3, concluded item 7, and then returned to item 3. You can consolidate all the proceedings that relate to the same item in one place.

- Number the pages and have a running header at the top of each one, giving the general context of the minutes, for example: "Minutes of March 15, 2002, Staff Meeting, Cameo Corporation."

- If the minutes are long and cover many topics (as the case may be with a meeting stretching over a few days), include a table of contents.

- Try a column system for a logical separation of topics, decisions, and action items. For example:

Topic	Decisions	Action
Staffing	To hire a new recruiter and a labor negotiator.	Rose Elliott to contact HR and report on progress at the next meeting.

Adopting Minute-Taking Standards

How can you avoid the free-for-all syndrome, whereby the secretary succumbs to orders by outspoken members and records whatever they demand? Instead of depending on a book on minute taking, adopt minute-taking standards to suit your group.

To become compelling, the minute-taking standards should be approved as a policy of your organization. This is the best way to establish clarity and consistency, and to avoid arguments on what should and what should not be included in the minutes. This section covers:

- The process for approving minute-taking standards
- Areas to address in your adopted standards

Process for Approving Minute-Taking Standards

The process of approving minute-taking standards can be as follows:

1. Preliminary standards for minutes are developed. These standards can be based on this chapter, or another book on minutes, or a survey of what your members prefer.
2. Sample minutes, based on the preliminary standards, are prepared.
3. The standards and sample minutes are circulated to the members for feedback.
4. Member feedback is used to revise the standards.
5. The revised standards are presented at a meeting for approval.

Given this inclusive process, members will have a greater understanding, appreciation, and ownership of the standards for minutes. From that point onward, there will be no more free-for-all and no more demands on the secretary that are not covered in the adopted guidelines.

Areas to Address in Adopted Guidelines

The main areas that should be addressed in your standards for minutes are discussed here. Feel free to modify the standards to suit your group's needs. The areas are:

1. Recording the basic parameters
2. Recording the processing of previous minutes
3. Recording the presentation of reports
4. Recording proposals (or motions)
5. Recording the results of a counted vote
6. Recording how individual members voted
7. Recording amendments
8. Recording the adjournment
9. Signing the minutes
10. Sample minutes

Recording the Basic Parameters

Start the minutes by including the basic facts about the meeting. They may include:

- The type of the meeting (regular, special, annual, reconvened, and whether closed or open)
- The name of the group
- The date, time, and place of the meeting
- Who chaired the meeting
- Who recorded the minutes
- For a large group: the overall attendance numbers, to verify the presence of a quorum
- For a small group: the names of those who attended, and, if desired, who was absent

Recording the Processing of Previous Minutes

Record the approval process for the minutes of previous meetings—that is, whether they were approved as read or circulated, or with corrections. If they were corrected, record the corrections in the minutes of this meeting so that absent members can correct their own draft copies. There is no need to resend the official (corrected) minutes to the members. They will pick up the corrections from the new set of minutes.

Recording the Presentation of Reports

The presentation of reports should be recorded as follows:

- Include the report's title and its originator.
- If a report was submitted in writing, refer to it in the minutes and file it separately.
- If a report was submitted verbally, record only the key points made.
- If a report was submitted for information only, there is no need for a motion that it be received. The fact that it was presented means that it was received. Suggest to your chair to save time and skip this meaningless procedure.
- If a report contains recommendations, record the decisions made on them and the actions to be taken as a result of them.

Recording Proposals

When recording proposals, the most significant things are:

- The precise wording of the proposal (or motion)
- The outcome (i.e., adopted, defeated, postponed, referred to a committee, etc.)
- Actions that were authorized to implement the decisions (Who will do what? By when? How will progress be measured?)

In the more formal meetings, when motions are made and seconded:

- If you insist, you may record the name of the mover of a motion, but it is suggested that you eliminate this practice or keep it to a minimum (see note below).
- There is no need to record the name of the seconder, since seconding a motion does not mean agreeing with it. Recording the name of the seconder would therefore be misleading.

Note on recording movers and seconders in minutes: Members often like to make or second motions in order to have their names recorded in the minutes as being there and doing something. These members may not like the former suggestions to delete names of movers and seconders. Nonetheless, minimize the number of names in the minutes because:

- The more names you record in the minutes, the more you entrench the notion of individual ownership. This notion is misleading, tends to fragment the group, and makes some individuals seem more important than others.

- Recording the mover's name makes no sense, since, after debate on a motion begins, the mover loses ownership and control over it. In addition, the mover may change his or her views about the motion as a result of the discussion and may even vote against it.

- Recording names of movers and seconders entrenches the notion that the only valid way of making a decision is by formally introducing a motion. As shown in Chapter 7, how a proposal is introduced is insignificant. What are significant are the precise wording of the proposal, the fact that it was opened for debate and amendment, and the outcome. A proposal can be introduced informally by the chair without being formally moved and seconded. A group's decision can also be facilitated by unanimous consent (i.e., by asking whether there is any objection to a noncontentious decision).

- Recording names consumes precious time. In typical meetings, the chair frantically looks for movers and seconders, and the secretary follows up: "What is the name of the mover? How do you spell it?" Recording names can also become a source of wasteful arguments in future meetings: "I didn't make this motion," or "My name was spelled incorrectly."

With these considerations in mind, simply record the motion this way: "After debate and amendment, the following motion was adopted (or defeated) . . ."

Recording the Results of a Counted Vote

If the result of a vote by voice or by show of hands is clear and conclusive, there is no need to count it. The minutes will then simply indicate that the proposal was adopted or defeated.

If, however, the vote was counted, the numbers should be recorded in the minutes:

- If the basis for determining the result is a majority of those voting, excluding abstentions, all you need to record are the numbers in favor and against the proposal.
- If you have a voting requirement of a majority of those present, record the number of the members present, then the number of those who voted in favor, and then the outcome—that is, the percentage, and whether a majority was achieved.

Recording How Individual Members Voted

It is horrifying to watch a large meeting when the chair asks: "Do those who voted against the motion want their names recorded in the minutes?" and a large choir responds with a resounding: "Yes!" It then takes 5 minutes to record the names. (And given that time is money, how much of a return is the organization receiving by investing these 5 minutes?)

Notwithstanding common practices, members do not have an inherent right to have their individual dissension or abstention recorded in the minutes. Allowing or encouraging such a practice can mislead people to believe that such members somehow become less responsible for the decisions made.

How one person voted is less significant than the collective wishes of the group. If the group voted in the affirmative (by the required majority), then a decision would be adopted and implemented. Otherwise, it would be defeated. That is all that matters. The focus of the records should be collective, not individual.

People often ask: "Does the recording of members' dissension or abstention give them some legal protection?" Conversations with several lawyers suggest to me that in most cases it is doubtful that your dissension or abstention (recorded or not) would give you legal protection. If you need legal advice on this issue, consult an attorney.

Notwithstanding the preceding statements and despite the need to keep the collective focus in minutes, there can be some perceived merits in recording how individual members voted on a small board or committee, primarily as a moral indicator. As another consideration, in political or publicly elected bodies (such as municipal government, school boards, or other public boards) there is some merit to wanting to go to the public in the next election and campaign on one's own voting record, as shown in the minutes.

With these thoughts in mind, it is suggested that you adopt the following guidelines:

- In large meetings, the votes of individual members should not be recorded.

- Small boards and councils should adopt their own guidelines on recording dissensions or abstentions. (Keep in mind that in some cases members don't have the option of truly abstaining from the vote. See Chapter 7.) An example of such a guideline is: "On any main motion, a member who has voted against the proposal or abstained from the vote may have her or his vote recorded in the minutes, provided that such member's request is made before the meeting is adjourned."

Recording Amendments

If an amendment to a proposal was introduced and the decision on the amendment was not made, you will need to record both the main motion and the amendment, and what was done with them (e.g.: "The motion and the amendment were not voted on but were referred to the Finance Committee for study." Or: "The motion and the amendment were postponed until the next meeting").

If, on the other hand, an amendment has been voted on, all that you need to record is the final wording of the proposal and the decision on it. Examples of how amendments are recorded are given in the sample minutes in this section, under "Member Consultation" and "Meal Service."

Recording the Adjournment

In the last paragraph of the minutes, indicate the time at which the meeting was adjourned. There is no need for a formal motion to adjourn the meeting, and the meeting can be closed by unanimous consent. All that the chair needs to say is: "Is there any other business to come before this meeting? (Pause.) If not, the meeting is adjourned." Even if there was a motion to adjourn (moved, seconded, and voted on), all you need to record is: "The meeting was adjourned at 9 PM."

Signing the Minutes

Minutes are ordinarily signed by the secretary. In organizations where there is an official secretary and a recording secretary, the person who holds the official title of secretary—and not the recording secretary—should sign them. Many organizations also have the chair sign the minutes.

The fact that the minutes are signed only indicates that the person signing them believes that they are accurate, not that they were approved. The minutes become the official record of the meeting only after they are approved by the members.

Sample Minutes

Minutes of the ABC Society Committee on Facilities

Present: _____

Absent: _____

OPENING:

The November 15, 2010, regular meeting of the ABC Society's Committee on Facilities was opened at 7 PM, at the society's headquarters, Meeting Room 1. Joan Smith chaired the meeting and Ellen Wright recorded the minutes. *The minutes of the October 18, 2010, meeting were approved with the following corrections:*

1. The word ``popular'' was misspelled on page 4, line 10.
2. Motion 5, on the purchase of furniture, included the words ``with all taxes.''

RENOVATIONS:

Evelyn Jones reported that she investigated the feasibility of renovations to Meeting Rooms 1 and 2 and recommended against them. A motion *"that this committee go on record as opposing the proposed renovations to Rooms 1 and 2"* was ADOPTED, the vote being five in favor and one opposed.

NEW INITIATIVES:

The report on new initiatives was received and placed on file.

MEMBER CONSULTATION (Note 1):

A motion was introduced *"that the committee urge the board to expand its consultations with the members regarding facilities."* An amendment was proposed to insert *"strongly"* before *"urge."* The main motion and the amendment were *not voted on,* but were *referred* to the staff for advice, with a request to *report back at the January 15, 2011, meeting.*

MEAL SERVICE (Note 2):

A motion regarding meal service for committee meetings was introduced. After discussion and amendment, the following motion was DEFEATED: *"That the committee recommend that the board approve a catered hot dinner for committee meetings."*

ADJOURNMENT:

The meeting was adjourned at 9 PM.

Note 1: The amendment was not voted on and therefore had to be recorded in the minutes.

Note 2: Amendments were voted on, but only the final wording of the motion is needed.

Minutes Approval Process and Its Meaning

By approving the minutes, the group certifies that it accurately reflects what took place in a previous meeting. Draft minutes, precirculated to members prior to approval, are not official minutes and should have a clear indication to this effect on every page. This discussion includes:

- A script for approving minutes of previous meetings
- Suggestions regarding the minutes approval process
- A suggested status indicator for minutes

A Script for Approving Minutes of Previous Meetings

The decision to approve previous minutes is typically one of the first items of business at the next meeting. This decision can be made by unanimous consent (without the formality of a motion). The chair says: "The minutes of the last meeting were circulated. Are there any corrections to those minutes?"

Corrections are usually approved by unanimous consent—that is: "Is there any objection to making this correction? (Pause.) The correction will be made. Are there any further corrections?"

If there are disputes as to the content of the minutes, they can be settled in several ways:

- The collective memory can be checked by a vote: "Those who believe that we approved $2500, raise your hand. Thank you. Those who believe we approved $2750, raise your hand. Thank you. It looks like $2750 has it."
- The secretary can be directed to review an audiotape or transcribed shorthand records of the meeting (if such a record exists).
- Ideally, such disputes can be prevented in the first place, by ensuring that proposals are clearly articulated several times at the meeting, before any votes are taken.

When there are no (further) corrections, the chair says: "There being no (further) corrections, the minutes are approved as circulated (or as corrected)."

Suggestions Regarding the Minutes Approval Process

Here are a few suggestions regarding the minutes approval process:

- Avoid asking: "Is there any discussion on the minutes?" This can lead to rediscussing decisions that have already been made at the expense of new ones. All you need to do is ask if there are any corrections. The objective is only to check if the minutes are accurate. It should be a simple process, and, if the secretary does his or her job well, it should virtually take no time at all.

- If the approval of the minutes could take time, try scheduling it for the end of the meeting, in order to avoid this administrative task from preempting the debate on new issues.

- When the minutes are approved, the draft copy should be edited, with the word "draft" replaced by "approved on _____" on every page. A copy of the approved minutes should be filed in the official records of the organization but need not be recirculated to every member. (Members can make corrections on their own draft copies.)

- There should be separate minute books (each containing the approved versions of the minutes) for separate bodies. As an example, for a membership-based organization, there should be separate minute books for meetings of the board, each committee, and the membership.

- Minutes are ordinarily approved by the body that held the meeting; for example, board minutes are approved by the board, and committee minutes are approved by the respective committee. It is a mistake to bring the minutes of a committee meeting to the board for approval. How can board members be asked to verify the accuracy of the minutes of a meeting that they did not attend?

  Exception: An exception to the above rule is the case of an annual general meeting (AGM). In this case, it is unreasonable to expect that members would remember what took place a year earlier, and their decision to approve the minutes would likely not be an informed one. Instead, the members should authorize the governing board or a minutes-approving committee to approve the AGM's minutes. The motion to achieve this goal would be as follows: "Resolved, that the board of directors be authorized to approve the minutes of this annual general meeting and to approve the minutes of future general meetings." If this practice is approved, the minutes of a previous general meeting could still be made available to members, but for information only, and as an approved document.

- There should be separate minute books for closed meetings. Such minutes should be approved at another closed meeting, not in an open meeting, in order to preserve the confidentiality of the proceedings and the decisions made.

- The group may, at some future time, decide to declassify the minutes of certain closed meetings, for example, if the subject no longer requires confidentiality. In such a case, the status indicator (see below) can be updated and the declassified minutes can be refiled.

- If errors are found in the minutes after they are approved, they can still be corrected by the members at a later time.

A Suggested Status Indicator for Minutes

Many organizations precirculate draft minutes to members so that they can review them prior to approval at the next meeting. In the absence of a clear indication of the status of the minutes, there can be confusion as to which are the official minutes and which are draft minutes.

Another difficulty is when the minutes of a closed meeting are circulated without a clear indication of the confidential nature of the proceedings. Other times, only the cover page is stamped "confidential," and, if an internal page is misplaced, it is impossible to tell that it is confidential.

To address these difficulties, it is suggested that you include a status indicator on each page of the minutes. The status indicator can be a stamp or a running header at the top or bottom of every page, and can show:

- Whether these are draft minutes or approved minutes
- The approval date, if the minutes were approved

- Whether the meeting was open or closed (e.g., the word "confidential" stamped prominently at the top of every page)
- Whether the minutes of a closed meeting were declassified, as well as the declassification date

Impacts of Freedom of Information and Privacy Legislation

Public bodies (such as a municipality, governmental agency, school district, regulatory body, or publicly owned corporation) may be subject to Freedom of Information (FOI) and Protection of Privacy (POP) legislation. The documents of such an organization, including minutes of meetings, are likely to be subject to public access requests. If so, the public body may refuse to release certain documents, based on criteria specified in the applicable legislation. For example:

- Documents containing legal advice, which is subject to attorney-client privileges
- Documents whose release could reasonably be expected to harm the economic interests of the public body
- Documents whose release would lead to an unreasonable invasion of a third party's personal privacy

Minutes should be prepared with public access requests in mind. Here are a few suggestions:

- Record only the action and key discussion points in an objective manner, and avoid recording conversations (who said what).
- Have a system whereby agenda items are classified prior to a meeting as open discussion issues or confidential issues (the latter being issues that the public body wishes to keep confidential and is justified in doing so under the legislation).
- Schedule open discussion issues on the agendas of open meetings. The proceedings of open meetings should be re-

corded in open meeting minutes, which should be filed in a separate open minute book and should be approved during open meetings.

- Confidential issues should flow into the agendas of closed (in-camera) meetings. The proceedings of in-camera meetings should be recorded in in-camera minutes, which should be filed in a separate in-camera minute book and should be approved during subsequent in-camera meetings.

- Open meetings and closed meetings should have their own separate agendas. If open issues and confidential issues need to be addressed on the same day, two separate meetings should be scheduled consecutively: an open meeting and then a closed one. The sequence of events should then be: The open meeting should be called to order, its agenda should be addressed, and, when the agenda is concluded, the open meeting should be adjourned. Next, nonmembers should be asked to leave, and, some time thereafter, the closed meeting should be convened.

- Minutes of in-camera meetings (whether they are draft minutes or approved minutes) should have a confidential indicator on each page (a running header or status indicator, or a confidential stamp).

Making the Secretary's Job Easier

The person recording the minutes often has a tough job, facing difficulties such as these:

- Members make vaguely worded proposals, expect the secretary to figure out what they are, and then criticize him or her for getting it wrong.

- Members do not conclude agenda items and do not bring issues to closure (e.g., a motion is proposed, but no vote is ever taken on it), leaving many loose ends.

- Members talk at the same time, making it impossible to follow what they are saying.

▪ Obscure technical jargon and abbreviations are used without explaining them.

▪ There is an expectation (explicit or implied) that the secretary should just sit there and take the minutes.

▪ Members come to the secretary after the meeting and demand that their statements be recorded in the minutes, or criticize him or her for not following their orders.

▪ The chair insists on making "minor adjustments" to the minutes, with the result being that they are inconsistent with what took place at the meeting.

A STORY TO PONDER: AN OUTBURST BY THE SECRETARY

Margaret, the secretary of a large organization, was a well-respected, well-liked, and calm-mannered woman. It would take a great deal to make her angry. However, during the organization's annual meeting, she was having a difficult time: The meeting was chaotic and confusing. The chair's performance was dismal, especially given the contentious issues at hand.

At one point during the meeting, the most unexpected thing happened: Margaret lost her temper, interjected, and said angrily: "Can someone tell me what's going on here? I can't record minutes when you're all over the map!"

There was a moment of silence as the members recovered from the shock and disbelief of seeing Margaret get angry. Then, because her outburst was so "off character," the members burst into laughter. But then something else happened: They got back on track and became focused and disciplined. They also remained on track for the remainder of the meeting. Who would dare make Margaret angry again?

Even the secretary can make a difference in a meeting. Do not wait until things are unbearable and do not try to remedy a difficult situation with verbal outbursts. You need to intervene in a constructive and appropriate manner, to create the conditions that will assist you in performing your task. See the suggestions on the preventive and remedial tracks.

The Preventive Track

Here are some suggestions for preventive work for the secretary: First, meet the chair on a regular basis, because she or he can be your most important ally. Your message to the chair should be: "I want to do my job well and serve the group effectively. Here is what I need you to do to help me achieve this goal." Specifically, request the chair to:

- Do whatever is necessary to ensure that proposals are clarified. The proponent or the chair can repeat them, or you, as the secretary, can read and confirm your understanding of them. This clarity must be established before a vote on a proposal is taken.
- Generally address only one issue at a time.
- Bring closure to agenda items and ensure that all loose ends are tied.
- Be sensitive to the task that you, as secretary, are trying to accomplish, for example, turning to you from time to time (and certainly before moving to the next agenda item) and asking if any clarification is needed before moving on.
- Establish the most appropriate way for you, as secretary, to alert the chair to a difficulty that needs to be addressed (e.g., by passing a note to the chair).

In addition to building a partnership with the chair, I suggest that you compile standards for minutes. Create sample minutes, and, after consulting with the chair, circulate them to the members for feedback. With this feedback, revise the standards and have them presented for approval at the next meeting. From this point on, you will follow these standards. If and when you are confronted by demands from an outspoken member to record something, you can say calmly and confidently: "Linda, I cannot record this in the minutes, because it is inconsistent with the standards that the members have approved. Here is a copy of these standards."

The Remedial Track

If, as secretary, you encounter difficulties at the meeting, or if you have a suggestion, you can intervene verbally or by passing a note to the chair, or by another method. Verbal interventions by the secretary would likely be inappropriate in larger or more formal meetings. Here are a few examples of verbal interventions:

- "Where are we on the agenda?"
- "I need to record the wording of the motion. Can someone help me out?"
- "Let me read to you the motion as I understand it, and you can tell me if I have it right."
- "My record tells me that a motion and an amendment were made, and that no decision was made on the motion."
- "Can you please slow down for a moment? I need to record the action items precisely: Who will do what and by when?"

Such interventions will not only help you take good minutes but will also enhance the quality and productivity of the meeting. Don't be surprised if some members approach you after the meeting to say how much they appreciate your efforts. Make your interventions nonthreatening and nonjudgmental, and intervene only if there is a clear need for them. Be sensitive to the chair and avoid being seen to undermine his or her authority.

Analysis of Really Bad Minutes

The following is an exaggerated version of bad minutes, and they are problematic in several ways. Review them in light of the information presented in this chapter and identify the weaknesses in them. An analysis follows the minutes.

THE BAD MINUTES

The November 15 meeting was opened even though some members said they were not going to come on time. Mr. Smith opened the meeting by telling the members it was entirely unacceptable behavior to even think of coming late and that if members don't want to keep their promises they should quit, plain and simple. He spoke with great eloquence, rarely seen in this usually quiet man before. The members were deeply moved by his opening remarks—as they should be—although it was not exactly their fault that the others were late.

Mr. Jones moved and Mrs. Humphry seconded that the minutes be approved, although they are hard to decipher and contain too much information. Lengthy discussion took place. Mr. Corrector said he was sorry for voting in favor of the motion on bicycle racks and moved to amend the minutes by striking out "bicycle racks" and inserting "car parking spots." The motion was carried with great enthusiasm, despite loud protests from Mrs. Jackson.

Mrs. Jackson insisted that it be recorded in the minutes how fed up she was with committee meetings, that she didn't think our guest speakers amounted to anything, and that every time she makes a motion she gets railroaded.

Mr. Jones reported that he had investigated the feasibility of renovations to the community center and that he thinks it's a terrible and awful idea. Mrs. Jackson said she disagreed, and that Mr. Jones is being a cheapskate, and that it's not his money that's being spent. Ms. Carter moved that the report be adopted. The members responded with deafening cheers and a hearty round of applause, much to the chagrin of Mrs. Jackson, who said that this committee doesn't know what life is all about.

Mr. Corrector moved that since the committee meetings are so long and members get hungry, the committee recommend to the board to authorize dinner. Mrs. Jackson seconded, but then moved to insert the word "hot" before "dinner." With a big smile on his face, Mr. Smith said that although it was a wonderfully terrific idea, the board will not agree to it. The amendment was adopted.

At 9 PM Mr. Smith said that he thought 5 hours was long enough for a meeting that didn't accomplish anything and that he was hungry and that his wife told him if he didn't come home by 9 he can forget it, and therefore he had no choice but to declare the meeting adjourned. Mr. Jones insisted that we needed a motion to adjourn. Mr. Corrector disagreed and Mr. Smith concurred.

The Analysis

Overall Problems

- Subjective interpretations by the secretary of what took place

- Poor writing style
- Irrelevant information and absence of relevant information
- Lengthy paragraphs
- Impression that the meeting is poorly run and the group is misguided

Specific Problems

- *First Paragraph:* Essential information is missing: Whose meeting was it? Where and when was it held? Was a quorum present?

- *Second Paragraph:* The members are attempting to change history (i.e., amending the minutes to reflect an amended motion, not the one that had actually been adopted).

- *Third Paragraph:* A free-for-all situation—an individual member insists on something being entered in the minutes and gets her way (anarchy, not democracy).

- *Fourth Paragraph:* There is no need to adopt the report. Instead, the committee needed to act on the recommendation included in the report (approve or reject the recommendation).

- *Fifth Paragraph:* The amendment was adopted, but what happened to the main motion?

- *Sixth Paragraph:* Was the meeting adjourned, and, if so, at what time?

9

The Virtual Meeting

Face-to-face meetings are expensive. In fact, in an increasingly competitive business environment, they are gradually becoming a luxury that organizations cannot always afford. You should conduct a cost-benefit analysis of your meetings:

- How much do they cost (money, time, resources, and human tolls)?
- How much value do they deliver?
- Is this value proportionate to your investment in them?

Your cost-benefit analysis will likely lead you to the conclusion that, at least in some cases, less costly and equally (or more) beneficial alternatives to meetings should be considered, for example:

- Meetings by phone (telephone calls, teleconferences, or audioconferences)
- Videoconferences
- Meetings by mail, fax, e-mail, or even news groups and chat rooms on the Internet

Alternatives to face-to-face meetings are explored in this chapter. They are referred to as virtual meetings. Specifically, the following topics are addressed:

- The advantages and disadvantages of face-to-face meetings

- The advantages and disadvantages of virtual meetings
- When to hold a face-to-face meeting and when to hold a virtual meeting
- Special issues to consider in connection with a virtual meeting
- Options for virtual meetings
- Examples of virtual meetings

Advantages and Disadvantages of Face-to-Face Meetings

Face-to-face meetings offer the following advantages:

- *More Interactivity.* Face-to-face meetings offer more communication dimensions. Members are able to see and hear one another in the same room. The full vocal and visual communication enables them to better understand and interpret what others are saying. Decision making can thereby be based on a more complete picture, and progress can be made more quickly.

- *Increased Responsiveness.* With everyone present in one room, it is easier to facilitate a dynamic and meaningful exchange of views. There are more opportunities to respond to questions about complex proposals and to address concerns about controversial or significant proposals.

- *Privacy and Security of Information.* In a face-to-face meeting it is simpler and easier to keep things confidential and to verify votes. Secret ballots are easy to administer.

- *Diverse Group Activities.* A face-to-face meeting offers more flexibility than a virtual one. With everyone present, it is easy to be creative and employ diverse activities and consensus-building techniques, such as breaking into small task forces, informal and fast-moving brainstorming activities, and intensive discussions of complicated case studies.

- *Group Cohesion, Team Spirit, and Social Interaction.* The face-to-face aspect offers a more substantial opportunity to build team spirit and cohesion, and to develop a group culture.

■ *Full Control and Accountability.* Members are guaranteed that they will see and hear all the discussions that lead to decision making.

Face-to-face meetings have the following disadvantages:

■ *High Costs.* Face-to-face meetings are costly (wages, expenses, meals, meeting room, preparation time, production of documents, travel time, meeting time, pre- and postmeeting stress, etc.). The investment in a face-to-face meeting does not always yield proportionate returns.

■ *Disruption.* Face-to-face meetings require individuals to disrupt their lives, set aside other work and personal commitments, and make their way to a meeting location (sometimes traveling long distances or fighting their way through rush-hour traffic). They sacrifice their time, may incur some personal costs, and their other duties and priorities may suffer.

■ *An Increased Potential for Hasty and Ill-Advised Decisions.* With all members present, things tend to move more quickly. This increases the risk of making poor decisions on the spur of the moment. It is more difficult to slow things down and make the decision-making process more measured and deliberate.

■ *An Increased Potential for Emotions to Overtake Principle.* The presence of both verbal and nonverbal dimensions in communications is a double-edge sword: Yes, it can lead to a better understanding of others, but it can also cause members to give more weight to emotional considerations, at the expense of common-sense principles and objective information.

■ *An Increased Potential for Adversarial Discussions.* With controversial issues, strong personalities, and pre-meeting adversity, face-to-face meetings are more prone to becoming battlefields.

■ *Reduced Personal Commitment.* In a face-to-face meeting, it is easy for the less assertive members to yield to dominant ones, defer to them for direction and ideas, and exercise less individual initiative, creativity, and independent thought.

Advantages and Disadvantages of Virtual Meetings

Virtual meetings offer the following advantages:

■ *Reduced Cost.* Without the requirement that all members be physically present in one room, the cost of travel, preparation and travel time, meeting room, and logistical details can be reduced substantially.

■ *Reduced Schedule Disruptions.* Members can participate in a virtual meeting from their offices or homes, and the disruptive impact on their work and personal priorities can thereby be reduced.

■ *A Tendency to Be More Focused and Task-Oriented.* Without being distracted by the many events, the fast-moving interactions, and the emotional tone in a face-to-face meeting, members can concentrate on the issues.

■ *Increased Individual Involvement.* With members being physically separated, a virtual meeting lends itself to more introspection and solitary thinking, and can thereby increase concentration and personal involvement. It has the potential of forcing members to be more creative, show more personal initiative, and be less dependent on dominant members for ideas or guidance.

■ *The Potential for Increased Communication and Consensus-Building Activities.* If you don't have to encounter the costs of a meeting to communicate with members, it may mean that you can afford to communicate with them more often.

■ *Reduced Likelihood of Adversarial and Chaotic Discussions.* The physical distance tends to soften personal animosities and the emotional tone of discussions, and to force members to focus on fundamental issues, objective principles, and the group's mandate.

Virtual meetings have the following disadvantages:

■ *Incomplete Communication.* In the absence of the vocal and/or visual dimensions, issues may not be fully understood and communication gaps may open. With this deficiency, members may not have the basis on which to make good collective decisions. This can also cause repetition and confusion, and may extend the duration of the virtual meeting.

■ *A Slower Pace.* In the absence of the vocal and/or visual dimensions in a virtual meeting, it takes more time to build the information base needed to make good decisions. (Conversely, this slowness may in fact be a blessing, and may assist in making the decision-making process more measured and deliberate. It is more difficult to rush things through in a virtual meeting.)

■ *Unique Challenges.* In a virtual meeting it is more challenging to maintain security of sensitive data, keep certain things confidential, ascertain a voting result, prevent voting irregularities, build team spirit and cohesion, and facilitate diverse discussion activities.

Choosing the Type of Meeting

Based on the advantages and disadvantages discussed, the type of meeting you choose (face-to-face or some form of virtual) will depend on the issues at hand and the purpose of the meeting. Face-to-face meetings will typically be needed in the following cases:

■ For controversial decisions requiring full interactivity
■ When complex or technical data must be explained, requiring the capacity to fully comprehend their verbal and visual aspects, as well as the full opportunity to ask questions
■ When sensitive data are to be exchanged or discussed, or confidential decisions are to be made
■ For large gatherings and conferences
■ For strategic-planning or team-building sessions, when diverse discussion activities are used
■ When there is a need to develop social interaction and get the members to personally meet one another

- When there is a degree of distrust among members and fear of compromising the decision-making process by having discussions and decisions made outside a face-to-face meeting
- When there is no provision in the governing statute, by-laws, or terms of reference for a virtual meeting
- When there is a statutory requirement to keep meetings open to the public (e.g., municipal government), in which case a virtual meeting would be impractical

Virtual meetings could be held to facilitate the following:

- Regular updates on progress or straightforward exchanges of information and ideas
- The presentation of a new policy
- Situations where the communication is mostly one-way
- Routine and noncontroversial decisions
- Urgent decisions, when no time is available to organize a meeting, or when doing so would be too costly and disruptive (as may be the case with a national board of directors)
- A purely task-oriented focus where there is no need for personal interaction

Special Issues to Consider Regarding Virtual Meetings

When considering a virtual meeting, attention should be given to these issues:

- *Governing Documents.* If your group is formally organized, check if your governing documents (bylaws, terms of reference) authorize decision making by the virtual meeting contemplated. If not, see if you can facilitate a decision to amend the respective document by including clauses such as the following: "Board meetings may be held by teleconference calls, videoconferencing, or other electronic means, provided that all members have been notified of such meetings, and provided that a quorum participates in them"; and/or: "A resolution in writing, signed by a majority of the directors, shall be as valid as a resolution adopted at a duly called board meeting."

▪ *Data Security.* Take the necessary measures to protect confidential information. This is particularly important with tele-conferencing, videoconferencing, and communications on the Internet or by fax. Ensure that the protective measures (techno-logical or others) are in place before the session begins and that the members understand them. Each member should be asked to confirm that only authorized members are in attendance at the respective location or are privy in any way to the information shared.

▪ *Verification of Voting Results.* Establish an airtight method of ascertaining the wishes of the members. Instead of the usual "Those in favor of the proposal, please raise your hand," you will likely need to poll individual members, one by one, ask how they vote, confirm your understanding (verbally or in writing), tally the votes, and only then declare the outcome. With controversial decisions, it may be preferable to ask members to send in their votes by fax, e-mail, or regular mail, along with their signature.

▪ *Voting by Secret Ballot.* This is not possible in a virtual meeting (given the need to verify that only eligible members have voted), unless you have access to a special system that is password protected and allows each member to vote privately (e.g., by punching digits on a touch-tone phone).

▪ *Overcoming Communication Deficiencies.* A virtual meeting does not offer the luxury of both hearing and seeing people speak. The facilitator and each member should be sensitive to this deficiency and compensate for it by:

—Establishing and enforcing discussion guidelines. Speak only after being recognized by the facilitator, and always open by identifying oneself.

—Communicating clearly and concisely.

—Replacing long and aimless statements by well-directed point-format comments.

—Speaking more loudly, enunciating clearly, using pauses

and varied vocal intonation to emphasize key points, to make up for the lack of visual communication.

—Using plain language, explaining technical terms and abbreviations, and confirming that everyone fully understands the issues before voting.

—Ensuring that members have equal opportunities to speak.

—Resisting the temptation to interrupt.

—Listening, listening, and then listening some more.

—Preparing thoroughly, reviewing documents, and researching issues.

—Clearly defining the purpose of the meeting, asking key questions, and making key decisions.

—Exercising a great deal of patience and self-discipline, to help keep the virtual meeting on track and on time.

Options for Virtual Meetings

The type of virtual meeting you choose will depend on your available resources. It will also depend on the purposes of the meeting, which may include some or all of the following:

- To give certain information (and answer questions about it)
- To receive information and progress reports and ask questions about them
- To discuss issues that the group is mandated to deal with
- To make decisions that will help in advancing the group's mandate
- To build organizational consensus and team spirit

These objectives can be achieved through the following forms of a virtual meeting, or a combination thereof:

- Meeting in writing (no audio and no visual dimensions)
- Meeting by conference calls (audio dimension but no visual dimension)

- Meeting by videoconference (both audio and visual dimensions)

Meeting in Writing

Using this method, information can be shared and consensus can be built via written communication, without members hearing or seeing one another. Here are several options to consider:

- Information is presented in written form (by fax, letter, e-mail, or live on the Internet).
- Members send their questions or views to every member. Alternatively, member responses can be sent to one person, who is designated to create a summary of the questions, the answers, and the apparent areas of agreement and disagreement.
- Follow-up documents are circulated to members, and further consensus building takes place.
- The written communication may be supplemented by phone messages.
- A face-to-face meeting can be held if and when needed.

Meeting by Phone

Meetings by phone give members the advantage of hearing—but not seeing—one another. There are two variations of these meetings:

- *Teleconference Call.* An operator arranges the teleconference among members in various locations. Some locations may have only one member, and the more central locations may have several members in attendance.
- *Telephone Consultation.* If the purpose is to give information, a facilitator can send a document and can then contact individual members by phone to answer questions. If, on the other hand, the objective is also to build consensus, the facilitator may circulate key questions and then contact members to discuss them.

Meeting by Videoconferencing

A videoconference enables participants to both see and hear one another. Members can respond to both voices and facial expressions, and can look each other in the eye. Although the setting does not offer the full flexibility and interactivity of a face-to-face meeting, it comes close. Videoconferencing technology is currently expensive. However, the investment may pay for itself over the long run by saving travel costs and reducing the impacts on individual schedules. The technology is also made available for rental by service bureaus.

Analysis of Examples of Virtual Meetings

Scenario 1: The Silent Meeting

Some organizations have used on-line forums to reduce meeting time and increase productivity. In one setting, participants sat at computer workstations in the same room, typing their thoughts on a subject for 30 minutes. A large screen in the front of the room displayed the results simultaneously, without identifying the writers. Participants could then categorize and rank ideas. This way everyone could "talk" while quickly learning on what areas the members were in agreement.

Scenario 2: A Large Staff Meeting

The objective is to explain a new policy, to make sure that every staff member has opportunities to ask questions, and to make sure that all members hear the answers to all relevant questions. By holding a face-to-face meeting, these outcomes could be achieved.

However, here are some familiar drawbacks: Schedules are disrupted. Some members need less information than others. Some members preface their questions by long preambles. The same questions are asked by several members. Those who hesitate to speak in public are effectively excluded. Time runs out before you can answer all the questions.

The virtual meeting alternative is to send the presentation (in concise and reader-friendly form) by e-mail, fax, or interoffice mail to all members, and request their feedback and questions by a certain date. The questions are then reviewed, a question-and-answer summary is prepared, and it is sent to all members.

The advantages of this approach are as follows: There is no disruption of schedules. Similar questions are answered only once. Lengthy preambles are omitted. Quieter members have a less threatening opportunity to get involved. Many more questions can be covered thoroughly. Much more is achieved than in a face-to-face meeting. The only thing lost is the social aspect of the face-to-face meeting.

Scenario 3: A Committee Decision

Your committee needs to develop a recommendation on a controversial issue. You want to make sure that the process is measured and deliberate, so you schedule a series of face-to-face meetings. The committee could achieve its objectives, but there might be a better way.

Consider building consensus through the following combination of written and phone communications, concluded by one face-to-face meeting:

1. Research the issues, define the questions that should be addressed, circulate them to the members, and contact them by phone to discuss their answers and check if you have covered the issues sufficiently.
2. Compile their feedback, send the summary to them, and request their opinions by a certain date (in writing or via a discussion with you on the phone).
3. Summarize the feedback, highlight areas of agreement and areas of disagreement, and then send them the summary.
4. Schedule one face-to-face meeting to resolve the contentious issues and finalize the committee's recommendations.

Note: This approach requires trust and confidence that you will not overtake or manipulate the decision-making process.

Scenario 4: A National Election

National organizations often hold their elections at their annual general meetings. Such meetings are typically attended by only a fraction of the members. Other national organizations hold their elections by mail ballot, without an opportunity to see and hear the candidates.

A virtual meeting alternative is as follows: A televised all-candidates forum is broadcast in selected meeting halls across the country and over the Internet. Members ask questions of candidates by phone, e-mail, or fax. They then vote by punching digits on phone keypads. The challenge is to ensure (electronically) that only voting members participate in the election. Of course, such a voting procedure would have to be authorized in the organization's bylaws.

10

Troubleshooting Guide

This chapter describes common meeting ailments (excluding procedural ailments, which are covered in Chapter 7), and remedial and preventive measures for them are suggested. This troubleshooting guide focuses on:

- General principles for interventions
- Facilitation ailments
- Agenda ailments
- Time management ailments
- Member commitment ailments
- Disorder and poor decorum
- Discussion quality ailments
- Logistical ailments

For each meeting ailment, you will find some or all of the following:

- The ailment, its symptoms, and possible root causes (where they are not obvious)
- Remedial interventions (how to cure the ailment if it occurs)
- Preventive measures (how to stop the ailment from occurring next time)

General Principles for Interventions

When faced with a meeting ailment and considering an intervention, keep the following principles in mind:

- There are times to intervene, and there are times to let go and allow things to take their natural course. Excessive interventions may worsen the ailment and may even cause a new one. For example: A digression from the agenda to relate a personal story is indeed against the rules. However, if it is brief, it can be harmless and may even offer the benefit of lightening things up. Intervening too fast can create unnecessary tension and rigidity at the meeting.

- Determine the root cause of the ailment before intervening and avoid impulsive reaction. The very same symptom may point to entirely different root causes. Choose the appropriate remedial or preventive intervention. You don't want to prescribe major surgery when an aspirin will do.

- Preventive interventions are generally preferable to remedial ones. Of course, you will not be able to anticipate every difficulty, but most problems are preventable.

- Assume that each member is a reasonable person, who intends no harm, and who genuinely cares about the organization, regardless of how disruptive and unreasonable a member may seem. This assumption must be a genuine and honest one. Pretending will not work.

- Make your interventions simple, brief, clear, focused, and principled. Avoid long and convoluted lectures. Just tell everyone what the difficulty is, what principle you seek to uphold, and what specific corrective action you are asking them to take.

- Use affirmative language. Say what you want members to do, instead of what you want them to stop doing. Instead of: "Don't speak without permission," say: "Please wait for permission to speak."

- Try ending your interventions with a question mark, thereby softening them and making them more consultative.

Instead of: "Stop rambling," try: "May I ask you to get to your point, please?"

- Use less of the word *I* and more of the words *we* or the *members*. Instead of: "I have to ask you to get back on track," say: "We need to stay on track."

- Balance the rights of the individual and the minority to be heard with the rights of the majority to rule. Good management is not about being nice and accommodating everyone all the time. It is about being principled. By being nice to one person, you may be not so nice to many others.

- How you say it is just as important as what you say. You may need to soften your tone of voice and facial expression. Conversely, you do need to sound confident, definitive, and unapologetic.

- Nonverbal interventions can be just as effective as verbal ones. For example: If there is a side conversation, you might just stop talking. The silence will likely compel the members to stop talking.

- If your intervention does not seem to work, seek directions from the group (instead of pitting yourself against the individual). Ask informally what the members want to do, or take a formal vote on how the difficulty should be addressed. For example: "Jack is requesting that the agenda be changed. What is the wish of the members? Those in favor of the change, raise your hand . . ."

- Use the carrot approach first and wave the stick only when absolutely necessary. Give a disruptive member every opportunity and incentive to participate constructively. In all likelihood, you will not need to resort to threats and accusations.

- Your ultimate "stick" should not be an order by the chair. Instead, the group should be asked to decide on remedial actions or penalties. For example: "What is the sense of the meeting? Is this language offensive or is it appropriate? Those who believe that this language is offensive, please raise your hand . . ." Or: "The member has repeatedly disrupted the meeting, despite being warned several times. Should he be permitted to stay or should he be asked to leave?"

- The chair does not have a monopoly on interventions. Individual members should feel free to help cure a meeting ailment if the chair does not do so. Keep the notions of shared responsibility and "suffering is optional" prominent.

Facilitation Ailments

The chair's role is crucial to the success of a meeting. Many problems in meetings can be attributed to poor facilitation or ineffective leadership.

Common Facilitation Ailments

Common facilitation ailments include a chair who:

- Shows no (or low) commitment to leadership duties.
- Does not prepare (or prepares inadequately) for meetings.
- Shows a lack of understanding of the organization's mandate, or fails to make it prominent.
- Is autocratic and imposes decisions on the group.
- Is too passive and hesitant to induce closure.
- Conversely, is always in a rush to close discussions and take votes.
- Unnecessarily interrupts speakers.
- Lectures or scolds members, and tells them what's good and what's bad for them.
- Is too formal, rigid, and stern.
- Dominates discussions and rebuts every statement made.
- Is nice and accommodates individuals, at the expense of the majority.
- Fails to clarify proposals and agenda items.
- Shows no respect for time: starts late, rewards latecomers with updates on progress, does not establish and enforce time limits, and consistently ends meetings late.
- Fails to listen or pay attention to the issues and to the members.

- Feels compelled to settle disputes unilaterally, instead of allowing the group to do so.
- Frames issues incorrectly, sometimes appearing to suit his or her own bias.
- Corrects the minutes for all reasons except to make sure they are accurate.

Root Causes for Facilitation Ailments

The root causes for facilitation ailments are usually:

- The varied perceptions that people have about the chair's role: Is it a position of power and control? Conversely, is it the chair's duty to always be pleasant and accommodating?
- The lack of good role models in the chair's position.
- Uncertainty about the roles of individual members in a meeting: Are they expected to sit back and let the chair run the show? What are they supposed to do when the chair is entirely ineffective?

Remedial Interventions

The best remedial intervention in a facilitation ailment is for individual members to express their concerns in a direct and principled manner, for example: "With respect, Mr. President, I believe that your primary role is to facilitate decision making, and not to impose decisions on us. With that in mind, that last decision should have been put to a vote, rather than being decided by the chair unilaterally." Or: "Judy, I am having trouble focusing on the discussion. Can you please remind us what subject and what proposal are being discussed right now?"

Preventive Interventions

To minimize the occurrence of facilitation ailments and reduce their impact, consider the following:

- Choose the right person for the chair's position, based primarily on the ability to lead (i.e., preside over meetings and build consensus), and not on popularity or being next in line.
- Establish an orientation manual and a mandatory training program for the chair, to emphasize the chair's roles and ethics, and to explain the chair's voting and debating rights (see Chapter 5).
- Establish an orientation manual and training program for members, to emphasize the notion of shared responsibility, and to entrench members' rights to intervene if there is a problem.
- Establish channels for members to offer feedback to the chair during meetings (e.g., by commenting on the conduct of each meeting before it ends) and between meetings.

Agenda Ailments

Ailment	Remedial Interventions What to Do Now?	Preventive Interventions How to Prevent It in the Future?
Inappropriate Agenda Item ``This issue is outside our mandate.''	Facilitate a decision to delete the item from the agenda, and save the time for mandate-related issues.	Refuse to include issues that do not relate directly to the group's mandate. No more free-for-all agendas!
Wrong Priorities Low-priority items are handled first or consume a lot of time. High-priority items wait until later, and ``later'' never comes . . .	Change the sequence of agenda items or the allocation of time. Hopefully, it's not too late to do so for this meeting.	Prioritize items when designing agendas. Establish a logical sequence and allocate time proportionately to the significance of items (80% of the time should produce 80%—not 20%—of the results).

(continues)

Ailment	Remedial Interventions What to Do Now?	Preventive Interventions How to Prevent It in the Future?
Reactive Agenda You spend most of the time reacting to what the world wants your group to do.	Discuss this issue with the members and collect ideas on what proactive components would make the agenda more meaningful.	Establish a schedule of proactive agenda items (based on a long-range plan), and schedule a few at each meeting.
Confusing Agenda Item It is not clear what an agenda item is and how it will be dealt with.	Explain whether an agenda item is for information or for decision making, how the discussion will unfold, and how much time has been estimated for it.	Give a clear indication on the agenda (or on an attachment) as to the nature of each item, the options for decision making, and the time allocated for it.
No Agenda A meeting was called hastily and without a precirculated agenda.	Start by clearly explaining the purpose of the meeting, the need for its urgency, and the agenda.	Never do this again (or, at least, make it the exception, not the rule), since this practice is very annoying and unsettling.
Crowded Agenda There are too many issues on the agenda, which means that you will inevitably hit rush hour.	Estimate how much can be realistically achieved at the meeting, drop or postpone some items, and deal only with the ``must do's.''	Scrutinize agenda items, estimate how much time they will require, and ensure that the scope of the meeting is realistic. Feel free to say no to items that can wait.

Surprise Agenda Item Last-minute additions to the agenda hijack the focus of the meeting.	Members can vote to refuse to address last-minute additions to the agenda, or demand the reason for their urgency. Schedule last-minute additions after scheduled items have been concluded, unless the group decides otherwise.	Entrench the notion that last-minute additions to the agenda should be the exception, not the rule, and that, as a general rule, pre-scheduled items are discussed first.

Time Management Ailments

Ailment	Remedial Interventions What to Do Now?	Preventive Interventions How to Prevent It in the Future?
Presenter Goes Overtime A guest presenter goes overtime. Other agenda items could suffer as a result of this.	Interject: ``Excuse me, Professor Higgins, but, in light of our time constraints at this meeting, how much more time do you need?''	Establish time limits with your speaker and how you will indicate that time is running out.
Never-Ending Statements A member doesn't seem to know when and how to end a statement.	``Jack, we have many issues to deal with. Your point is made and we need to move on. Judy is next.'' Or: ``If you had to say it in one sentence, what would it be?''	Opening script: ``We have a busy agenda and we need to be efficient. Please keep your comments brief and focused.''
Time Limits Violated In a formal meeting, a member wants to	``Sir, in fairness to others, your 3 minutes are up. We	Give them advance warning: ``1 minute left; 30 seconds left;

(continues)

Ailment	Remedial Interventions What to Do Now?	Preventive Interventions How to Prevent It in the Future?
speak longer or more often than agreed to.	need to make sure that the rules are followed consistently by all members." Or: "Madam, you've already spoken, and we need to hear from first-time speakers first."	time is up." The signal can be vocal (raising your volume slightly for the "Time's up"), or via timing lights, or even by a bell!
Late Start The chair waits until everyone arrives before starting the meeting.	Options: Start anyway, with less significant items. If it is counterproductive to start (e.g., no quorum, or a snowstorm), ask those who are there what should be done next.	Make sure the start time is reasonable. Announce a social and networking time to precede the meeting. State your intention to start exactly on time.
Late Ending The meeting continues past the established closing time. Some leave. Others stay (resentfully), but their subsequent commitments suffer.	The chair or a member interjects: "In fairness, our scheduled closing time is here, and members have other commitments. We should adjourn now, and continue the meeting another time."	Establish a realistic agenda for the meeting and allocate time for major items. Start the meeting on time and give members periodic progress statements on time: "We have 5 minutes left for agenda item 6."
No Ending Time Scheduled	"When should we aim to conclude the agenda? Is 4 PM reasonable?	Estimate an ending time, have it printed on the agenda, and facilitate a decision on it at the start of the meeting.

Early Ending The meeting is about to end early.	It is not a crime to end a meeting early. You can break the good news to the members and quit while you're ahead.	If your estimate of the required time was too generous, budget more realistically next time. Conversely, if you rushed through and the quality of the decisions suffered, slow down next time.
Late for a Scheduled Item The scheduled time for an agenda item has arrived, but another 15 minutes is needed to facilitate a natural closure on the previous issue.	Halt the discussion on the current item and facilitate a decision on whether to extend the time for it (possibly at the expense of the next item).	Allocate time realistically, monitor the clock as you go along, and give members progress statements on how much time they have left for an item.

Member Commitment Ailments

Ailment	Remedial Interventions What to Do Now?	Preventive Interventions How to Prevent It Next Time?
No Preparation Members open the premeeting packages at the meeting itself.	If an informed decision cannot be made, facilitate a delay, e.g., a reading recess, followed by a question period; or postponement to the next meeting.	``Based on the discussion, it seems that some members prepared more than others. Would everyone please prepare next time so that future meetings can be more focused and efficient, and so that we can make better decisions?'' Or: Speak to repeat offenders between meetings.

(continues)

Ailment	Remedial Interventions What to Do Now?	Preventive Interventions How to Prevent It Next Time?
Quiet Members Members show no interest in the discussions (not speaking; being preoccupied with another task).	If they have nothing to contribute, see if they can be relieved of the burden. Otherwise, facilitate activities to engage them in discussions, e.g., ask each person to consider a key question for 3 minutes and then poll them at random.	Establish the mandate of the group and the role of each member in fulfilling it. Have private discussions with difficult members to discuss how to increase the relevance of the meetings to them and raise their commitment levels.
Postmeeting Debates No one says much during the meeting and proposals are ''rubber-stamped'' without questioning. But then there is a break, and the real debate begins . . .	If it becomes apparent that a stupid decision was made, see if it can be revisited when the meeting resumes.	Next time, emphasize in your opening comments the importance of their comments and that ''There is no such thing as a stupid question, except perhaps the question you don't ask . . .''
Broken Promises A member consistently offers reasons for not completing assigned tasks.	Reassign the task to someone else, unless the member can reassure the group that it will get done.	Shift essential tasks to more reliable members. When a task is given, confirm it verbally, record it in the minutes, and follow up with a phone call to check on progress. Offer time management training.
Tardiness and Early Departures	Ask Johnny what the problem is and	Be selective and choose only individ-

Johnny arrives late and seems anxious to leave.

whether he can focus on this meeting. If this is not possible, he may as well leave. (If he is not there in spirit, he may as well not be there at all.)

uals who should be a part of the group. Emphasize the importance of consistent attendance. Contact members like Johnny to find out about any pressures they may have.

Absences

Rachel is absent from a meeting without notifying you.

Call Rachel, tell her she was missed, and ask for the reason for her absence. Then ask her to let you know in advance whether she will miss a meeting.

Check if there are any problems with your system of notifying members of meetings. Request that members confirm their attendance (or absence) ahead of the meeting. Run meetings that no one will want to miss.

Same Volunteers Always

You ask for volunteers and always get the same people.

Don't look for volunteers at random, but say: "Cathy, could we interest you in this assignment? We all know that you are a busy person, but we will help you in any way. What do you think?"

Make the work of the group more interesting and enticing. If a member's workload does not allow for meaningful participation, it may be good to question the need to have him or her in your group.

Falling Asleep

Members are falling asleep, especially in the afternoon or after a heavy meal.

Ask them to stand up and stretch, or go for a brisk 10-minute walk in the rain! Facilitate parts of the meeting standing up. Pick up the pace of the meeting.

Plan the next meeting to be shorter, better focused, more interesting and engaging, and more fun. Avoid hot and heavy meals.

Disorder and Poor Decorum

In this table, no specific preventive interventions are given, since the same would apply to all of the given scenarios: Establish the rules for the meeting, and, if needed, reinforce them at the start of the meeting.

Ailment	Remedial Interventions What to Do Now?
Chaos Everyone is talking at the same time.	"Can we have only one person speaking at a time?" Or: "Can we agree that a member will speak only after being recognized by the chair? Great, now let me establish a speakers' lineup. Please raise your hand if you want to speak and I will take your name down."
The Hanging Hand A member raises his hand and does not put it down.	"Esther, I saw your hand and added your name to the speakers' lineup. You can put it down now."
The Frown A member is frowning, or appears puzzled, troubled, confused, or frustrated.	As soon as there is an opening in the discussion, ask: "Mel, is there a problem?" Or: "Helga, what do you think?"
Barging In Jack barges in when Joan has been recognized to speak.	"Jack, could you please raise your hand if you want to speak? (Pause.) Joan, go ahead"; Or: "Hands up, please"; Or, in a large meeting, say: "In fairness to everyone, could members who want to speak please line up at the microphone?"
Domination The discussion is dominated by two outspoken members; or a member has many follow-up questions.	If the participation is helpful and no one seems to be bothered by the domination, you can let it continue, at least for now. However, at some point you will

need to intervene: ``Ron, we need to hear from members who have not spoken. Are there any first-time speakers on this issue? How about you, Tom?''

Interruption
Tom interrupts Jenny in midsentence.

``Tom, may I ask you to let Jenny finish? If you want to respond, I suggest that you jot your thoughts down and share them when you get your turn to speak.''

Side Conversation
Graham and Leslie whisper or conduct a side conversation while Josh is speaking.

``Josh, can you pause for a moment? Graham and Leslie, is there a problem?'' Or just wait silently until the two stop. Or say: ``Can we have only one meeting at a time?''

Digression
A member talks about an unrelated issue.

``Ron, how is this related to the item on the agenda, which is the proposal to renew the lease for our premises?'' Or: ``Bob, could you please save your vacation stories for break time?''

Stubborn Nagging
A member stubbornly pushes her point, even after a vote on a proposal is taken.

``Thank you Jane. In fairness to the group, the decision on this issue has already been made by a majority vote. We have other issues to deal with, and we have to move on.''

Verbal Abuse
A member uses offensive language in the discussion, or attacks another member's motives or personality.

``Sir, can you please tone down the language?'' Or: ``In fairness to others, can you please keep good decorum and use language that is appropriate in debate?'' Or: ``Can we please speak on the issues and avoid personal criticisms?''

Heckling
A member is being heckled.

``Members, no one will argue with your right to disagree with

(continues)

Ailment	Remedial Interventions What to Do Now?
	others. At the same time, we need to give the member who is speaking the same respect and attention that we want when we are speaking. Thank you.''
Insensitivity A member uses a term that is insulting to one culture or tells an off-color joke.	``Before we go any further, I have a word of caution. I suggest that we be careful with the words we choose and the jokes we tell, because some of them may show insensitivity to one culture or another.''
Patronizing Paul, a longstanding member, says: ``Come on, guys, don't you realize that _____. Be serious.''	``Paul, all of us appreciate your long-term experience with this organization. At the same time, we need to listen and carefully evaluate new ideas, and avoid dismissing them too quickly. Sally, do you want to elaborate on your idea?''
Hidden Agenda Larry's participation puzzles you. There appears to be something he is not saying.	``I must say that I am puzzled by the twists and turns of events, and I wonder whether certain things have been left unsaid. Am I right in any way? Can someone help me out?''; Or: approach Larry at the next break for some feedback.
Adversarial Tactics Adversarial tactics are used before a meeting: lobbying, manipulation, intimidation, threats.	Remind members that, after the decision is made, they will need to work together to serve the same organization. Urge them to avoid tactics that they may regret later.

Discussion Quality Ailments

Ailment	Remedial Interventions What to Do Now?	Preventive Interventions How to Prevent It in the Future?
Predictability Discussions are predictable, reflecting no visionary thinking outside the box. (If it isn't broken, why fix it?)	Be brave and dare to introduce novel ideas, and recognize these enemies of creative thinking: "We've tried it and it didn't work"; "I have three reasons why it won't work." It's much easier to be a critic than to be a creator.	Initiate discussions about the quality of the group's decision making. A clear vision and persistence do work, so don't give up too fast. The battle against intransigence and entrenchment in the status quo must be won.
Last-Minute Reports Several reports are received late, giving no time to review them, and making it difficult to make informed decisions.	If the related agenda item cannot wait, call a break and give the members time to read the report. If the agenda item can wait, suggest that it be postponed.	Ask members to plan their time so that this practice is minimized. Ask members to support report writers by giving them needed data on time.
Premature Solution Mode A member proposes a solution (or a motion) prematurely, but the problem has not been fully explored.	"Jerry, can you please wait with your idea for the time being? It seems like we need more time to define the problem before we discuss solutions."	Before opening a complex issue for discussion, explain how it will unfold: problem definition, criteria for solutions, exploring options, selecting the best option, deciding on implementation.
Premature Closure A decision is rushed	"I know that our time is running short,	Allocate and manage time more care-

(continues)

Ailment	Remedial Interventions What to Do Now?	Preventive Interventions How to Prevent It in the Future?
through and it seems futile to raise a concern in the face of the steamroller effect.	but I have one concern about this idea and a simple way of addressing it. Here is the concern . . . Here is the solution . . .''	fully so that you can proceed in a measured and deliberate manner without needing to rush.
Repetition Discussion is repetitive.	''Does anyone have anything new to say, and, if not, shall we bring closure to this issue? We have a busy agenda and need to move ahead.''	At the beginning of the meeting, encourage members to be efficient and avoid repetition.
Narrow Interests Promoted A member promotes the interests of an affiliated group, at the expense of the interests of the full organization.	Remind the member of the duty to serve the entire organization, and that the interests of one group or another must yield to the broad interests.	Develop a member orientation package and organize training programs for new members, to establish their roles and responsibilities.
Hesitancy to Criticize Members hesitate to question and scrutinize proposals.	''I sense some hesitancy to criticize or ask questions, when this is exactly what we need to do. There is no such thing as a stupid question, and criticizing an idea is not a personal attack.''	In your opening remarks, emphasize that questioning and scrutinizing ideas is part of due diligence. Teach members to give criticism in a way that is easy to receive (principled, objective).
Critics, Not Creators A member articulates very clearly	''Are there changes that you could propose to address your	Involve potential critics in developing proposals. Have

what is wrong with a proposed new policy.

No Positive Reinforcement
Members are too quick to criticize but are very sparing with their accolades.

concerns? If you don't have any now, would you bring some ideas to the next meeting?''

Start recognizing effective participation: ''Thank you, Gene, for preparing such a detailed and comprehensive report. How about showing our appreciation to Gene with a round of applause?''

them presented as preliminary and clarify that ideas for improvement are welcome.

Develop a program to celebrate member achievements and group successes. Recognize task-related milestones or non-task-related events (birthday, new baby?).

Nitpicking
Members nitpick at words, propose amendments, and shift the focus of discussions away from the main issues.

''It's great that you want the words to be exactly right. I am concerned, however, that we are spending a lot of time on words, at the expense of discussing the principles at the core of this decision.''

Talk to nitpickers between meetings and offer them feedback. It may also be productive to involve them as devil's advocates before the meeting, when proposals are drafted.

Technical Jargon
Technical jargon and abbreviations are used and members appear confused.

Interrupt the presenter: ''Excuse me, but do you mind explaining what _____ means?''

Ask presenters to use plain terms and listener-friendly language. Request lists of terms and abbreviations.

What Are We Voting On?
The proposal to be voted on has not been clearly stated.

''Before we vote, can we clarify the precise wording of the proposal?'' The proposal can be clarified by the chair, the secretary, or anyone else.

Ask the proponent of a motion to submit it in writing. Whenever possible, proposals should be written out and included in the pre-meeting package.

(continues)

Ailment	Remedial Interventions What to Do Now?	Preventive Interventions How to Prevent It in the Future?
Many Abstentions Members hesitate when they raise their hands to vote.	"Put the brakes on" and say: "Is there a problem with this proposal? I sense some discomfort about it. It may be better to delay the vote, rather than make a decision that we may regret. Does this make any sense?"	Ensure that proposals are clear and balanced, addressing as many needs and concerns as possible. Suggest that members work to improve the quality of the decisions instead of abstaining.
Aimless Statements A member speaks with no clear focus, or starts with a long preamble and only then gets to the point.	"I am having trouble following. Where exactly are you going with this?" Or: "What exactly is your point?" Or: "If you had to say it in one sentence, what is your opinion?"	Teach members to use the sandwich approach: Tell them what you'll tell them ("I am in favor of this idea"); tell them (elaborate in concise point form); and then tell them what you told them (recap: "Therefore . . .").
Aimless Overall Discussion Several ideas and issues are raised, but in a random order, and with no focus.	"You seem to be raising several points so far: First _____. Second _____. Third _____. Shall we address them one at a time? How about starting with _____?"	Map out each agenda item: Outline the questions that need to be addressed, the key decisions that need to be made, and the time allocated for the item.
Deadlock There are three distinct proposals, with	Facilitate a decision to skip to an easier topic and return to	Prior research of issues may reveal some interesting so-

no apparent agreement on which is best. The discussion is not going anywhere.

this one later; or suggest a break when each member can team up with someone who has an opposing view, and look for a solution that would be better than either one.

lutions that are unlikely to emerge in an interactive discussion.

No Follow-Up Established
A proposal is approved, but implementation duties are not assigned.

``Before moving to the next agenda item, we need to establish who will do what and by when. I can suggest duties and schedules, and you can tell me if you agree. Is that acceptable?''

At the beginning of the meeting indicate that upon making a decision the group may also need to decide on how it will be implemented. Ask the group to remind you to do that if you forget.

A Small Setback
A temporary setback (or a failure in one area) causes the group to negate progress made in other areas.

Acknowledge the setback and its impact, while reminding the members of the broader perspective, including successes and achievements.

Establish the same notion with the group at its formation stage or before the meeting.

Logistical Ailments

Ailment	Remedial Interventions What to Do Now?	Preventive Interventions How to Prevent It in the Future?
Poor Audibility Members point to their ears or say: ``Can't hear you.''	Speak up, and ask others to do so too; or ask them to stand up or come to the	Arrange for a room with good acoustics and with no noise distractions (e.g.,

(continues)

Ailment	Remedial Interventions What to Do Now?	Preventive Interventions How to Prevent It in the Future?
	front and face the group; or insist on the use of micro- phones. From time to time, ask: ``Can everyone hear?''	loud fan, a disco next door). Have pretested micro- phones.
Nonfunctioning Au- diovisual Equipment The lightbulb in the overhead projector is burnt out, or there is no electricity in the outlet, or there is no screen.	Try fixing it, but, if you can't, carry on with- out it; or skip to an- other item while the technician works on it. (You can't afford to waste prime time on logistics.)	Arrive early and test every piece of equipment.
Catering Glitches The refreshments or meal is late, or the wrong food has ar- rived, or not enough, or too much.	Arrange for some- one to check things out and take correc- tive action. Advise the members of the delay and facilitate a decision to con- tinue with the busi- ness.	Communicate your expectations to the caterers clearly and fully. Ask them to confirm their under- standing of your needs and whether they can indeed meet them. Have a contingency plan.
Visual Distractions Members are dis- tracted by those who enter or leave the room or get up to grab a coffee, or by the sun shining in their face.	Do what is needed to eliminate the dis- traction, e.g., move the head table or the refreshment table to the other side; or close the curtain to block the sun.	Anticipate problems and take corrective action before the meeting begins.
Restlessness Members appear	Ask what the prob- lem is and address it.	Plan enough breaks. (``The human mind

restless or physically uncomfortable.

If members have been sitting for too long, take a break. If the room is too hot or too cold, take corrective action.

will absorb only as much as the human seat will endure.'') Before the meeting, make sure that the room temperature and ventilation are comfortable.

Room Too Large or Too Small

Check if another room is available (in the same hotel or at another location close by). If there is none, ask the members to assist you in making the best of an imperfect situation; or suggest rescheduling the meeting.

Estimate the number of people who will likely come and select the appropriate room size. Have a contingency plan ready in case of an uexpectedly high turnout.

Index

About the Author

Eli Mina, M.Sc., P.R.P., is a professional speaker, consultant, and meeting facilitator who runs a unique consulting and training practice out of Vancouver, Canada. Since 1984, he has offered his clients interactive workshops and seminars, and has served them by chairing contentious meetings, demystifying and humanizing the rules of order, and mediating large-scale disputes. Mr. Mina's clients come from business, municipal government, school districts, credit unions, regulatory bodies, labor unions, and the nonprofit sector.

Mr. Mina holds the designations of Professional Registered Parliamentarian (PRP) and Certified Professional Parliamentarian (CPP). However, it took more than these elaborate and wordy titles to develop this book. Eli has earned his reputation and credibility through a sensible and wholistic approach to problem solving, being consistently able to look beyond procedural formalities and uphold the fundamental principles of fairness, equality, and common sense.

Contact information for speaking engagements and consulting assignments:

Phone: 604-730-0377   Fax: 604-732-4135
E-mail: eli@elimina.com   Web site: www.elimina.com